The Counterfeit Coin Story

by

Ken Peters

To Rory
with thanks
Ken Peters

Published by Envoy Publicity

for Gill

ISBN 0-9543487-0-2

Photography by Ken Peters and Gill Askew

Book designed by Ken Peters

Published by Envoy Publicity
8 Kings Road, Biggin Hill. Kent TN16 3XU

Typeset in Bookman and printed in Great Britain by
Thanet Press Limited, Margate, Kent

Contents

Author's Note

My thanks go to the following coin experts and enthusiasts whose help and suggestions have been much appreciated:

Mark Blackburn, Colin R. Bruce II, Alan Cherry, Chris Denton, the late Patrick Finn, Jim Furner, Henry Kim, Koray Konuk, Phil Mernick, Ron Payne and Douglas Savile.

I am also grateful to the FitzWilliam Museum for permission to publish photographs Gill and I took of prime examples of counterfeits held in the Museum coin cabinet.

The story of coin counterfeiting is an uneven one, leading to an apparent imbalance in period coverage. This is particularly the case with the epidemics where more interesting happenings occurred than usual, and with the Anglo-Saxon period, where considerably less occurred.

The subject in all its facets is too vast for one book, so this story, of necessity, has been told from the British point of view. It is the first book to be published as part of The Counterfeit Coin Library. Other titles are listed at the back for those interested in delving deeper into the fascinating, murky world that was, is and will continue to be *coin counterfeiting.*

1

Two and a Half Thousand Years of Deception

All the evidence points to the appearance of counterfeit coins in the fifty years following the invention of coinage in the seventh century B.C. As the coins were made of specific amounts of precious metal to specific sizes, the forgers gained their profit by reducing the size of their copies or by reducing the precious metal content and topping up again with base metal. This could be achieved in different ways. Firstly, by mixing precious and base metals and casting the molten result into moulds made from genuine coins. Secondly, by coating or plating a base metal core with precious metal. This was then struck with false dies or with official dies being misused by moonlighting mintworkers. Some dies would have been stolen from mints by internal or external thieves. Occasionally, someone would exploit carelessly discarded plates. A third approach was to create an alloy that looked like precious metal but contained none. This too could then be cast or made into flans to be struck.

There does not appear to have been any significant time when counterfeiting was not occurring in all the centuries from the first crude efforts right up to the present where you may be reading this in unconscious possession of a dud pound coin. But amongst all this endemic counterfeiting, there have been occasions when it has risen to epidemic proportions. In Britain the greatest of all epidemics occurred in the first, third and fourth centuries A.D. and in George III's reign. Each had the same core reason - an insufficient supply of small change by the governing authority of the time. Each was ended by the arrival of a good supply of official coin. In the first epidemic, the failure of Rome to provide enough bronze coinage following the invasion of Britain in A.D. 43, led to a flood of Claudian copies.

This contemporary plated sixth stater, showing on its obverse a Griffin with tunny beneath, and on its reverse, a square punch, roughly quartered, is from Kyzikos, Mysia. It dates from around 600 to 550 B.C., at the dawn of coinage. It is of plated electrum, probably with a silver core. Its weight of 2.17 gm compares to a genuine weight of 2.70 gm. 10.5 mm.

BRASS FARTHINGS

Downturns in available small change exacerbated by sudden upsurges in trade produced similar epidemics of forgeries in the seventeenth and eighteenth centuries, with the addition of tokens that traders issued for local use as small change. A pattern then established itself with the initial acceptance of these imitations, for convenience, being followed by a clampdown when it dawned on the powers of the day that they were, to coin a phrase, being short-changed. In 1658, Salisbury City Council described the practice as "..the great and general abuse....by several persons....presuming without any authority to cause certain brass farthings to be stamped...for their several lucre and private gain." The expression "not worth a brass farthing" came from this time, and probably also "filthy lucre".

PASS THE PARCEL

This 1993 £1 forgery with clear test scratches on its surface, has a special place in the author's examples, as it was given to him in change for admission to, of all events, the London Coin Fair.

Once currency counterfeits enter a monetary system, human nature keeps them moving, because those who have been fooled into accepting them may well then recognise them as fakes, but feel disinclined to suffer the loss themselves. If the forgeries are around in sufficient numbers, and are being passed to and fro by people increasingly aware of their true nature, then a degree of unofficial acceptance can occur. At various times in the past, even officialdom has concurred in the situation, sometimes legitimising them, with a lower value than their genuine counterparts, sometimes trying to call them in, with offers of lowly recompense. Professor Mattingly quotes an instance: "The emperor Probus was determined to enforce Aurelian's currency reform and to drive the illegal moneyers out of business...Hoards of *bad* coinage went into the ground during his reign...doubtless to prevent their having to be surrendered at unfavourable rates, and in the vain hope of a change in government policy." Such hoards are now being found by metal detectorists.

The life of a circulating coin waxes and wanes; therefore so will that of a counterfeit coin, particularly as new issues have always seemed to stimulate counterfeiting.

MOTIVES

Greed is the dominant motive for most forgery, but it is not the only one. Other motives include a desire to 'show off', to have a go at authority, to plug official gaps and in many cases in the past, just to survive, when no other way seemed possible.

Nearly all U.S. coins are known to have been counterfeited. On the evidence of the author's collection alone, most British coins have also been counterfeited, either contemporaneously or subsequently. "Nobody would forge such a low value coin for such a little profit". This has never been true, as the thousands of false Georgian half-pennies testify. Volume production makes it worthwhile for the criminal. Even to-day, in Britain, counterfeiters are making a profit selling batches of forged £1 coins for 10p each! The buyers do have to provide their own gold paint however, to finish off these unconvincing cast lead-alloy efforts.

COLLECTORS BEWARE

The initial targets for forgers making 'collectables' were early Greek silver staters, Roman sestertii and medallions. These 'collector' counterfeits do not occur below a certain value/interest level. To give an extreme example, no one has yet thought it worthwhile to counterfeit the common Roman radiates to sell to collectors. It is difficult to establish exactly where this line can be drawn, as some of the more prolific counterfeiters of the past seem to have included in their productions, the occasional common coin, perhaps as an exercise of their skills or to disarm buyers by having such for sale as well as rare and 'valuable' coins. Fakes for tourists are the poorest efforts falling in the collecting group, as there is a clear presumption that tourists know nothing and can therefore be easily fooled.

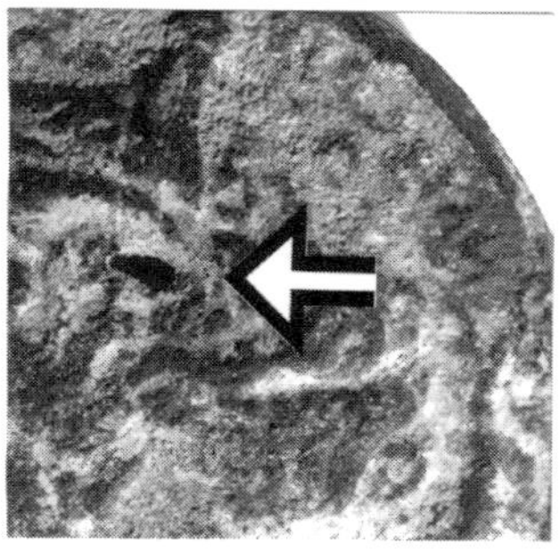

As a tourist in Egypt, the author bought this 'coin' from the Arab with the scarab (which was also a fake). The enlargement shows a blowhole in the metal, revealing it to be a cast copy, and not a genuine struck coin.

GENUINE

CONTEMPORARY FAKE

Athens new style silver tetradrachm, c.150 B.C. 31 mm.

Struck in bronze and then plated in silver. 27.5 mm.

2

Greek Beginnings

To act as recognizable units of barter, i.e. coins, little bean-shaped blobs of electrum, a naturally occurring alloy of gold and silver found in Lydia's capital city river, were punched on one side with the snapped end of a nail. This accidental design could never be imitated exactly because of the random pattern of the break. The other side at first bore just Anvil marks and then the marks of hand punches. It took a hundred years for double-sided designs to appear on coins, the first being by Athens.

Scholars have divided the evolution of early Western coinage into seven periods:

1	600-480 B.C.	Archaic
2	480-415 B.C.	Transitional
3	415-336 B.C.	Finest Art
4	336-280 B.C.	Later Fine Art
5	280-146 B.C.	Decline
6	146-27 B.C.	Continuing decline
7	27 B.C.- A.D. 268	Imperials

ARCHAIC

It was around 560 B.C. that Kroisos (Croesus) of Lydia made his change to bimetallic currency. Lesbos was then producing base silver coinage (billon). By the fifth century B.C., the regal coinage of Macedonia had split into two standards - top quality export coins at high purity and internal usage coins with the silver content reduced firstly to 95% and then down to 76% by the addition of copper.

TRANSITIONAL

Billon coinage was issued by Mytilene 480-450 B.C. and much of the later coinage of Elymais was of debased silver. A base silver coin was issued by Kolchis, Asia Minor in the fifth to fourth century B.C. Bronze coins first appeared around 450 B.C., in Sicily, and became widespread towards 350 B.C. From then on they replaced the inconveniently small fractional value silver coins.

FINEST ART

By c.400 B.C. artificial electrum had come into use. Increasing the permitted amount of silver to gold, gave coin-makers illegal profits. The agreement for alternate issues of electrum coins to the same standard, between the three cities of Mytiline, Lesbos and Phocaea,

GENUINE

MODERN FAKE

Syracusan decadrachm, style of Euainetos, 400 B.C. 38 mm.

Nineteenth century forgery, with poorly styled dolphins. It was acquired by the FitzWilliam in 1891, and thought for some years to be a Punic imitation because of the style. 38.5 mm.

Ionia, therefore embodied the death sentence for anyone found tampering with the official standard.

LATER FINE ART
A Greek tetradrachm of Lysimachus, 321-281 B.C., is described (in SNC 7/36) as the first coin to depict a human head. Its contemporary forgery is thus the first to copy a human head design.

DECLINE
Ae26 bronzes of Micipsa (148-118 B.C.) were sometimes struck in lead. Both Demetrios II (145-140 B.C.) and Antiochos VI (145-142 B.C.) issued bronze coins with serrated edges, probably as a deterrent to counterfeiters.

CONTINUING DECLINE
Orodes II coins (c. 57-38 B.C.) had a standard reverse inscription that was copied for the duration of his dynasty. Later die-engravers however, with little or no knowledge of Greek, copied blindly, leading to almost illegible versions.

Cleopatra VII's tetradrachms (51-30 B.C.) became increasingly debased during her reign. Hermaios (c. 41-0) debased his silver coinage towards the latter part of his reign, ending up with just bronze coinage.

Thracian tetradrachm, after 148 B.C. As GCV. 1/1635, except that Dionysos has been replaced by Herakles on the reverse with a corresponding legend change. Silvery, slightly crude appearance. The type was imitated by Danubian Celts of the interior. Wgt 11.90 gm. 32 mm.

IMITATION
Once the first coins bore recognisable designs, imitation followed and has persisted ever since, but it has meant different things at different times and places. The early imitations were not intended to deceive. They were a natural result of people adopting a new procedure with no available experience, combined with a logical assumption that familiar looking products would be more easily accepted by the populace.

Throughout the early history of coinage, there were waves of coin imitations by associated and peripheral countries, states and cities. Many can look like counterfeits. The first barbarous imitations of genuine coins (of Lydia), were struck (possibly by the Cimmerians) within a few years of the originals. They are electrum thirds, twelfths and twenty-fourths, showing a lion's head in outline, and a square punch impression on the reverse.

An early fifth Century coin of Motya in Sicily has designs based on a Himera coin on the obverse and a Segesta or Syracuse coin on the reverse. Another has a Syracuse coin obverse and an Akragas coin reverse. There was a similar lack of originality in the coins of Naxos. Philip II's gold stater became the staple unit of trade from the mid-fourth century B.C., spreading out from Greece and spawning imitations all across Europe and eventually into Britain. The successive copying gradually corrupted the original design.

A Lampsakos fourth century obverse type is a close copy of the contemporary Athenian coinage.

GENUINE

CONTEMPORARY IMITATION

Regular silver drachm of Sinope, c. mid 4th century B.C. 19 mm.

Imitation struck by Ariarathes, Persian satrap, c. 360 B.C., whose name appears in Aramaic under the dolphin. 18.5 mm.

A Tarsos coin was the prototype for Mazaios' coins (331-328 B.C.).

Many 'Philisto-Arabian' (Palestine) coins of the early fourth century B.C. were versions of Athenian coin designs.

Examples of imitation occur across the whole spectrum of Greek coinage. A Zagaba reverse type on a fourth century coin very closely copies a Syracusan tetradrachm of the late fifth century B.C. A mid-300's Zeugitanan tetradrachm has an obverse type very close to the Syracusan original. A Lysimachos Ar Hemidrachm of c.310 B.C. is based on coinage of Philip of Macedon. A late fourth century tetradrachm has an obverse based on Alexander III's coinage. Sophytes' silver stater (c.300 B.C.) copied its obverse from a Seleukos I, Nicator coin which had copied a Persian satraps' coin. An Arabian Gulf Ar tetradrachm (struck on a folded hammered flan) imitates Athens' popular helmeted head of Athena on the obverse and owl on the reverse.

Spink refer to numerous second century B.C. imitations, of poor style and rough execution, of the coins of Histiaia. A Hyspaosines tetradrachm of 125/4 B.C. appears to have been derived from an Euthydemos coin.

The Danubian Celts of the interior copied coins of Thasos, and Pelagia. Gortyna, Knosos, Kydonia, Hierapytna and Olonte all issued imitative coins.

Greek silver drachms were extensively imitated by the Celtic tribes. These barbarous versions became more common than their Greek originals. Many more examples could be quoted.

EARLY COUNTERFEITING

One of the coins on display at the British Museum's 'Money Under the Microscope' Exhibition held in 1994 was a Lydian plated forgery of 546-541 B.C. A silver-cored electrum coin of c.575 B.C. was shown in the Museum's August 2000 Illegal Coins Exhibition. Polykrates, the tyrant of Samos (532-521 B.C.) was said by Herodotos to have bought off the besieging Spartans in 525/4 B.C. by fooling them with a ransom of staters that were in fact electrum-coated lead counterfeits. This may be an apocryphal tale, but these contemporary fakes exist and are described in Spink's catalogue, as: Naked Herakles kneeling l./ two oblong punches - *counterfeit stater in lead, originally plated with electrum* - £2,500! The description suggests that only coins with no precious metal coating left have survived. There are various obverse types.

Greek plated coins started appearing around 450 B.C. (silver wrapped round copper cores and then struck). Because of a silver shortage after the Peloponnesian War, Athens issued silver-plated bronze tetradrachms in 407-406 B.C. Aristophanes mentions this in his play 'The Frogs', describing the coins as "brassy counterfeit pretences." Amyntas III (393-369 B.C.) silver-plated his coinage to stretch his silver supplies. All early Greek plated coins, bar these two

Thasos type.
This silver plated tetradrachm is either a rare contemporary Thasos counterfeit, a copy by the Eastern Celts - tribes of Danubian and Balkan areas - Transylvania, or a counterfeit of a copy. Head of Dionysos wearing crown of ivy leaves and grapes/ Herakles with club and lion-skin. Virtually all the silver is intact. It has an unusual curved exergual line. There are two small test cuts on the obverse. Wgt 14.54 gm. 31.5 mm.

exceptions, are now classified as counterfeits by most numismatists. The opposing view is that these silver-plated, copper cored coins appear to have been struck on official dies, making them most likely either official issues, or 'moonlighting' products of the mint staff. An alternative explanation of the apparent use of official dies is that the counterfeiters hammered genuine coins into die faces to make their dies. The silver-clad coins have a thick (100-200 microns) silver layer over a copper disc. Because two shallow cups are put together, the edge-plating is doubled in thickness.

GENUINE

Silver tetradrachm of Alexander III (the Great) (336-323 B.C.), Pella, Macedonia. 27.5 mm.

Zeus holding up an eagle and staff.

CHEATS PROSPER

The tale of Polykrates of Samos raising the Spartan siege of 525-4 B.C.with a ransom of electrum-plated lead cored counterfeits of the contemporary Samian electrum coinage, is lent credence by several surviving examples.

CONTEMPORARY & LATER IMITATIONS

Silver tetradrachm imitation, Philip III Arrhidaeus (323-317 B.C.). 25.5 mm.

Lightweight silver tetradrachm imitation. Danubian Celtic. The first century A.D. 28.5 mm.

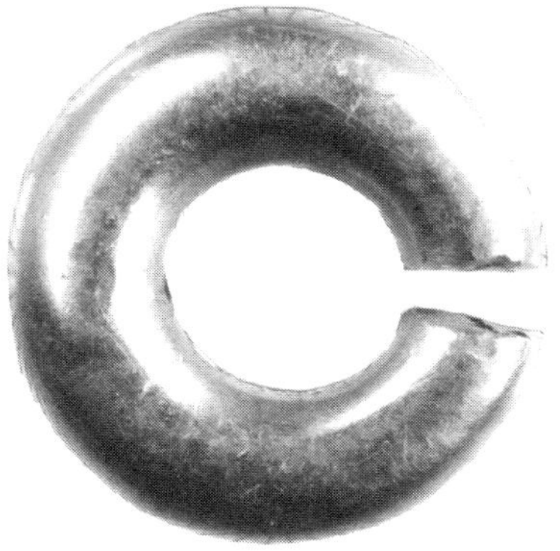

Durotriges tribal gold-plated penannular ring money. The soft patina to be found on this and on other examples suggests long use, supporting the concept that they were used as currency. Various dates are attached to them - 700 B.C. (Joan Taylor, 'Bronze Age Gold Work of the British Isles); 1,200 to 100 B.C. (Van Arsdell); 1,000 to 750 B.C. (Peter Northover).

The external appearance is of a gold ring, with a 15 mm external diameter; 6 mm internal. Both its weight (5.6 gm) and magnified examination reveal its plated nature. In the inner part, there is a slight crease and a tiny flap of gold lifting up from the copper or bronze core. A pure gold ring would not have the unevenness discernible on the two terminals - the result of the bronze slightly expanding over three thousand years. Those found to date fall within the range of 15 mm to just over 20 mm external diameter and 5 mm to around 8 mm internal. This plated example was found near Stanbridge, Wimborne in Dorset in the late 1990's.

3

Celtic Tribal Platers

FALSE RINGS
The plain type of Celtic gold rings (up to 12 gm and 16 mm), found in British contexts from c.1200 to 100 B.C., may have become a form of money somewhere along the way. Plated examples of these rings, assuming they were neither official nor semi-official, may be Britain's first counterfeits, unless, as one view has it, any monetary function only commenced in the second century B.C., long after coins and their counterfeits had appeared. *See left.*

CELTIC METALLURGY
Celtic metalwork reveals an impressive knowledge of alloys and the methods of mass-production, applied to their coin production in various metals:

1 copper alloy with high level of tin - potin coinage.
2 bronze.
3 silver, showing a green patination where the copper alloyed with it is high.
4 gold with silver or copper.
5 gold with silver and copper.

Examination of plated copies of the Continental Gallic War type, c.60 B.C., showed that they had been made by heat bonding gold sheets to silver cores.

IMITATIVE BEGINNINGS
Many of the Celtic coins of Central Europe and Asia Minor were imitative, copying coins of Alexander III, Philip II and III of Macedon, Lysimachos of Thrace, etc.

The prime example of this imitative process was Philip II's gold stater depicting on the obverse, the head of Apollo and on the reverse, a Biga (two horse chariot). It became the most popular coin of its time and was extensively and barbarously copied by the Helvetii and Celtic Gauls, finally arriving in Britain (c.125-100 B.C.) as the Belgae tribe's large flan version of the original work of art. All that was left of the original chariot after centuries of copying, was a stylised horse and a solitary wheel. Britons then copied these imported copies. The Westerham type stater follows the design of the Gaulish Atrebatic coins.

Gallo-Belgic A Ambiani gold stater, c.150 – 50 B.C. Very thin, with a brightness to the gold that shows this to be a modern counterfeit aimed at casual collectors. Wgt 4.4 gm. 25 mm.

Forgery of a Tincomarus stater - COM.F / TIN. 18 mm.

Because it was found in Britain, a rare Iron Age die, for a Gallo-Belgic stater obverse, may well be the work of a forger.

The Celtic tribes having most contact with the pre-invasion Romans, tended not surprisingly to be most influenced in their coinage designs. Some such as the British Trinovantes produced very direct copies of Roman originals on their silver and bronze coinage. In the late first century B.C., there was an increase in this copying of Roman prototypes, particularly of Roman Republican denarii. As experience in coin production grew, so did originality in design.

POTINS

A Massalia Greek coin (c.200-49 B.C.) depicting a charging bull, is the most likely prototype for the Kentish coins popularly known as potins, but now often referred to as cast tin-bronzes. Potins were cast in moulds or strips and then given a tin wash to make them look like silver coins. Clay moulds for these crude British products were found in the 1930's at Colchester in Essex. They were designed to turn out many at a time. Quantity casting slabs are known in various combinations. One from Verulamium has seven neat rows of seven, plus an add-on one to make the round figure total of fifty.

It was once thought that potins were cast in wooden moulds. If they were pure tin coins it might be possible, but they comprise mostly copper, and wooden moulds could not have been used with a molten bronze alloy. This particular alloy also is too brittle to make striking likely. An investigation to confirm or refute these points was carried out by Hedges and Robins[HE], using metallographic examination of a typical potin, backed up by X-ray fluorescence spectrometry and X-ray diffraction. Their results indicated a cast coin of approximately 75% copper and 25% tin with a metallic structure suggesting a pre-heated refractory-type mould. If made from clay, a wooden 'master' may have been used to imprint the design into the mould, thus leaving the wood marks previously interpreted as being the actual mould itself.

METROLOGY

Potins seem to have had no strict weight standard, unlike the coins of Tasciovanus and his successors, which show a particularly consistent standard of weight and gold content.

With the exception of potins (c.100 B.C.), coins were struck between dies on cast flans. Concave trussels allowed the flans to be positioned more easily. Gold and silver coins could be struck with bronze dies, but bronze coins, unless on very thin flans, required the more technologically demanding iron dies.

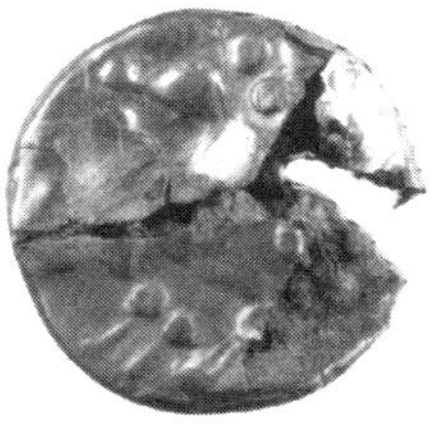

Over the centuries, corrosion has caused the bronze core to expand and burst through the gold skin of this plated Celtic stater. 18 mm.

COUNTERFEITING

Celtic coinage has been extensively forged, both contemporaneously and in modern times. The contemporary forgeries are almost entirely plated, with gold-plated staters on bronze, or occasionally silver cores, dominating. These were struck with forged dies, although there is a body of opinion that says genuine dies were used and official status must have applied to plated coins. By their often comparatively uncirculated condition, it is clear that many were spotted soon after manufacture, and discarded, supporting the *unofficial* status viewpoint.

Haselgrove**HA** lists all single and hoard Celtic coins found in Britain between 1977 and 1982 that were known in 1984. Of the total 1,968 gold and silver coins, 86 were plated, i.e. 4.37%. Coincidentally, these comprised exactly 43 gold and 43 silver. Around 0.5% only of the hoarded Celtic gold and silver coins found were plated, as opposed to 9.5% of non-hoarded finds. This strongly suggests that the Celts could recognise most of the counterfeit coins around and exclude them from their savings. An odd contradiction to this is a small hoard found in 1932, at Birling, near Eastbourne, Sussex. It comprised three staters and two quarter-staters - all gold-plated. The staters were Dubnovellaunus and a Gallo-Belgic E, Wonersh type. Perhaps a collector of other people's rejects.

The average of under 5% plated for all the above finds shows how exceptional are the Celtic coins found at the Hayling Island temple site in Hampshire:
Gold-75% plated; silver-46% plated. This amazingly high proportion may possibly be due to selective offerings, i.e. get rid of the dross on the gods. Having seen donative gold leaf covered boxes from votive sites, I am sure that some Celts undoubtedly thought they could fool their gods. Alternatively, plated coins may have been produced specifically for ritual deposition as purely symbolic votive offerings.

Verica silver-plated unit, A.D. 25-35, Cavalry duo. Celtic warrior with oval shield COMM.F/Celtic warrior with spear. Only three examples are known of this so far unpublished variant of VA 530.1. This piece was found near Winchester in 1995. Wgt 0.73 gm. 12 mm.

Chris Rudd, the well-known Celtic coin dealer, believes that many Iron Age plated coins were official issues because of those which appear to have been made with the identical dies used in striking gold or silver coins, due perhaps to a temporary shortage of gold or silver bullion. There are alternative possibilities. The use of the same dies could have arisen if the moneyers had been 'moonlighting'. Or official dies could appear to have been used if genuine coins were employed as hubs for dies.

All 36 Roman denarii recovered from Hayling Island were plated. None bore bankers' marks, but there were plenty of cuts, stabs, scratches and pricks. All but two were pre-A.D.15. There may be political reasons behind the occurrence of plated denarii on Celtic sites, just as counterfeit Celtic coins turn up on Roman sites. Were the occupied trying to fool the occupiers and/or vice versa?

John Collis**CA** highlights an interesting phenomenon relating to the plated forgeries of the gold coinage of Cunobelin. He points out that they seem to have been recognized in antiquity, but not by everyone. The bar charts he has constructed from excavation records, show that on other than market sites, around 30% of the gold coins that have turned up are plated. This is probably a reasonable indication of the number of forgeries in circulation at the time, exaggerated to some extent by the discarding factor for coins no longer able to fool anyone. Where better to pass on the forgeries than at a busy market.

Some pieces, such as this modern copy of a stater, have a 'too good to be true' look. 19 mm.

Sure enough, the incidence of forgeries to genuine gold coins found at market sites is almost 50:50 at major markets; but far larger, over 90%, at minor markets. One interpretation of this striking difference could be that the risk of detection was high at major markets and low at minor ones. If this interpretation is regarded as valid, then it could be applied to undefined or newly located market sites, i.e. a high percentage of forged coins suggesting a minor Iron Age market and a low percentage a major market.

4

Rampant Roman Counterfeiting

The concept of MONETA, a goddess of the Mint, gave Romans a measure of reverence for coins, the products of the Sacra Moneta. So forgers had to overcome or ignore religious scruples to ply their trade. But then scruples of any sort have never seemed to be one of their problems and counterfeiting was endemic throughout the Roman era. In this time there were three great epidemics of counterfeiting, which are generally considered to have arisen because of genuine coin shortages. These occurred in the first, third and fourth centuries A.D. All three followed a pattern of weight reduction.

Moneta is depicted striking coins on this bronze medallion struck by the Royal Mint.

From 287 to 325 there was an official Roman mint in London, and for a short while another with the initial letter C which may have stood for Camulodunum (Colchester). Almost always, the products are well designed and produced, with the tail side precisely inverted from the head side, something to look for when checking coins. In Dr. Kent's view[KE] all other coins made in Britain during the Roman occupation are clearly and visibly forgeries. There were cast coins - usually good imitations when genuine silver and large bronze pieces had been used for the moulds, and die-struck coins which ranged from good to incredibly poor down to the minuscule barbarous minimissimi. No one could have been fooled by these, so they must have been thought of as necessary evils. In the epidemics, imitations approached and sometimes exceeded the number of genuine coins in circulation. Forgeries were so common on the continent in the first century A.D. that according to Tacitus (germania V), the Germans preferred the old, familiar Roman coins, particularly the biga and serrated edge types.

Some still cling to the view that silver-plated Roman coins are official products. If so, where are the die-links between plated and genuine? Their absence is convincing evidence that all plated examples are contemporary forgeries. Pliny categorised them as such. Anyone still supporting the official idea should read Crawford's article on the subject[CR]. Most plated examples can be clearly recognised as forgeries for reasons of style, garbled legends, wrong control marks, wrong die-axes, wrong pairings of obverse and reverse. Coins that at first appeared to be identical have proved to be different when closely examined - different die-breaks, different diameters. A silvered lead Republican denarius could never have been official or even semi-official. Roman law, promoting the rejection of false money, would have rebounded on the State if it had been producing such pieces itself, so it is unlikely, particularly considering that evidence from Roman hoards shows that the people of the time knew how to winkle out plated pieces from their savings. Crawford quotes the Cosa hoard of over two thousand silver coins without one plated piece, compared to a fifty-fifty recovery rate of solid v plated pieces from the Cosa site. The 3,000+ silver coins of the Beachy Head hoard (A.D. 196-c.266) excluded the contemporary forgeries of the time - a wave of base imitations of the debasing denarii - showing that their nature was clearly known and such pieces were recognisable to the hoarder.

Contemporary Roman examples can be found of most ancient approaches to forgery - cast, plated, cliché, degraded precious metal, pewter, lead, lightweight, etc.

CAST AND PLATED

Cast counterfeits occur throughout the Roman period. Where they were made in the same metal as full-value genuine pieces, they had to be lighter to provide a profit. Not so, where the genuine coins did not contain their full value of metal.

The Roman plated coins were all struck after being plated. Plating was effected in various ways: silver foil envelopes, silver soldered on copper cores, hot-dipped in silver-alloy; also by fusing granules or foil to the surface. Dr. Kent's[KE] opinion of the dies that have survived from this period is that they could all be forgers' dies.

This weak attempt at a Janus as is comparatively recent, unlike the bulk of Roman counterfeits which are contemporary.

ROMAN BRONZE COINAGE

The Romans started their metal currency with Aes rude (chunky bronze lumps), evolving into Aes signatum (cast bronze slabs bearing designs and signatures) and then large, coin-shaped discs - Aes grave - usually depicting Janus and the prow of a galley. Initially these cast pieces weighed around 300 gm, dropping over time to c.17 gm and finally being struck on cast flans. By the late Republican period, they were only slightly larger than pre-decimal pennies.

The term First Brass signifies sestertii and Second Brass, dupondii and asses. Some official sestertii and dupondii were made from badly mixed metals, resulting in their present look of copper streaks and corrosion beads. Britain was a particular centre for the production of forged lightweight asses of Claudius, clearly inferior to the Imperial bronzes. Throughout the history of counterfeiting, copies that were not meant to defraud, but to fill needs, tended to start poorly and then go downhill if produced over a significant period. The Claudian as copies depicting Minerva typify this.

Cast asses were prolifically produced in southern Britain from soon after the Roman invasion, up to the Severan period; also at the time of the Tetrarchy, as shown by the number of moulds found for casting folles' copies.

The phenomenon of the bronze coinage in the third century was the barbarous radiate, copying the issues of Tetricus I and II, Claudius

Gothicus, etc. These were mainly struck as were those in the next century, imitating Constantine I coins and the prolific commemoratives - URBS ROMA and CONSTANTINOPOLIS. Following these came a rash of copies of GLORIA EXERCITUS soldiers and standards type. The ensuing epidemic of the false FEL TEMP REPARATIO/Fallen Horseman coins included over-stamped GLORIA EXERCITUS copies.

Constantius II's large Ae2 coins were forged in quantity in the West. Many were "almost void of silver" according to Cope, who considers that forgeries made from the fabric of official coins might be expected to contain a slight silver content. Copying then subsided to endemic levels and copies of later rulers such as Magnentius are scarce. Some late minims bear a resemblance to Saxon sceattas.

Rust breaking through this Mark Antony denarius has revealed its iron core.

IRON COUNTERFEITS

To have sufficient coinage to pay his Legions, Mark Antony lowered the silver content. It is possible that the iron cored denarii that turn up were his last resort in this endeavour to make a little go a long way. Iron, coated with bronze or brass, was used by some forgers to fake Roman bronze coinage as cheaply as possible.

ROMAN SILVER COINAGE

Denarii were extensively counterfeited, with plating being more popular than base-metal casting, particularly of Roman Republican and Imperial denarii to c.A.D. 64 and again in the third century. They are often light, hybrid, struck on white metal instead of silver, giving them a base look, and with eccentric die-axes. Some had iron cores.

Because of the reducing profit for the counterfeiters, the gradual official debasement that then ensued may have caused the noticeable lessening of silver forgeries. With Septimius Severus's debasement of A.D.193, the silver content fell below half. Despite this, Severan dynasty denarii were popular targets. Silver-washed coins can be found with no trace left on them of the original silver deposit, giving them the appearance of bronze coins.

FORGED ROMAN DENARII

Die-struck

Cast

VOTIVE COPIES?

Cast tin copies of early Imperial denarii found in the Thames and a remarkable group from a well on Bar Hill could be specially-made offerings to the Gods. Some Claudian copies are thought to have been made in the third century A.D. for the specific purpose of throwing them into rivers being crossed, to placate the river god.

Starting with Trajan Decius, denarii were occasionally restruck as antoniniani.

ROMAN GOLD COINAGE

Contemporary counterfeits are rare, although some examples are known where false denarii dies have been used to produce supposed gold coins. Aurei have been frequently counterfeited in post-Roman times. Some can reveal themselves by having signs of wear, yet with their fields showing mint lustre. Hill lists and illustrates 140 Becker counterfeits of Roman coins of which 84 are gold. A number of these were also struck in silver.

Roman aurei fakes were emanating from Beirut in the early 1990's. They were pressure cast in pure gold. The design is not quite as sharp as genuine pieces, and the colour is slightly different.

FAKE-SPOTTERS BEWARE

Roman mintworkers formed a class which, once entered, could not be left. The variable quality of mint-workers and of complete Mints, pose problems when considering if coins are genuine. Probable engravers' errors cover a multitude of anomalies: "*Mintmark quite anomalous but absolutely clear; just conceivably an engraver's error.*" R.I.C. Vol. VI, p. 537 quotes the mintmark PLN rendered as DLN. It is thought that the workers allocated the reverse design and lettering cutting were the least skilful, and so more mistakes could be expected in these areas. Bad striking can change the appearance of genuine coins. Ineffectual striking can fail to spread the flan and so result in under-sized coins which are, nevertheless, genuine. Careless double-striking can create incomprehensible legends. Different weight pieces can emanate from one set of dies. Official retooling occurred to change portraits. The Roman lead alloy coins that occasionally turn up were probably plated fakes originally.

Large, variable weight Ae medallions, emanating from Rome alone, may have been mementoes for people visiting the Rome mint.

The only forgeries in quantity of brass and copper Roman coins are contemporary casts. But choice sestertii attracted higher-grade efforts aimed at collectors. Much higher in some cases, which can be their downfall, as they can look 'too good to be true'. Also the odd detail can look wrong. Modern forgeries of Roman coins range right back to the chunky bronze Aes Grave pieces.

CAST OF THOUSANDS

A display case in the Museum of London is devoted to coin-casting Roman forgers, showing some of the coin moulds they left behind.

A mould was simply made by pressing a genuine coin into damp clay. Molten metal would then fill the mould. An illustration in this display shows a family group busily engaged in this nefarious activity.

A Roman coiner's den, containing a mould and a quantity of forged Roman coins, was uncovered at Halton Chesters, near a fort on Hadrian's Wall.

ROMAN REPUBLIC

The earliest contemporary Roman forgeries were the plated copies of silver Republican denarii which approached epidemic proportions. From 124 to 37 B.C., examples are known of plated denarii in the names of almost every Republican moneyer.

Plated hybrids are known for Fannia 1a (obverse of Porcia 1, struck at the same mint at the same period), Plaetoria 8 (appropriate name!), P. Carisius and L. Mescinius Rufus.

Cassia 11 denarii may all be contemporary forgeries as only plated examples have been found to date. There are barbarous imitations of Considia 1b denarii.

With his Porcia 11 quinarius. Porcia copied coins issued by his namesake over 40 years earlier.

Many Roman Republican coins bear Bankers' marks, not so much to test for plating as to indicate approval. Checking for plating involved cuts or stamps of symbols, or letters penetrating the coin surface sufficiently to confirm solidity or reveal plating. Some plating was so good that test cuts did not break through[SE]. Counterfeited stamps appear on counterfeited coins! The Edsdon Hoard contained eight countermarked legionary denarii of Mark Antony. These punched or gouged marks were made either on the obverse or on both sides of the coin. The use of stamps had faded away by around A.D. 100.

Volteius denarius of the Roman Republic. c.78 B.C.
This is a contemporary copper-cored silver plated counterfeit. Laureate head of Jupiter with a Temple of Jupiter Capitolinus reverse; M. VOLTEI M.F. below. Good style, with most of the plating still intact. It is almost certainly a product of skullduggery at the mint, rather than an unofficial counterfeit. 19 mm.
RSCV Volteia 1.

HAYLING ISLAND TEMPLE
The Roman plated coins found at this Temple site in Hampshire were free from Bankers' marks or the regular stamps used in other parts of Britain. The deliberate damage to be found on them took the form of striking, bending, stabbing, cutting, breaking, scratching, pricking or snapping off pieces.

Some silver Roman Republican denarii, c.100 B.C., have serrated edges, hence the name serrati. This design may have been to deter counterfeiting, but many examples exist of plated serrati. Genuine pieces were only struck at an Italian provincial mint. The early serrated bronze coins do not resemble denarii serrating, having the look of blobs added to the edge rather than a series of edge cuts.

A plated brockage Republican denarius is quoted by Sellwood as an example of official production, because a forger would not issue such. The counter-argument to this is that it may have been lost or left by the forger for a variety of possible reasons.

ROMAN REPUBLIC FORGER'S DIE
A bronze-headed pile with iron back and stud (on sale in 1998 for

£500), was made to reproduce a copy of the reverse of a denarius of L. CAECILIVS METELLVS, issued in Spain, c.96-75 B.C.

MARK ANTONY (44-39 B.C.)
No one wanted to hoard Mark Antony's low silver denarii, so they kept circulating and are thus normally found in very worn condition. It is doubtful if any authentic specimen exists of Legionary coins LEG.XXIV to XXX. Some genuine legionary denarii have been tooled to produce such varieties.

FIRST CENTURY A.D.

Roman bronze coinage was imitated in Britain throughout the Roman era. In Gaul from c.10 B.C. to A.D. 70, barbarous, mostly underweight, local copies of Roman bronze coins proliferated.

AUGUSTUS (27 B.C.-A.D. 14)
Production of plated denarii was particularly widespread during the reigns of Augustus and Tiberius. They were sufficiently well plated to give quite a good ring when dropped.

TIBERIUS (A.D. 14-37)
Tiberian plated denarii had around 20% silver to 80% copper. Some had pewter cores. There are frequent barbarous copies of the 'Pontif. Maxim' denarii of Tiberius. At Auxerre in Gaul and elsewhere, apparently genuine 'Pontif. Maxim' coin dies have been found. This may have been the result of pillaging troops stealing the dies from the mint.

CALIGULA (Gaius) (A.D. 37-41)
In Caligula's time, a number of local mints issued coins, mainly aes, in a semi-barbarous style and fabric, but imperial design. These are frequently found on Western sites. They may have had Roman Government authority, or have been tolerated by the Government, just as tokens were at times in more recent centuries. Notably the small copper quadrans were not copied during the reigns of Caligula and Claudius.

Caligula was so abhorred that his coinage was recalled after his death, leading to a coin famine that Spain, Gaul and Britain rectified with crude bronze unofficial coinage.

This bronze cast, purporting to be a sestertius of Caligula, is a nineteenth century product. It shows a seated Pietas, and is probably a copy of a sixteenth century Paduan fantasy Roman. 38 mm.

British copy of an S.C. Minerva type Claudian as. 26 mm.

Contemporary British copy of an as of Claudius - with a bruiser's face. LIBERTAS AVGVSTA SC appears on the reverse. 27 mm.

CLAUDIUS (A.D. 41-54)

Following the invasion of Britain in A.D. 43 to Nero's re-opening of the Lyon Mint in 64, Britain was short of the imposed coinage, imported from the Rome mint. Local enterprise, or perhaps wholly or partly the Roman army, filled the gap so thoroughly that Claudian copies often outnumber the genuine pieces found on British sites. They do not seem to have spread farther north than York. Coventina's Well contained just 20. Copies of asses that are well-executed and weigh 10 to 11 gm may be authorised products. Those poorly made and below 10 gm are almost definitely counterfeit.

The Minerva as prototype, by its simple, elegant style, lent itself to imitation, so it is not surprising that Minerva copies are by far the most prolific, followed by asses with the reverses CONSTANTIAE AVGVSTI S.C. and LIBERTAS AVGVSTA SC. Also, to a much lesser extent, dupondii and sestertii.

It is possible that at least half of the asses in circulation in Britain were local copies, and of these, three-quarters were Minerva imitations - in all stages of degradation. Although Minerva dominated the imitations, Spes walking right with flower and Ceres seated were quite popular design choices. Hoards show that copies of this time were still in circulation for a hundred years after Claudius's death. A bronze hoard[SU] found in the early 1960's in Worcester comprised one commemorative as of M. Agrippa and nine Claudian copies with six different die-axes. Wear suggested years of circulation. Weights vary considerably. These copies may well have been produced long after the issue of their prototypes. With most copies, the absence of 'P.P.' shows the originals to have been the A.D. 41 types, Claudius having been given the title Pater Patriae in A.D. 42. The copying went on to A.D. 64 and the absence of copies of later Claudian types is a strong indication that they did not arrive in Britain from the Continent in any significant quantities. Claudian copies are also common in Gaul suggesting that Britain was not the only under-supplied part of the Roman Empire. Die-links have been found between British and Continental copies. All types crop up in British, Gallic and Spanish contexts, poorly made, some with blundered legends, and ranging from semi- to completely barbarous workmanship. Gloucestershire has provided many examples of the poorer types. Several clearly defined styles have been detected, suggesting a regular issue from local mints. There is evidence of a Claudian as counterfeiting centre in Camulodunum (Colchester).

SESTERTII

Copies of sestertii are far less common than asses. The stamp TI.AV, found on some imitative sestertii, may have been put there to legitimise them.

PLATED ASSES

There are copper/bronze plated asses of the coins of Claudius, Antoninus Pius and Septimius Severus, Some are cliché-made with lead cores, but the more common are hot-dipped iron cores. These marginal profit counterfeits can be found with test cuts.

British copy of a Claudian bronze sestertius. Good quality obverse, but the reverse, Spes advancing left, is crude. Clearly two different hands have been at work. 35 mm.

GRADED BARBARITY

Sutherland devised a useful framework for grading the markedly different levels of barbarity to be found in Claudian copies. In general, as copies tend to emphasise the wide triangle of the eye and on the reverse, a spindly Minerva has often drifted from the centre of the design.

GRADE	DESIGN	LEGEND	WEIGHT (11 gm)
1	near original	correct or nearly so	c.9 to 10 gm
2	coarser	correct or nearly so	c.7 to 9 gm
3	noticeably barbarous	degrading	c.4 to 7 gm
4	noticeably barbarous	degrading plus mirror-image in part or entire	c.4 to 7 gm

Sutherland considered that the Grade 1 types might be products of the Roman military requiring coin to pay the troops. In his Colchester report, Kenyon considered the barbarous asses of Claudius to be official. The jury is still out on this.

DENARII
Counterfeiting of denarii peaked in Claudius's time with four in five plated. The plating is thicker at the edges than at the centre. They have copper alloy cores with a very occasional iron-cored example from A.D. 52. There was also a high incidence of plating with Claudius Drusus and even more so with Domitilla.

Although many denarii were well made, some close to the genuine ones in quality, even to a brow line being visible on Claudius's bust, they are lighter than the full silver coins - 2.7 to 3.1 gm instead of 3.5 gm. Some soundly plated denarii look and feel like cast coins.

Crude, probably cast Romano-Iberian imitation of a Claudian as, Minerva type. Found in Spain. 23 mm.

THE ST. SWITHIN"S HOARD
A hoard[SY] found prior to 1856 at St. Swithin's Lane, King William Street, London, comprised 89 plated denarii, from c.90 B.C. to c.A.D. 43. Some had copper cores, the rest iron. The considerable number of die-links, with one group containing 26 pieces, has to mean that this was a forger's hoard, not examples collected at random from circulating currency. The technique of using genuine coins to create the false dies is evident from the worn look of the earlier pieces.

THE WAVENEY HOARD

This hoard, found in 1996/7, comprised over 160 plated denarii of Claudius, plus one each of Augustus and Tiberius. All were made by striking hot copper flans wrapped in silver foil to provide a thick silver cover. Some show the edge of the foil. The hoard was found in the Iceni area, at Waveney, with Norwich being the nearest big town. Probably deposited in A.D. 47-51.

The evidence for this being a forger's stock awaiting circulation, or for recycling if they had not come up to his quality control standard, is firstly the lack of wear, although some deterioration appears to have arisen because of metal waste accumulation on the dies. Also, there are no test cuts, some obverse legends are irregular, eg. T.CAVD CAESAR & TI CLAV CAESAR, hybrids occur, they are underweight and the die-engraving is inept. So far no links with any other plated denarii have been found, yet die calculations show that the large number of dies used to produce the coins in the hoard represent a huge potential coinage output. Reece classifies it as an important find, possibly indicating the presence of a Roman Fort.

Two of the Waveney hoard coins of the same design but struck from different dies. 17 mm.

Orna-Ornstein and Kenyon detail comparable hoards of plated denarii in their report on this hoard[OR].

WANBOROUGH

Of 63 denarii found at this Roman Temple site, five were plated, the latest being Claudius.

In a survey of 2,752 denarii from 21 hoards found in Britain between 1985 and 1991, only four were plated.

NERO (A.D. 54-68)
Nero reopened the Lyon Mint and the coin shortage that arose in Claudius's reign ended soon after. Significant levels of the semi-barbarous imitations of Imperial currency disappeared from c.A.D. 64. The base coinage mint of Lugdunum established in Nero's time is the most likely reason for the rapid decline in counterfeit production. Few Neronian aes copies have been found in Britain. His Victory asses deteriorated from 8 gm to 4.7 gm.

A strange method of production found in a counterfeit from Norfolk[BR] had the external silver-plating round the bronze core, supplemented by a central silver disc.

OTHO (A.D. 69)
No copper or bronze coinage was produced during his brief reign (95 days). This was too great a temptation to forgers, who accommodatingly filled the gap. Paduan examples are known. Even his genuine coins, of gold and silver, had a false content - his wig!

VESPASIAN (A.D. 69-79)
His 'eagle' design as was a popular target for forgers.

TITUS (A.D. 79-81)
THE IVDAEA NAVALIS FANTASY bronze as of Titus[TA] was probably faked shortly before or during 1836, the year of its supposed discovery at Pont-sur-Yonne, near Sens, France. The obverse inscription is TCAESIMPAVG-FTRPCOSVICENSOR, with IVDAEA NAVALIS SC on the reverse, which shows a figure seated under a palm tree, with his back to the 'spoils of war'. A genuine piece may have had the word CAPTA tooled into NAVALIS.

TRAJAN (A.D. 98-117)
The restored coins of Trajan, thought to have been issued c.107 A.D., may all be false. Designs are nearly all of Republican coins, plus Pompey and Octavian/Augustus. The reverse legend is IMP. CAES. TRAIAN. AVG. GER. DAC. P. P. REST. On the assumption that these coins are genuine, and that they seem to celebrate the past of Rome, Trajan has been considered the trailblazer in using numismatics as an aid to history.

A Restitutio silver denarius of Trajan in the Republican style, struck by Carl Becker, a notorious, early nineteenth century forger. 20.5 mm.

A superb contemporary plated imitation of a silver denarius of Claudius. This rare reverse shows a spear-carrying Roman soldier standing on top of a battlemented wall. On this is the legend IMPER RECEPT (Imperatore Recepto), a reference to the Praetorian Guard, who made Claudius emperor. The structure represents a Praetorian camp. 19 mm.

SECOND CENTURY A.D.

The debasement of silver coinage in the second century meant there was much less return for the same effort of counterfeiting, which probably accounts for the decrease in plated coinage. There is an opinion that an official casting mint existed in Britain in Hadrian's time. A group of cast copies of Nero to Hadrian types was found at Sulis Minerva, Bath; date of manufacture estimated as c.A.D. 122.

Hadrian (A.D. 117-138) denarius. Laureate head right, HADRIANVS AVGVSTVS COS 111, Victory standing right, holding palm. This is probably contemporary with its barbarous style reverse linked to a good obverse, perhaps struck with a stolen die. RSCV 358b. 17.5 mm.

COIN PRODUCTION
'Hubbing' may have been used at this time, particularly the die-producing technique whereby a master-punch produces a basic face that can then be worked into a final portrait. Evidence for this is in the way different portraits match each other in size and detail.

HADRIAN (A.D. 117-138)
Plated denarii, including hybrids, occur. Some are clearly barbarous. Also cast denarii and asses. Cavino the Paduan created a Hadrian sestertius in the sixteenth century. *(see Chapter 13)*

ANTONINUS PIUS (A.D. 138-161)
There was a plentiful supply of coin from Antoninus Pius's time, with Rome his only regular mint. Barbarous imitations occur which may be the output of irregular provincial mints.

In Britain, sestertii were fairly plentiful, with dupondii and asses in short supply. By his time, through to the Severan era, cast aes copies were widespread. Strange, slightly barbarous aes showing a crying Britannia, seated on rocks with a hand against her face, have been found in some numbers. They could be either forgeries or the poor efforts of a semi-official travelling mint, possibly commemorating the building of the Antonine Wall.

An extremely rare barbarous copy of a sestertius of Marcus Aurelius, A.D. 161-180. The reverse shows Salus seated left, COS III. 30 mm.

Cast denarii have been found at many British sites. Plated denarii exist for all but the most obscure of the second century emperors and their wives. Marcus Aurelius's wife, Faustina Junior, was a popular target *(see page 30)*. Cavino found a gap and produced a 'sestertius' depicting Antinous, Hadrian's favourite playboy!

SEPTIMIUS SEVERUS (A.D. 193-211)
Severan issues of A.D. 193 were better than later issues, and were more counterfeited. Old denarii were officially over-struck in this reign. A rare base gilt counterfeit is known of a Severus aureus.

Forgers' coin moulds have been found in Britain and on the Continent. Most are of Severan denarii, sometimes made by pressing worn denarii into the moulds. He had his silver coinage debased to just over half silver content and A.D. 198 saw a wave of base imitations of this debasing denarius, plus cast senatorial aes copies.

Faustina Junior silver-plated denarius. Reverse shows VENVS standing left holding an apple and rudder around which a dolphin is entwined (RCV. 1484). This thick plated example on a slightly oval flan, has its plating intact. Some blunderings of legend, but it was well struck on an even flan with good surfaces, and has bold detail and a skilful portrait. Wgt 3.36 gm. 18 mm.

Faustina Junior silver-plated denarius. Reverse - FECVNDITAS, standing right holding sceptre and child (RCV. 1495). Thickly plated example with the plating still intact. Well struck on an even flan with good surfaces. Portrait of good style, with just some blundering of legends. Wgt 3.20 gm. 18.5 mm.

Faustina Junior denarius. Silver-plated on copper alloy. Sound, thick plating. Obverse of good style; reverse PVDICITIA, standing left, altar at feet (RCV. 1483). Bold and clear detail, with a pleasant portrait, but some blundering on the reverse legends. 18.5 mm.

They fade out with Gordian III (238). They are mostly identifiable by their very light weight and sharp edges.

JULIA DOMNA
Counterfeiting evidence found in the settlement adjacent to Housesteads Roman Fort includes a Julia Domna coin mould found outside what seems to have been a coiner's den. Another mould was found at a different part of the site. Genuine denarii of Julia Domna, Septimius Severus's wife, minted at Laodicea. often seem to have a 'filmy' surface suggesting that part of the issue may have been cast.

Galley copies exhibit considerable weight fluctuation and irregular legends.

CARACALLA (A.D.198-217)
Counterfeit denarii are common, mostly plated, but with some cast base metal pieces.

This is one of three hybrid plated silver on copper alloy denarii of Caracalla (A.D. 198-217), that were all found in Wessex. ANTONINVS AVGVSTVS /PRINC. IVVENTVTIS. Prince standing holding branch and sceptre with trophies (standards) behind. Its hybrid reverse is of Geta. RIC 38A. RSCV. 502a. The plating is still intact, and it has a good portrait, but the legends are of barbarous style. Another hybrid of unknown provenance, combines Caracalla (ANTONINVS PIVS AVG) with Septimius Severus (PART. MAX.P.M. TR.P.X.) These Severan dynasty hybrids appear to be peculiar to Britain. They may be the product of a semi-official mint travelling with the Severan party whilst on their British campaign. 17.5 mm.

COUNTERFEITS CAN TALK

Several books have been written to illustrate the wide range of information that can be derived from coins. Contemporary counterfeits offer most of the same advantages, with similar limitations. Just as a coin cannot exist before its known date, nor can its copy, so the copy also has dating value when found stratified. Counterfeit coins can also be sources of information not obtainable from genuine ones. For instance, the existence of many coins is known only from forged copies, no originals ever having been found. The historical fact of the third century Roman, Sponsianus is known solely from one gold barbarous coin.

THIRD CENTURY A.D.

In this century, denarii were extensively counterfeited. They were base looking, light, hybrid, and had eccentric die-axes. Many were made in white metal masquerading as silver. False denarii dies were also used for supposed gold coins. The phenomenon of the bronze coinage in this century was the barbarous radiate, copying the issues of Tetricus I and II, Claudius Gothicus, etc.

LIMESFALSA c.200
Lightweight cast copies of Roman aes, dubbed 'Limesfalsa' by Kubitschek, were thought at one time to be exclusive to Pannonia, but examples have been found at Caerleon and elsewhere in Britain. These seem to have started in Antonine times and are recognisable by being thin, small, consequently underweight and of particularly poor metal. Sharp edges resulting from the removal of sprues are another giveaway sign. One specimen, analysed in the 1960's, was found to have a copper content down to 2/3rds, with over 10% tin and approaching 20% lead, plus a trace of zinc.

Weight reduction was achieved mainly by using thin flans, but also by trimming the originals or the casts. Genuine aes range from 9 to 12 gm; Limesfalsa from 2.2 to 4.25 gm. Boon set half genuine weight as the upper limit for classifying cast copies as Limesfalsa.

Clay moulds were used, employing at least two different production methods:

1. Impress genuine coin between small pads of clay. Pile up the pads in a column and stack two or three columns together. This method necessitated breaking the moulds to extract the coins. It was popular in the Severan era for producing base denarii.

2. Use two large slabs of clay - one for the obverse impressions of original coins, the other for their reverses. The resultant 2-piece mould could be re-used. Boon[BO] illustrates the traces that can sometimes be found on coins made by these methods.

Obverse half of a clay mould for a denarius of Septimius Severus.

Continental Limesfalsa seem to have been more sestertii than asses, whereas Caerleon examples are almost entirely the latter - of Domitian, Trajan, Faustina II and Commodus, and dupondii of Elagabalus and Antoninus Pius. These Caerleon Limesfalsa have a high lead content (c.19%), greyish-green patina and occasional white 'lead' spot flaking.

Possible Limesfalsa from other sites include asses of Hadrian, Mamaea and Geta, Mamaea sestertii and Faustina I and Marcus Aurelius dupondii.

FALSE DENARII

By Caracalla's reign (A.D. 198-217), the silver content of a genuine denarius was barely 40%. Counterfeit denarii, cast in base metal, became common. During the first half of the third century, plated denarii crop up all over the north-west of the Empire. Britain, Central Europe and Egypt saw the spread of cast copies of denarii from c.238.

THE ANTONINIANUS

In 214/5, Caracalla introduced the antoninianus, probably at two times the value of the denarius, despite being only 1.1/2 times the weight. Some antoniniani were overstruck on denarii. The silver content dropped to c.15%. By 220, inflation had set in. Nearly 30 antoniniani were needed for a purchase that would have required just one denarius fifty years' earlier. The antoninianus continued to be debased. To reduce the coppery look of such a low percentage of silver, the coins were pickled - a process of heating and quenching the coins in a bath thought to have been filled with human urine. This effectively removed the oxidised copper from the surfaces of the coin, leaving a deceptive covering of silver.

In Gallienus' time (253-268), the silver in his antoniniani dwindled to just 3%, resulting in a bronze or copper coin with a slight silver wash, the lowest level of debasement possible whilst still providing the appearance of a silver coin. Its size also diminished and its value ratio to gold dropped to 700:1. Not surprisingly, hoarders of the time concentrated their savings into the older denarii. The variability in size and appearance, the later issues being often badly struck, make the separation of regular from irregular difficult. This may account for the apparent scarcity of Gallienus copies found in Britain, apart from some later pieces with animal reverses.

By 270, the silver content of antoniniani was about 1%. Coins from 268 to 274 now look bronze, although they were probably all silver-washed originally.

Unofficially plated antoniniani mark the end of a plating era until the fourth century.

SMALL CHANGE O.K.

No Roman law specifically forbade the forgery of copper until the fourth century, *providing* they were not silvered to pass as antoniniani and were just used as small change.

COUNTERFEITERS' MANUFACTURING METHODS

Casting was the usual method in Britain in the first part of the third century for copying regular coinage. Moulds paired each side of hard-fired clay discs, about a centimetre larger across than the coins. The coin to be copied was impressed on to a disc, and the pair of discs channelled so that when fixed together, molten metal could be poured through an inlet hole and the air driven out through an outlet hole. This produces two sprues (also known as jets or stubs).

COIN MOULDS
Clay moulds have been found bearing designs of Septimius Severus, Caracalla, Geta, Julia Domna, Plautilla and Severus Alexander. Hybrid cast coins also occur, e.g. Julia Domna/Severus, Geta/Elagabalus. Over 300 coin moulds, c.250, for producing cast denarii, were found near Blomfield Street in the City of London (1988). They were made by pressing genuine coins into soft clay which was then baked hard. The casts were bronze with a high tin content to give them a similar look to the half-silver alloy coins they were copying. Another mid-third century Roman London forger, of fake denarii and copper alloy coins, dumped over 700 moulds into the city ditch.

A number of moulds for cast copies of folles of the Tetrarchy have been found. Struck copies superseded these in the following century.

The Eastern issues of Severus Alexander (222-235) were thought by Dr. Pink of Vienna (1935) to have been produced either by some revolutionary party or (less likely) a company of forgers, and not by any official Antioch mint.

MASQUERADE

A Severus Alexander denarius tooled to give it a crown so it could masquerade as an antoninianus, was found in the Mattishall, Norfolk hoard *(NC 1969, 142).*

Issues of Gordian I & II (238), are rare, but both cast and struck forgeries exist. Also, Gordian III coins have been tooled by modern counterfeiters to resemble his predecessors' designs.

There may be no genuine sestertii of Aemilian (252-253). Many types that would be interesting if genuine, turn out on examination to be either hybrids or coins of other reigns, with obverses tooled to look like Aemilian.

Unlike most of his numerous predecessors on the Roman throne in the third century, Valerian (253-260) made serious efforts to combat the forgers of his day.

BARBAROUS RADIATES

BEGINNINGS & ENDINGS
At the end of the second century, a new type of obverse bust appeared, showing the emperor wearing a radiate crown. It became the most popular design of the third century and imitations, because of their generally poor nature, have been dubbed barbarous radiates, abbreviated for convenience to br's. They were produced by unofficial individuals or groups of moneyers at irregular mints around the Roman Empire.

Barbarous Radiates

The skill levels of the engravers of barbarous radiates, range from on a par with mint engravers of the time, down to abysmal. As can be seen, the following illustrations are in descending order of competence. The top right piece compares so well with the genuine antoninianus opposite it, that a moonlighting mintworker is a possibility.

Genuine antoninianus. 17 mm.

Reasonable Claudius II type bust but with an odd legend - CHILIEM. 19 mm.

Tetricus I. Bust and crown appear to have been engraved separately. 14.5 mm.

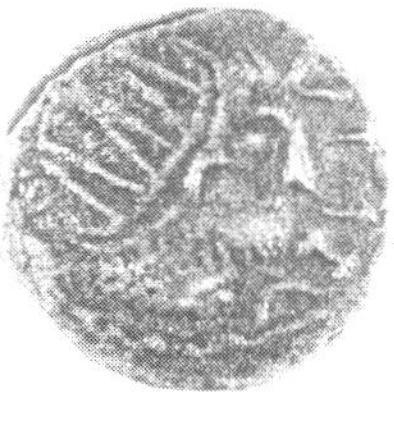

Yet another strange legend - VIII. 15.5 mm.

A skilful forger has produced a bust to rival genuine pieces. 17 mm.

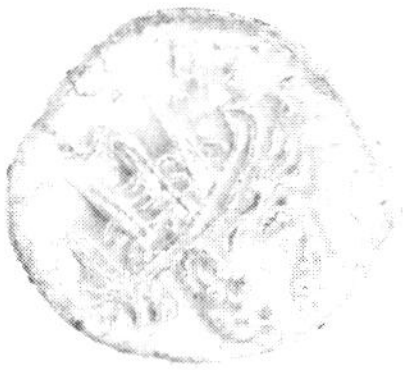

Another odd legend - LYETC. 16 mm.

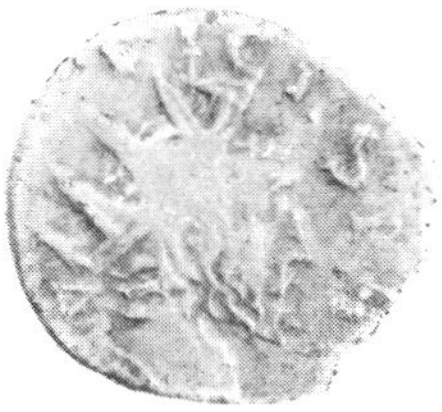

Tetricus. The cruder the design, the larger the crown. 16 mm.

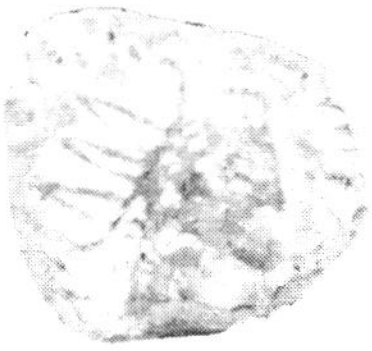

Irregular shaped flan. Childlike attempt at a face. More old Steptoe than Roman Emperor. 14 mm.

reverses

It is noticeable that, whatever the individual skill level, barbarous radiate engravers almost always took more trouble with their obverses than with their reverses.

Reasonable attempt at a reverse figure. 17 mm.

Figure running left. 18 mm.

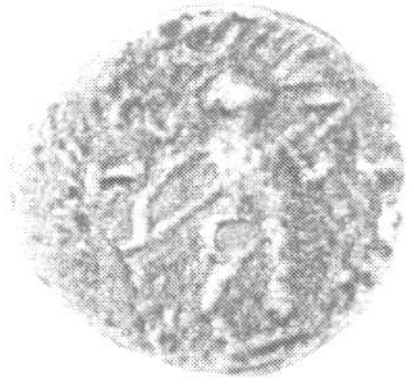

Unconvincing warrior. 16.5 mm.

Crude, standing figure with short legs. 17.5 mm.

Spes type 'Lowry' style figure. Tetricus I. 14 mm.

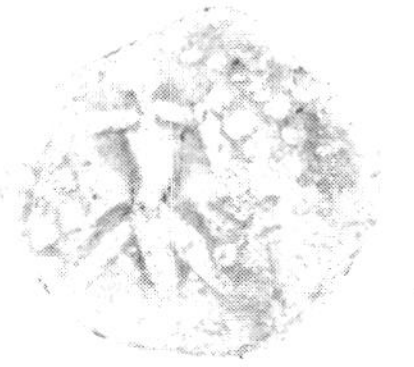

Lead imitation of an antoninianus. The metal used and the crudeness of the figure suggest that this may have been a contemporary toy coin. 15 mm.

HYBRID

Tetricus I/Gallienus imitative antoninianus hybrid. Tetricus I style obverse. Gallienus reverse imitating HIPPOCAMP & NEPTVNO CONS AVG legend. The reverse die was clearly meant for a smaller flan. 20 mm.

flans

The flans of normal radiates vary from round to slightly oval, but barbarous flans have much greater variety, including quite eccentric shapes.

Tetricus I antoninianus inscribed TITIIICVS and struck on an oval flan. 22 x 20 mm.

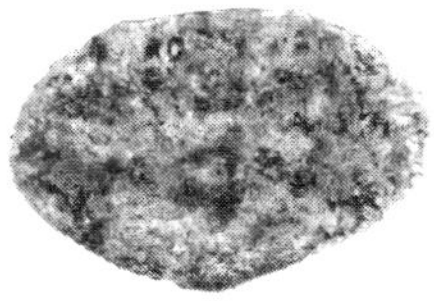

Undersized oval flan. 16 x 12 mm.

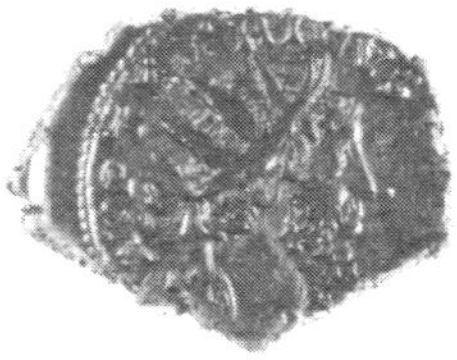

Tetricus I - IMP TETRICVS - on a pentagonal flan. 19 x 15.5 mm.

Br's are believed to have started in Gaul in 263 and in Britain some five or six years' later, spreading also to North Africa, Germany and Spain. Peak production occurred between 268 and 274, tailing off by 280-281. Mattingly puts the end at 282. In his 1988 thesis, Davies[DA] estimates the production period in Britain as being from the late 260's to the late 270's.

Die-links have shown numerous coins from the same dies, turning up in both Britain and Gaul. The cross-Channel movement of these barbarous copies probably eased off as production increased in Britain. Some British products drifted back to Gaul. Gallienus copies are common there. Minims were more a British phenomenon, but were not unknown in Gaul. Most are copies of copies. A time estimate for the occurrence of minims is from 275 to 287.

Some sources and dates of production are known. Cast coin counterfeiting at Whitchurch was going on at roughly the same time as cast counterfeiting elsewhere, probably between 260 and 270.

Br's occur over-struck on regular radiates or other br's - not on later pieces.

These imitations ranged from close facsimiles to extreme barbarity. Die-struck almost completely replaced cast during the barbarous radiate epidemic, probably around the mid 270's. Crudely engraved efforts appeared, often with nonsensical reverse legends. This was not surprising as to make a profit out of such poor originals, the forgers turned out really dire products. When these in turn were used as models by other forgers, the decline led to 6 mm diameter scraps. Although not unknown in France, these small pieces, dubbed minims, were more a British phenomenon. Usually minims of 13 mm to 6 mm diameter have simplified and/or stylised designs. How could anyone have been fooled by these abysmal efforts? The only logical answer is that no one was and they were accepted as necessary evils. It is not always correct to assume that the baser the copy, the later it was made.

Eventually, there were more barbarous than genuine coins in circulation. In particular, the common reverses for Tetrici and Claudius II Consecratio issues were subject to widespread copying in Britain and Western Europe. Some pieces are overstrikes on coins of Tetricus and Gallienus. The styles range from better than genuine pieces, to awful. A poorly executed radiate crown gives away many of these. Partially underweight coins are considered by Weder**WE** to have emanated from moonlighting Roman mint workers through a twenty- year period from 270. In a review of Göbl's book, (*NC 154*, pp. 243-66) Markus Weder says he has "noted that many of the smaller illegal coins of the mint of Rome have their edges carefully filed". This filing produces a rounder coin than the genuine ones; later clandestine Rome mint emanations showed heads closer to Aurelian types than Claudius II. An example is known of a piece bearing a Probus reverse**WE**. Inappropriate marks occur, e.g. XXI. One puzzling antoninianus, with a Neptune reverse, is in base silver equal to Claudius's better legitimate issues.

Counterfeiting subsided when Carausius assumed power in 287. There then seems to have been a lull during Constantine I's reign, followed by a resurgence of counterfeiting with the appearance of 'diademed' copies and minimissimi around the end of the fourth century. Minimissimi went down to 4 mm diameter. There is no evidence that the barbarous radiate (third century) and FTR (fourth century) epidemics overlapped.

CAUSE OF THE EPIDEMIC

There are differing views on the reason for the br epidemic. One explanation is that there was a coin shortage and a metal shortage, leading to shrinking coin sizes and a debasement of the coinage, so more were needed for everyday transactions, resulting in widespread forging when official supplies could not keep up. By 270, 28 coins were needed to make what in 215, would have been just a single coin purchase. Against this, Boon says there could never have been a shortage of 'orthodox' radiates and another explanation must therefore be found for the epidemic. It might be because of a need for small change denominations below the lowest-value official coins. But Boon's view is that all radiate units had the same value as the regular antoniniani regardless of size. Perhaps they were locally made in defiance of the centrally imposed government coins. Blanchet (1940) thought that they were struck at unofficial, but not secret or counterfeit mints. There appears to have been some toleration of them by the authorities.

A 9.5 mm diameter minim with casting sprue.

Base-metal cast antoniniani radiates produced by Claudius II (268-270) and Tetricus I & II (270-273) were imitated in large numbers by unofficial mints in both Gaul and Britain and turn up frequently in British hoards of the period. A Divo Claudius example is known of an

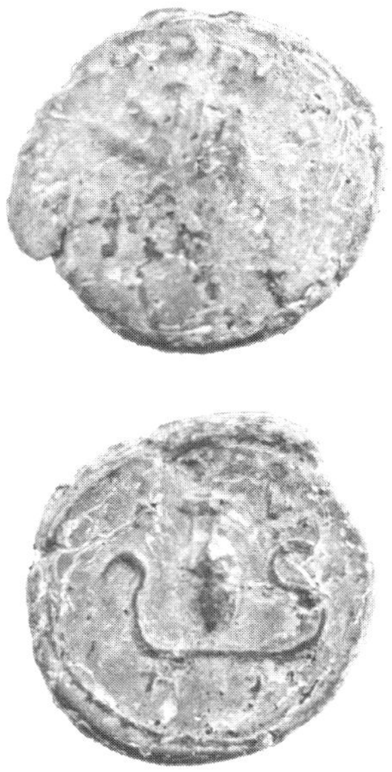

Counterfeit mule of Victorinus and Tetricus I or II. Radiate bust right of Victorinus ///TORINVS ////; reverse - Tetricus II implements type with jug. 16 mm.

official obverse die being used with a poorly made false reverse die. Divo Claudio irregulars tend to have a high lead content.

Cast copies of Victorinus (268-270) and the Tetrici are rare. Some, said to be linked to the earlier, Severan tradition of counterfeiting, have emanated from Whitchurch. The number of more or less barbarous coins of Victorinus is small compared with the Tetrici, but is evidence of irregular mints using his name during or after his lifetime.

From the mid 260's, low levels of 'small change' were issued so imitations proliferated in Aurelian's time, particularly base-metal cast antoniniani.

Probus (276-282) was the last 'radiate' emperor to be barbarously copied. His repressive measures to eradicate free enterprise minting were, no doubt, the reason for the clearly observable rise in hoard burying at this time.

British sites do not seem to have produced any br's imitating any originals later than Probus. The subsequent Carausian copies are different and never diminish in size in the way that the radiate copies do.

QUALITY OF COPIES

Degeneration of design is revealed by the copyists misunderstanding the copies *they* are copying. Such is the variety thus produced that some br designs seem to resemble coins of following centuries. This is now regarded as purely co-incidental and the consensus of opinion is that br's are a phenomenon solely of the late 3rd century.

UNOFFICIAL MINTS

As early as 1949, Philip Hill was saying that there was considerable evidence for unofficial mints, including die-identities and mintmarks. There was not an official mint in Britain until Carausius.

Analysis of forgeries in third century hoards has revealed pieces with a unity of fabric and technique pointing to a possible production centre at Caistor St. Edmund, Norfolk.

According to M. Blanchet (Rev. Num. 1940, pp. 79-80), regionally located Continental 'design schools' have been observed. Original barbarous coin workshops have been found at Autun and Eprave. All this points to systematic approaches to imitation manufacture, and not entirely the assumed individual, ad hoc production suggested by

A MINER OFFENCE

Counterfeiting material was found around a hearth deep in the Roman lead-silver mine at Draethen; two antoniniani (Claudius II and Tetricus I), two hammered and cut coin fragments, four blank flans, cast rod sections and a number of small metal pieces.

the poor end products. Remarkably, with so many types to choose from, there are invented reverse types. Hoards have shown that the forgers produced their copies soon after the issue of the genuine coins.

There are considered to have been just two official mints in Roman Britain, both under Carausius (287-293) - L (Londinium) and C (possibly Camulodunum). Sometimes the same die would be used for striking copper and gold.

Coins which bear no reverse legend, or badly blundered ones, or legends made up of mere circles must be considered the products of irregular mints. They are minor compared to the irregular issues of Gaul. Carausius was not widely imitated. Technically competent but clearly barbarous copies exist of the later Carausian coins on large flans. Imitations tended to have a recognisable face. They never dwindled to minim size.

Forgery, generally, seems to have faded out by 290. Copies of Allectus coins (293-296) are comparatively rare. There are certainly fewer barbarous copies than with Carausius.

GHOSTS OF THE PAST

Silver imitations, inscribed GLORIA ROMANORVM, that are probably at least two hundred years' old, represent the only evidence for the existence of a gold solidus multiple of the late Fourth Century emperor Arcadius.

FOURTH CENTURY A.D.

From the introduction of the plated, silver-bronze follis of Diocletian (294), there was a surge of cast counterfeiting. The British Museum has moulds for coins of Diocletian, Constantius I and Galerius. Early counterfeit folles, also known as laureates, were cast. These 'laureate' moulds are much commoner in Egypt than in Britain or Gaul. The eastern mints were producing increasingly illiterate and incomprehensible pieces, thereby encouraging counterfeiting, which was considerable. Many of these eastern fourth century forgeries were made from casts of genuine coins, and so were undersized. Often the channel sprues are still visible.

The appearance of siliquae in the early fourth century prompted 'traditional' plated copies, plus low grade silver and lightweight counterfeits. Clipped false siliquae are known. There is evidence to suggest that cast counterfeiting of denarii and antoniniani was occurring at the same time as struck fourth century laureate copies.

THE CONSTANTINIAN ERA

For some years into Constantine I's reign (307-337), forgeries were uncommon. They began to increase from 318 to 330, stimulated by the introduction of the centenionalis to replace the follis, starting with the VICTORIAE LAETAE PRINC PERP types. Whenever unfamiliar coins were issued, forgers seized the opportunity to foist copies on the public. On this occasion, both struck and cast copies appeared. By the 320's, struck counterfeits were replacing cast.

The struck counterfeits of this period fall into two distinct groups:

1. Quite well engraved albeit slightly coarsely, and clearly under weight.
2. Poorly engraved, of low weight and carelessly produced.

VRBS ROMA, CONSTANTINOPOLIS and GLORIA EXERCITVS were popular choices with contemporary forgers. GLORIA EXERCITVS and two soldiers holding standards became an extremely common coin throughout Europe, and was copied in quantity. There is a modern Beirut forgery of it, so good that only seeing a batch of identical pieces convinced an experienced dealer that they were not genuine. There were fewer contemporary copies of the single standard type.

Examples are known of Fallen Horseman copies overstruck on every regular Constantinian Ae 3/4 from 330 to the mid 350's, but not on later types such as SPES REIPVBLICE (c.358-361), so the copies were clearly contemporary with their prototypes.

Many irregular coins occur during this long reign. Coins are suspect where STR mintmarks appear as just ST. An intaglio image, laureate

DEN OF INIQUITY

A Roman counterfeiter's den was found at White Woman's Hole, an isolated cave located in Asham Wood near Leighton in the Mendip Hills of Somerset.

An archaeological excavation revealed counterfeit material for Romano-British coins of the Constantine period. It comprised around 200 coins, together with flans, coin fragments, bronze droplets and cast rod sections. It was a deep cave, but the counterfeiting material was found in the daylit part near the entrance. There is no evidence to say whether it was a hiding-place.

bust Ae4 in cast lead, made by pressing a real coin directly into the disc, may have been made as a toy or novelty for a Romano-British child.

The Argenteus is a rare coin, infrequently copied.

The twentieth century Geneva Forgeries include numerous pieces imitating the coins of Martinian (324) to fool collectors *(see Chapter 13)*.

In the 330's, apart from low or no supplies of coinage, the supply of only high values also led to aes being counterfeited. Minims began re-appearing. Flans were sliced off small, cast cylindrical rods - a production method started in the third century, but mainly used in the fourth century. The flans were usually smaller than the dies.

BARBAROUS
These barbarous coins of the late Roman period are considerably enlarged to show the crudeness of the portraits.

AFTER CONSTANTINE
From Constantius II (337-361) to 367, false gold coin was a problem. There were many FTR/FH copies in this period. Most imitating after Constantine, in the period 337 to 364, occurred in Britain and Northern Gaul, perhaps because these particular provinces were poorly supplied with official coinage.

Coins inscribed FEL.TEMP.REPARATIO (FTR), meaning the return of better times, appeared c.348 to commemorate the 1,100th anniversary of Rome. They were around to 357/8 and were widely distributed in Britain as were their copies, which reached epidemic proportions. On more than half the excavated Romano-British sites, there are as many and often more copies than genuine FTR's.

A popular design to be copied from the FTR series is that showing Victory guiding a galley carrying the emperor, often found cast or die-struck. But, topping the huge output of barbarous coins in the fourth century, are those pieces copying Constantius II's silver-bronze half-centenionalis - FTR - with the 'soldier spearing fallen horseman' design - FH. This may be because the copyists considered that the image represented locals killing a Roman horseman, although it was probably intended to represent a Roman soldier spearing a Persian horseman. Copies are so prolific that studies have been possible revealing correlations between them and original design variants. These show that some have been swamped with copies whereas with at least one type, there is so far, no known copy.

The fallen horseman's attitude and appearance are the main variants: he can be seated by his horse; clutching its neck; lying along its back - with Phrygian cap, diademed or bare-headed - with or without beard. There are also shield variants. If the horseman has his hand extended behind him, it is copying a Gallic mint type (reduced weight coinage - 353-354), rather than the earlier type. Copies range from good to abysmal.

FTR copies were produced not long after the introduction of the official coins, proliferating after the regular size reduction of 353.

MOST BARBAROUS
Late Roman minimissimi – and we think 5p's are too small.

In the late 1970's, Kent[KE] noted that the Brean Down excavations had shown clearly that even the smallest of the late Roman imitations were contemporary with their c.354-358 FTR prototypes.

The degeneration to tiny counterfeits went even farther than the barbarous radiates, which did not fall below 6 mm diameter. Minimissimi appeared in the fourth century, with weights dropping to 0.3 gm, and sizes down to 4 mm dia. In the most extreme examples, the amount of metal in one genuine coin, 2.5 gm, could be used to produce up to eight of these minuscule copies. Despite their minute size, there were still scraps of design struck on to them, suggesting strongly that they were passing as units of currency.

They were made by cutting from drawn-out rods, which provided roundness, but often had a weak centre resulting from the drawing out process. Sections of cast bronze rod were found at White Woman's Hole. Cast rod was also found, together with minim blanks, at Draethen, South Glamorgan.

METAL CONTENT
Trier mint coins of the period 348-350 can contain more than a quarter of their weight in lead, to the extent that patches are sometimes visible on the coin surface. FTR originals have some silver content, unlike their copies. FH design types may have been well-plated, as a silver copy is known.

East End[HI] and Ickham finds suggest that there may have been a counterfeit production centre in east Kent.

Lyndey Park, Glos. produced a barbarous FTR mint-marked COL, which may have come from an unofficial mint-site at nearby Glevum where there was a Colonia. From Maiden Castle in Dorset, a similar coin was found with the mintmark PLN which would mean a London origin, but the official London mint had closed down over twenty years before this design appeared, This is strong evidence for an unofficial mint in London. At least one other PLN barbarous Fel Temp has been found.

The prolific FTR-FH copies are rarely die-linked, pointing to an enormous production. Hoards show that most copies were being produced soon after the issue of their prototypes.

OVERSTRIKING

Initially, both genuine and counterfeit overstrikes occurred. Overstriking in quantity is an almost exclusively British phenomenon (354 - c.358), with just some occurring in North and East Gaul.

Around 355, pre-348 coins falsely overstruck mingled with the usual struck forgeries. They were particularly on Constantinian coins such as the Ae3 two soldiers and standard, to change them to FTR/FH designs. Some undertypes include early FTR designs. The Heslington hoard has 296 overstruck on official coins and just one on another imitation. At White Woman's Hole, radiates were being converted into 4th century copies.

Some 15 coins of the 350's all from Britain have been found so far for a mysterious ruler, CARAUSIUS II (354-358?). This may be just a fanciful forger's poetic licence. Die-linking ties most of them together, strongly suggesting an individual source.

A Constantius II FTR derivative. A crude laureate bust is backed by a naive attempt at the fallen horseman type. 16.5 mm.

Laureate copper alloy minim. Bust right. Reverse - soldier spearing fallen horseman. 12.5 mm.

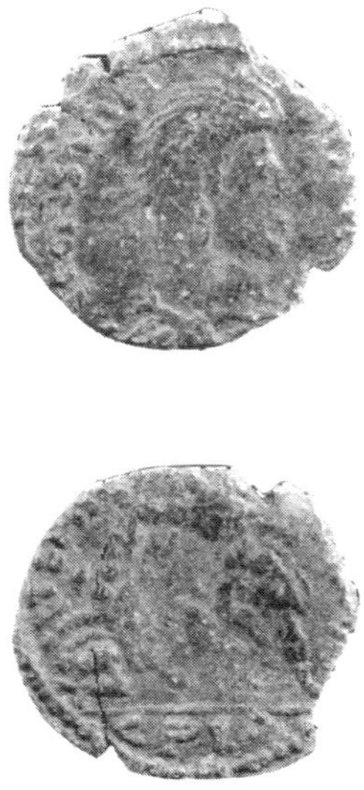

Constantius II. Fallen horseman derivative minim. Classic type. 13.5 mm.

In the second half of the fourth century (c.358), forgers turned to the siliquae as being more profitable to copy than bronze coinage. A large number of irregular reduced siliquae, often base or plated, occurred during the reign of Julian II (360-363).

Counterfeits of Valentinian I (364-375) and Valens (364-378) only occasionally appear. There are slightly more of the small bronze Theodosius I (379-395) pieces. A few may have drifted in to Britain from the Continent. From Gratian's time (367-), cast and struck copies of the common ae2 Reparatio Reipub design showing the Emperor raising a kneeling woman, and holding Victory on a globe, were fairly common on the Continent, but not in Britain. Heavyweight cast examples strongly suggest that the official coins were overvalued for their metal content. By Valentinian II and Theodosian's reigns, at the end of the fourth century, the attempts to pass off the official coins as silver ceased, and they became a standard bronze coinage which was rarely, if ever copied. Some late-fourth century gold coins were imitated in gold-plated copper.

There is a die, made by Karl Becker, a notorious nineteenth century counterfeiter, for a solidus, used by him for Arcadius (395-408), Constantius III (421) and Johannes (423-425), which were, as one numismatist said, "unlikely subjects for forgery" *(see Chapter 13).*

The Arcadian type CONCORDIA AVG (GG) was liberally imitated. Many lightweight and degraded style silver coins arose during Honorius's reign (393-423). Roman coins were imitated in Germany in the Roman period when official issues were scarce.

Coin forgery was by this time endemic in Africa, Egypt and Dalmatia to fill local demand.

FIFTH CENTURY A.D.

It is now generally accepted that, following the departure of the Romans from Britain in 410, the use of coinage in Britain had ceased by c.420. The idea, once widely held, that barbarous copies of Roman coins were produced in the fifth and sixth centuries is now considered erroneous. The current, more substantiated view, is that they were all produced initially, very soon after the introduction of the originals that they were imitating, continuing in some cases until after the originals had been superseded, but with nothing like the longevity previously attributed to them.

Britons returned to barter, and for some time, there was no point in ciunterfeiting coins. It is likely that, when coinage once more appeared, Roman coins were the main prototypes, as Saxon sceattas bear a noticeable resemblance to some late minims.

On the continent, Roman coin production continued.

Rare barbarous style silver siliqua of Julian II. Diadem bust right. The reverse shows VOTIS V MVLTIS X in wreath with an LVG (retrograde) mint mark. An oddity, appearing to be struck in good quality silver and to be of full weight. Portrait and legends are passable but are undoubtedly barbarous. 16.5 mm.

Julian and Jovian coins are known to have been tooled into Jovinus. (411-413). Modern copies also exist, plus fantasy pieces.

There are quantities of contemporary and ancient imitations of THEODOSIUS II's (402-450) gold coinage, some combining earlier obverses with later reverses. Modern forgeries also exist. So far, all genuine examples have officina numbers, so absence of a number is suspicious. A Theodosian coin tooled into a Majorian is known. There are some modern forgeries of the light miliarenses. Ulrich-Bansa quotes what he considers a Cigoi forgery of a rare Ae4 SPES ROMANORVM of Eugenius in Theodosius II's name (393-394 - Roma), to be found struck in silver and also in bronze. Johannes (423-425) Rome bronzes were frequently poorly struck and a nineteenth century Cigoi copy of a SALVS ROMANORVM type clearly got its wrong mintmark TR (not TRM) from a worn original *(see Chapter 13)*.

Fraudulent Roman weights were a problem for Marcian (450-457) and others.

5

The Anglo-Saxon Lull

Early Anglo-Saxon Period

c. 630-c. 775

The later Fifth to the early Seventh Century in Britain saw virtually no coinage circulating as currency. English coins restarted around the 630's and the first coins of this period, gold thrymsas, followed the styles of continental coins or obsolete Roman coinage, one example being a gold imitation of a Helena bronze. During this century, gold coins debased until the coinage had devolved into silver, silver sceattas appearing around 650. Their designs initially were poor imitations of old Roman types, but they developed into a new style that was, in its turn, copied in the Low Countries. It is considered probable that sceat mules and variants are contemporary forgeries. In the late 700's, the silver sceattas were debased until they became just brass or copper. Up to Offa (757-796) almost all inscriptions were letter jumbles copied from Continental coins.

Contemporary Anglo-Saxon plated forgeries occur, but are not in the quantities that start from the thirteenth century. It is difficult to separate the official coinage from contemporary imitations for this period. Those struck from counterfeit dies are more deceptive than modern forgeries. They are amongst the rarest of all contemporary counterfeits. Presumably Æthelred II's draconian laws against the practice indicate that it did go on, but little evidence remains. The threat of death or hand lopping would certainly deter many, but not all.

The Kentish rulers successfully excluded continental copies from their kingdom, unlike less advanced parts of Britain. In his analysis of the general type of B111 sceat, c.725, Metcalf[ME] points to the odd fact that most of the surviving specimens are copies. Many of these are thought to have emanated from Frisia. Eighth century England and Frisia freely copied each other's coin designs. Coins of Pepin were forged in Frisia, almost certainly after Charlemagne came to the throne, so Metcalf considers that these British sceattas may also have been copied after their official counterparts had been superseded by Type 37.

Significant collector forging of Anglo-Saxon coins started in the 17th century, and took off from the mid-18th, continuing into the 19th. At the start of the 20th century, they were being made in silver, to match the originals. Nearly all modern Anglo-Saxon forgeries are in silver. They are rarely of sceattas. Popular targets have been Offa, Cynethryth and Coenwulf. The cast efforts are fairly easily spotted, being generally of variable quality, often with giveaway stylistic differences. Anglo-Norman coins were sometimes used as flans.

SCEATTAS

Although called sceattas, they were pennies. Due to their range of silver content, some so base as to be virtually copper, it is difficult to pass firm judgement on dubious copies. There may have been instances of semi-official local production.

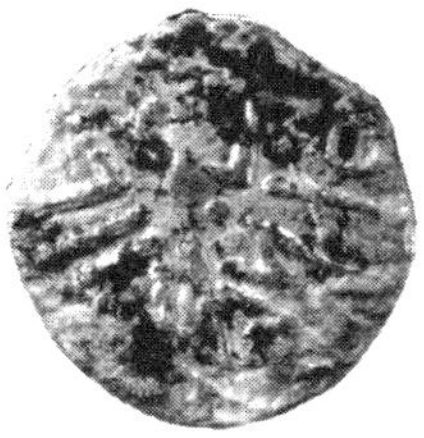

Rare sceat mule from the early Anglo-Saxon period (c.600-775). Series R/Type 51. Plated base metal contemporary copy. Radiate bust right, runes in front/Saltire standard, pellets in angles. 12 mm.

Modern fakes are cast or struck. Some are silver-plated on a lead core. The cast efforts are mostly overweight and are often revealed by tests to be made from Rose's metal. This combination of lead, tin and antimony or bismuth was popular with forgers because it has a melting point lower than that of boiling water. It provides thereby an unusual test that is destructive if the piece is a Rose's metal fake, but non-destructive if not - boil it in a saucepan!

A 1905 report speaks of lead and cast forgeries. Despite the different weights of genuine examples, mid nineteenth century cast forgeries still usually show up as being far too heavy. One forger of that time produced a number of dangerous copies of Anglo-Saxon coins[BLU]. By the start of the twentieth century, Anglo-Saxon forgeries made in silver, to match the originals, had become the biggest problem for collectors. Coins of Northumbria seem to have attracted their own band of forgers.

THE BOLTON PERRY HOARD

The Bolton Perry Hoard of 1967, comprising ninth century Northumbrian coins, included 397 derivative regal out of a total of 1,775. They imitate or stem from the coins of the Northumbrian kings Eanred, Æthelred, Redwulf and Osberht. Nearly all fall in the third period of the hoard, outnumbering the genuine coins in that period. Those few in the first two periods can be accounted for as mint errors and contemporary forgeries that would normally be expected of an Anglo-Saxon coin issue. Something different was happening with the third group with its garbled legends and inferior workmanship, irregularities in inscription and type, and die-links. Irregular flan and reduced weight coins increase towards the end of the series. These may be private products filling an official gap.

The hoard also included two continental imitations - an Edward I penny, with style, metal and weight all wrong, possibly by Gui de Dampierre, Count of Flanders, or from the Flanders region. The other is a version of a standard Meraude sterling of John the Blind (1309-1346).

STYCA
Lead forgeries of Styca exist which are reputed to be of 1860 London manufacture. The FitzWilliam museum has casts that have been made from genuine coins of Æthelred II (841-4) and Eanbald II of York (796-808).

In the late seventh and early eighth centuries, there was a Frankish practice of edge-cutting Merovingian Deniers, presumably to test for plating. This is rarely found on English provenanced coins. Perhaps the English of the time were more trusting.

(left) genuine mid 7th century Anglo-Saxon gold thrymsa. 10 x 11 mm. (right) modern fake, exposed by too high gold content. 11 mm.

THE HEWORTH 'HOARD' HOAX

In 1812, a hoard of coins bearing the name Ecgfrith was reputedly dug up in Heworth, Jarrow, Northumberland. Of the 23 coins said to have been found, four only seem to have survived. These were struck from one pair of dies. X-ray fluorescent examination of the coins' surfaces shows the metal to match that of George III halfpennies. Ecgfrith, other wise unknown, stands revealed to all except the most pedantic as a nineteenth century hoax.

MIDDLE ANGLO-SAXON PERIOD

c. 780-973

The first Anglo-Saxon pennies (c.780-800) were copies of the denarii of the Franks. In the early Ninth Century, the designs of Continental coins continued to appear on English coins. For example, the ship-type penny of Æthelstan I of East Anglia (c.825-40) is a close copy of a Louis the Pious denier that is itself derived from an Allectus issue. Offa's coins were imitative (one famous coin copying an Arabic original) and were in their turn imitated on the Continent. An East Anglian coin of this time is clearly copied from the famous Roman wolf and twins design.

From at least Æthelstan I's time, the circulation of foreign coin was forbidden. Exceptions that were allowed from time to time, and given official sterling equivalents, promoted the widespread use of coin balances and weights.

Offa, King of Mercia (757-796), restored the quality of coinage to 95%+ silver content, with his silver penny that remained *the* coin in Britain for the next five hundred years. The voided cross design that evolved along the way facilitated cutting pennies into halves and quarters to provide small change. This cutting habit extended to clipping off bits of silver to resell as bullion or reuse for counterfeiting coins, despite the severe penalties. The silver penny settled to a weight of 24 grains.

Around the start of his reign, there was considerable contemporary forging of his silver coinage. Offa fakes are deceptive, more so than other Anglo Saxon forgeries. In the 1950's, a modern counterfeit of an Offa penny appeared, bearing a runic reverse legend.

In Alfred, King of Wessex's time (871-899), there was much official debasement of the silver coinage. Silver content could range from 29% right down to 11%, making the occasional counterfeit difficult to spot. One of the reverses on an Alfred coin, c.886-892, is copied from a Roman original. Alfred's London monogram penny, probably issued around 880 rather than 886, was imitated by the Vikings. These imitations of his coins reveal themselves by their illiteracy, light weight and anomalous style.

Imitation Alfred coins were hand-struck in white metal on the Royal Mint's stand at the 1924 British Empire Exhibition, Wembley, and sold well for 6d each. Specially engraved dies were used that closely copied Alfred's London monogram type; so much so that, despite coin catalogue warnings, Museums are still asked if they are genuine.

Imitation Alfred penny, struck at the British Empire Exhibition, Wembley, 1924.

Coins of Edward and Æthelstan were the most counterfeited in this period.

Unearthed in Norfolk, a group of struck contemporary counterfeit silver pennies of Edward the Elder (899-924) had a fineness of metal directly comparable to the prototypes, suggesting strongly that these were the main metal source. They were necessarily of low weight in order to make a profit. The blundered legends and poor style confirm their counterfeit status. Research by Norwich Castle Museum has revealed that coins from the same dies had been found in Rome.

A number of coins of Æthelstan (924-939) occur with blundered legends. Some of these are contemporary forgeries.

Eadred (946-955) ordered that after his demise, gold mancuses should be struck. None has ever been found; nor has any forger yet 'created' one.

A modern die-struck copy in pewter of a penny of Eadwig, King of Wessex (955-959); moneyer Oswald. 1.5 gm. A product of Trevor Ashmore who has been a prolific creator of unmarked ancient coin copies. 21 mm.

THE VIKINGS

c. 885-954

The Hiberno-Norse coinage appears to have been unsophisticated, seemingly aiming only to reach a standard sufficient to make the coins acceptable at home and abroad when compared to Anglo-Saxon prototypes. Weights kept reasonably close to the prototypes without achieving their precision. One or two examples suggest that the silver content probably maintained a 94%+ level, as did the Anglo-Saxon pennies. The style of these Viking imitations varies tremendously from close to gross.

Pecking on Viking imitations indicates that this coin testing method was being used in Britain in the late 9th century.

A poor lead copy of a St. Peter coin (c.919-925), one of the English coins of the Hiberno-Norse Vikings. 24 mm.

LATE ANGLO-SAXON PERIOD

959-1066

Comparatively few late Anglo-Saxon and early Norman contemporary counterfeits are now known, although they must have been around at the time, as St. Dunstan, the tenth century Archbishop of Canterbury (and patron saint of the author's old school), would not start Mass until the latest batch of dishonest moneyers had been hanged.

In this and the following century, continental coins were not allowed to circulate in England. Mints converted them into English coins.

Imitations were widespread, particularly in Ireland, the Continent and Scandinavia, where Vikings brought back and re-used English coin dies[JE]. Sweden's first known coinage (c. 994-c.1022) copied

Replica penny of Cnut, 1016-1035. No replica marks! Wgt 1.11 gm. 17 mm.

Anglo-Saxon issues of Æthelred II[BLA]. The 1924 Igelosa Hoard from Skane in Sweden included Scandinavian copies of Dublin imitations of Æthelred II's English long-cross pennies.

A penny of Cnut (1016-1035) (Brooke 3) from an altered reverse die (Wynsige, London?), of very light weight and unusual fabric, may be one of the few surviving examples of a contemporary Anglo-Saxon plated forgery.

The Hunterian Collection had (now missing), a false coin[SC] of Harold I (1035-1040) with the legend 'WATHLOS ON LINIC'.

LEAD STRIKINGS

Lead impressions from official mint dies are known for Edward the Confessor's Helmet type and William II's last coin type[ST]. Trial-pieces, customs tallies or weights?

6

Post-Conquest problems from the Continent

The extreme penalties of the times, brought in by William I (1066-1087) - swingeing fines and brutal mutilation - could be a factor in the comparative rarity of contemporary forgeries. A general lack of skill to produce plausible results may also have contributed. At the start of the twentieth century, very few were known, but a number have since come to light, to which must now be added a rash of modern copies, particularly by Edward Emery *(see Chapter 13)*.

In the reign of Henry I (1100-1135), control of the mint weakened and forgeries became a constant problem, despite attempts to curb them. The public took to cutting pennies to ensure that they were not plated counterfeits. Also many refused to accept these damaged coins. This became such a problem that 'ready-cut' coins were issued, (c.1107-1108) forcing the public to accept all such. This lasted until 1127-1128.

Some sixteen years' later, poor coinage still abounded and mintworkers were adjudged to be the perpetrators, leading to them being called to Winchester, where many were deprived of a hand and a testicle. Modern evidence suggests that they were innocent, taking the blame for forgers' products.

The coinage was improved to combat forgery and then gradually declined again, a feature of coinage production throughout the twelfth and thirteenth centuries. The presence of the moneyer's own name on his products was significant, not only in deterring him from forgery but also in encouraging him to track down anyone else who might be tempted to take his name in vain. When moneyers' names ceased to appear on the coinage, the incidence of counterfeiting seems to have risen.

In the civil wars during Stephen's reign (1135-1154), mints fell into the hands of rebel barons, who struck barbarous versions of Stephen's coins. Many of the crudely struck main and baronial coins of this Stephen/Matilda civil war period are completely unidentifiable, making them unlikely candidates for modern counterfeiting. Neither has the author yet been able to trace any contemporary counterfeits from this time, although the poor nature of Stephen's coinage makes it difficult to decide what might be genuine, imitation or forgery. Matilda's coins were poor, hand-engraved and of low weight. Crude dies were used with degenerate reverse legends. Some Stephen dies were deliberately damaged and used to produce defaced coins. The irregular issues of this period are not counterfeits in so far as the issuers claimed to have the right to mint their own currency, be they Baron, Queen, Bishop or Duke. There was a popular trend to produce pennies with decreasing percentages of silver. A counterfeiter's obverse die exists for a penny of Stephen & Matilda (c. 1141) *(Baldwin's)*.

The Cross-and-crosslets coinage of Henry II (1154-1189), nicknamed Tealby because of the huge hoard found at Tealby in Lincolnshire in 1807, replaced Stephen's coinage which had become a mixture full of substandard and irregular pieces. It was of crude style, compared with preceding and following coinage, and so could easily be taken for copies or forgeries. Alphonse III of Portugal is reported to have been a Tealby copier.

Genuine Tealby. Lincoln, bust D. 19 mm.

The difference as can be seen here is that the forgeries were even cruder than the originals

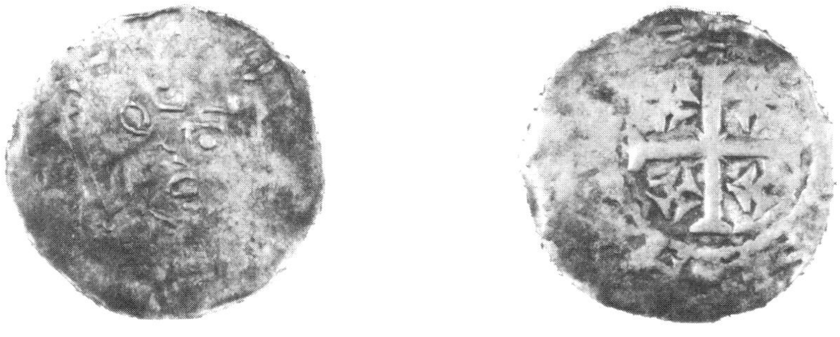

Contemporary Tealby counterfeit. 20 mm.

Good weight and metal, but unlike all illustrated Tealbys, the eye-nose triangle is not isosceles; also an irregular method of striking and a 'clumsy' die. The eyes and mouth have strayed so far as to hardly resemble a face.

Pennies exist with tooled reverse inscriptions[ST]. These appear to have been the work of moonlighting mint employees, intent on producing lightweight coins from purloined dies. The moneyer and mint names have been altered or obscured so the crime could not be traced back to source; a wise precaution when death or mutilation awaited those caught. One example reveals a moneyer trying to change his name to that of another moneyer.

King John's mint issued a penny 'poise' for weight checking, always a useful method of sorting the good from the bad.

In 1180, Philip Aimer of Tours designed the voided short-cross penny, a slight improvement on the Tealbys, The two arms of the cross on the reverse made it far easier to cut the coins into halfpennies and farthings (fourthings). Philip's success was brief, as accusations of fraud led to his early dismissal. Short-cross coinage lasted for nearly seventy years, but despite this, imitations are not common.

13TH CENTURY

GOLD

For five hundred years, there was only silver coinage. Then in 1252 the city of Florence introduced a gold florin. This became so popular that it was extensively imitated. The obverses all showed St. John the Baptist, but the reverses often revealed their new origins. For forgers, the advent of gold coinage was a double-edged development. On the one hand, a gold coin took no more effort to make than a silver one, but offered much more potential profit. On the other hand, a gold coin would be much more closely examined before being accepted.

Foreign gold coins, such as Bezants, Oboli and, to a small extent, Augustales, circulated in Britain in the thirteenth century. Forgers have often chosen to copy such coins because people would generally be less familiar with them and thus less able to spot fakes of them. This is the most likely explanation for the Continental dies that have been found in the Thames.

Epidemics of clipping often led to a recoinage to restore confidence and attract more bullion to England. It was sometimes accompanied by a weight change. The recoinage of 1247 saw the short-cross design of the reverse replaced by that of the long-cross, deliberately designed to discourage clipping. Each stem of the cross extended to the edge of the coin. Removal of the end-flare would thus make obvious any clipping. Any coin without all four cross-ends was illegal.

14,000 silver pennies of Henry III were found in 1969 at Colchester, Essex. This enormous hoard included about 20 laminated forgeries (up to ten of which were cliché-type). They were described as "in undoubtedly official style", but were not considered to have been struck with official dies, due to the variety of prototypes they represented.

Continental Sterling

During the early thirteenth century, because of their popularity, English short-cross pennies were being copied on the Continent by counts and clerics. These imitations tended to have similar reverses but diverse obverses. The copying grew and can be divided into three main phases. Firstly, the short voided cross phase (c.1205 to 1245) mostly in the Westphalia region, between the rivers Rhine and Weser. Secondly, the long voided cross phase (c.1247 to c.1279) in the Low Countries. Thirdly, the long single cross phase (c.1279 to 1300), also in the Low Countries, which followed the introduction of Edward I's new penny of 1279, and its popular acceptance around Europe, particularly with rulers in the Low Countries, northern France and Germany.

The difference between the similar sterling copies and the exact ones is that the latter were initially almost entirely up to the English silver standard. The commonest of the exact copies bear the names of English mints, London (LON DON) and Canterbury (CAN TOR). When they also carry English obverse legends, they can be hard to spot. There was a good reason for this. They were made primarily to save continental merchants from having to pay a minting charge for turning their coin into sterling, when they came to Britain to trade*. So they needed coin that would pass in Britain. Wren says that the early types were not underweight, so although they were imitations, no one was really losing out, except for the government not getting its minting revenue. They were used on the Continent as normal currency.

EASTERLING PROBLEMS

"(The) Easterling good money was in short time so corrupted and clipped by Jewes, Italian usurers, called then Corsini...and Flemings, that the King (Henry III), by proclamation, was inforced to call in old money, make a new stamp, and to erect exchanges, where the weight of old money was exchanged for new, allowing thirteen pence for every pound, to the great damage of the people, who...received...of the bankers scant 20s. for 30s...

DECLINING VALUE

But underweight coin then appeared of rather baser metal than the English sterling coins of 92.1/2 % pure silver. They were called Esterlings or Easterlings, with those replacing the King's crown with a chaplet of roses being called Crockards. Others, from ecclesiastical mints, showed a tonsured or 'polled' head and were therefore nicknamed Pollards. Crowned head types were dubbed Coronati.

When the silver content of the Continental imitations had dwindled down to half and sometimes even less, they were exchanged for good English pennies. With the silver from these, a greater quantity of Continental sterling could then be produced, for exchanging once again, creating a profit circle.

In Edward I's time, because of their assumed base alloy and light weight, the foreign coins flooding into Britain were named as 'false', and had attracted even more nicknames - Brabants (from Brabant in the Low Countries), Croccodone, Eagles, Lions (or Leonines), Mitres, Scaldings and Sleepings (or Dormientum).

**The thirteenth and fourteenth centuries saw a booming English economy in wool, sold to the Low Countries.*

(top) Penny of Henry III of England (1216-1272). 16 mm. (bottom) Imitation by Henry II of Kuinre, Low Countries (1263-1294). 17 mm.

(top) London penny of Edward I (1272-1302). 18 mm. (bottom) Imitation by Robert de Bethune of Flanders (1305-1322). 17.5 mm

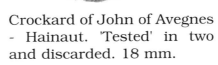

Continental copy of a long-cross penny, with a notably crude cross. Wgt 0.99 gm. 17.5 mm.

Crockard of John of Avegnes - Hainaut. 'Tested' in two and discarded. 18 mm.

Continental copy of an Edward I long cross penny by Guy de Dampierre, 1280-1305. Mysterious legend. Wgt 0.87 gm. 18 mm.

ROUGH JUSTICE

"Money so refined was (7 Ed. I.) by stealth transported and counter-feited; and forraigne coynes, called Mitres, Lyons imported in such quantity, that they were forbidden by procla-mation, and 280 Jewes executed at London, for clipping the King's coyne. Afterward (28 Ed. I.) Crocards and Pollards were decried downe to an halfe penny; Rosaries, Stepings, and Scaldings forbidden."

By the 1290's, for every English sterling struck, there were possibly as many as ten continental sterling. By the late 1290's, they were so debased that few people would accept them.

In 1299, with The Statute of Stepney, Edward I made the crockards and pollards circulating in England - to be identified by the absence of a crown in the design - legitimate but only worth 1/2d. each. In natural consequence, examples have been found with a crown scratched on. Halving the value was a clever move, because although they did not contain the full value of an English penny, they did have more than half, and so were melted down in great quantities, thus reducing them as a problem. Despite this, the outflow of good English silver pennies continued, and so within a year, foreign sterling was completely demonetised and could only be converted to sterling at Exchanges. Many of the continental sterling coins were reminted at provincial mints between 1299 and 1302. Thus the problem of crockards and pollards had largely been solved. By 1307, there was to all intents and purposes no problem. It was not too many years however, before once again prolific continental copying of the English pennies was occurring; Black Money, Lusshebournes (with crowned heads), Rosaries and Turneys. It was much less of a problem with Scottish and Irish issues, except for Scottish groats.

"(Edward I) called in certaine counterfeit pieces, coyned by the French, called Pollards, Crocars, and Rosaryes, whereupon was then made this echoing barbarous verse:

Laude decoreris, nostris sterlinge gereris,
Crocar est, æsque perlis, fugias, as rite teneris."

After the introduction of the long-cross penny by Henry, the next step to curb clipping was to remove the need for any legitimate cutting, by the issue of silver halfpennies and farthings. These tiny coins can look counterfeit because of blundered or illegible legends. Edward I (1272-1307) also added a groat (or 4d piece), making the coinage more user-friendly than it had been for hundreds of years. Despite this, small change deficiencies seem to have started after 1300 and pennies were still being cut into halfpennies and farthings in the 15th century.

Forged coins in Edward's reign were described as being of bad weight and alloy, cast in tin and other metals, pure copper, pewter or lead between leaves of silver. Enigmatic sterlings are probably contempo-rary counterfeits. Edwardian forgeries recovered from Bell Wharf on the Thames were found in a context contemporary with their genuine counterparts. They are almost always of low silver content, frequent-ly down to below 50%. That forgers should bother to copy these (around the mid 1290's) and also the crockards and pollards (c.1296/1297) instead of concentrating completely on the English sterling, may have been because their debased efforts compared better. They chose common designs.

Forgers in the late thirteenth century were adept at obtaining silver for their products by clipping genuine coins so delicately that the minute amounts removed from the edges could only be detected by weighing.

JETONS

Use of the same detail punches reveal that some medieval English jetons (reckoning or casting counters) were made at the same place as the coin dies. This explains their resemblance to coins of Edward I and II. But for the central hole, silver-plated examples could have been mistaken for regal coins. It is possible that the hole was meant to prevent this misuse. An alternative suggestion has been that it was merely a scribing hole. Whatever the reason, it helps differentiate them from counterfeits of the time.

By the middle of Edward II's reign (1310-1320), the reaction on the continent to Edward I's closed-door policy had meant that in order to slip them through, continental imitations had got closer to the English originals.

In Edward III's time (1327-77), Edwardian pennies were still circulating widely in Europe, particularly in north Germany and the Low Countries. By the mid-fourteenth century, lower quality imitations from these areas were once again causing problems. It was said of Edward III (in Fabyan's Chronicles - c.1350) that *"he dampned certayne coynes of money, called pollardes, crocardes, and rosaries and caused them to be broughte unto newe coynage to his great advantage."* He achieved this 'dampning' with a re-imposition and widespread enforcement of hanging and quartering for the importation of Lusshebournes, the popular name of the time for quantities of base metal coins flooding in from Luxembourg.

LUSSHEBOURNES

Two contemporary commentators, Piers Plowman and Chaucer, had this to say of these notorious imitation sterling pennies:

From THE VISION CONCERNING PIERS PLOWMAN (passus XV)

"As in lusshe-borwes is a luther alay, (bad alloy)
And yet loketh he lyke a sterlynge,
The merke of that mone is good, Ac the metal is feble."

From THE PROLOGUE TO CHAUCER'S THE MONK'S TALE, 74

"God woot! no lussheburghes payen ye!"

7

Golden Reflections

The design of the French gold coin called an Agnel, which circulated in the thirteenth and fourteenth centuries, was imitated by both Edward III and Henry V in the Anglo-Gallic series. It was a prelude to gold coin copying of an unacceptable nature, where intent to deceive was the prime motive. This first manifest itself when the Wool Trade was used to try and bring in English gold coinage to Calais, by making English staple merchants legally required only to accept English nobles in payment for their wool. The unforeseen result of this was that from 1388 Flemish mints began producing imitation English nobles slightly lower in weight and fineness[MU]. Richard II (1377-1399) countered these threats to his coinage with wool trade restrictions.

Parliament, under Henry IV (1399-1413), banned all Flemish nobles in 1401 and they eventually tailed off by 1402. By this time though they formed a significant part of the gold coin circulating in England, possibly as much as twenty five per cent. The problems posed by this situation were solved by a drop in the regal weight standard in 1412 from 120 gr to 108 gr. Edward III and Richard II nobles were officially clipped to this lighter weight standard so that they could continue in circulation as currency and the Mint started issuing bronze check-weights for this denomination.

With official clipping showing the way, it is not surprising that Henry IV's reign was plagued by illegal clipping. Counterfeiting was rife, and there was widespread use of small value foreign coins such as suskins, doitkins and the base-metal galley-halfpence (galyhalpens) from Venice. These were about the size of the contemporary English halfpenny, but of much poorer alloy, providing half or less value of silver. They were denounced at various times between 1402 and 1423.

In 1406, there started an influx into England of *"false money of Scotland, resembling the coin of England and of false alloy."* A succession of unsuccessful Statutes (1409, 1411 etc.) was introduced to prevent this.

The Low Countries' imitations of Henry VI gold nobles, Edward IV and Elizabeth I gold ryals were fairly close copies using fine gold. Most copy the annulet issues of the London mint[WO].

The Ryal and its copies

In the fifteenth century, Edward IV's ryal was popular on the continent because of its high gold content. The Netherlands in particular, took to it, and when it was replaced in England by the angel, they started producing their own ryal versions, referring to them as rose-nobles. The Van Arkel family made their city of Gorinchem notorious by their output of these imitations.

Genuine ryal
of Edward IV.
35 mm.

15th century
counterfeit of
the ryal above.
37.5 mm.

Undated
Gorinchem
rose-noble
imitating
the ryal.
36.5 mm.

Undated rose-noble imitation, possibly by the Van Arkel family.
37 mm.

Genuine shield

Utrecht shield
(see below left)

Undated rose-noble from Utrecht (1600-1601). The legend TRAIECTEN, meaning Utrecht, and the coat of arms on the shield identify the issuer.
36.5 mm.

Contemporaries may not have been able to tell coins struck on local dies from counterfeits. A genuine York mule had been holed in the way forgeries were treated. Doitkins, Galley halfpence from Venice, O'Reyleys and Suskins continued to circulate. Worn deniers could easily be mistaken for English sterling. In 1469, Charles the Bold's Burgundian double patard was made legal tender in England.

> BLACKE MONEY
>
> "Blacke Money (what that was I know not, if it were not of copper, as *Maile* and *Blacke-Maile*) was forbidden by King Edward the Third, upon paine of forfeiture thereof; and gally halfe pence, brought hither by the Gallies of Genoa, who had great trade in Englande, was eftsoones prohibited by Parliament, in the time of King Henry the Fourth. *Sufkins* and *Dodkins* by King Henry the Fifth, and *Blankes* by King Henry the Sixt."
>
> 15th CENTURY REPORT

The WYRE PIDDLE HOARD**AR1** was found in Worcester in 1967 and comprised 219 fifteenth century silver coins, including 7 counterfeits. There were three Henry VI counterfeits - two groats and a penny and four Edward IV, all groats. All were lightweight, and two were visibly base. They were all hammered from dies cut in the same way as genuine coins of the period. Some punches were used on different designs, suggesting a common source for these forgeries.

The FISHPOOL HOARD of 1,237 gold coins, found in Nottinghamshire in 1966, contained two gold-plated, base metal forgeries of annulet nobles of Henry VI. They are underweight and poorly designed. Cracks in the gold covering show their base-metal core.

During an excavation at St. Lawrence's Priory at Stamford in Lincolnshire (July 1969), a hoard was found in a pit in a plaster floor. It comprised clippings of fourteenth and fifteenth century coins up to coins minted soon after the 1464 standard weight reduction. Heavy coinage pennies weighed 1 gm, reducing with the light coinage issue to 0.8 gm.

Edward IV's second reign (1471-1483) saw a rash of contemporary forgeries and Continental imitations. Low Countries' imitations of the noble were quite common, but can be identified by style differences. Similarly for his London mint rose-noble (ryal), roughly copied in the Netherlands throughout the sixteenth century. The best-known source was the Van Arkels of Gorinchem.

Many mules exist, e.g. Edward IV/Henry VI groat with both sides differing from official dies and punches.

The BULL WHARF HOARD**AR2** found on the Thames foreshore near the medieval Queenhithe Dock consisted of hundreds of counterfeit pennies copying Edward IV's 1465-1483 light coinage.

The Bull Wharf hoard, from which examples are shown on the right, comprised over 850 imitations, c.1490-1500, of Edward IV light coinage, struck from just four reverse dies paired with one obverse die. The obverse inscription is ECARCUS CEI (G)RA REX. The reverses - one London - TAS CIVI CO(N CON); three York - 1. CIV TAS ERO RAC; 2 - CIVI TAS ERO RACI; 3 - (CIVI TAS) EBOB ACI. The reason for the hoard could be either accidental loss, a frequent happening with the jostling ferries crossing the Thames, or the urgent disposal of incriminating evidence.

Common obverse. 13-14 mm.

The coins are likely to have been made later in the century (c.1490-1500) and in London, judging by their uncirculated condition. Their weight (0.37 gm to 0.78 gm) and silver content (66% to 92.5%) show them to have been worth less than their bullion value, a necessary prerequisite for profit. They were struck from forgers' dies on flans too small for the design. This made them look like clipped coins, which may have been deliberate. Some show traces of corners, revealing that the flans had been straight cut from sheet silver and then rough trimmed to resemble a round coin.

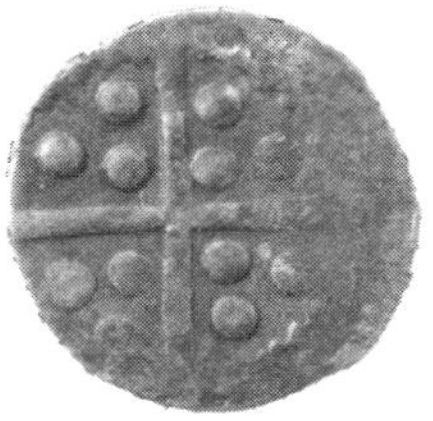

London type Wgt 0.46 gm.

They are exposed as false by metal, inscription, bust and weight anomalies.

Punches were used to create the dies on which they were struck, as with the official coinage of the time. Different letter sizes reveal the use of two different letter fonts, the larger of which appears to have been missing the letters B(R), D(C) and L(C), so for example, LONDON became CONCON.

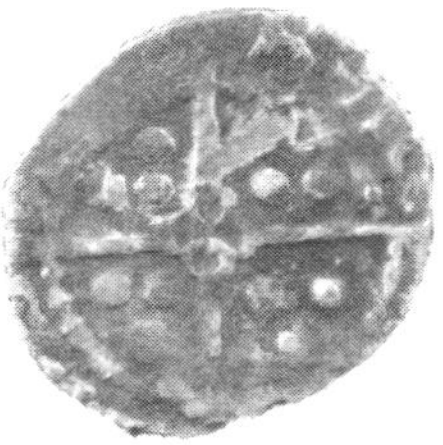

York 1 type Wgt 0.37 gm.

Official coins of the time had random die-axes. These hoard examples fell into groups depending on the reverse die being used. This could however merely be the result of the striker getting into a pattern on a particular batch and this hoard being lost or abandoned before they drifted apart.

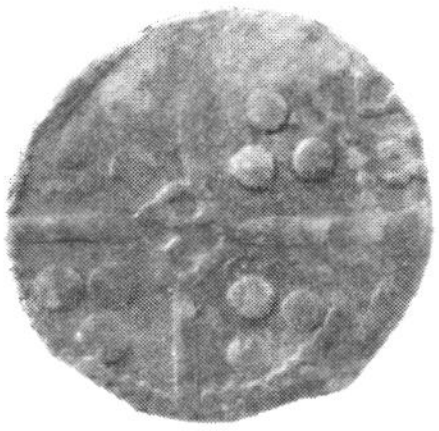

York 3 type Wgt 0.47 gm.

Richard III (1483-1485) had a brief reign that has attracted fantasy counterfeits.

CLIPPING THEIR WINGS

The Act of 1504 declared that clipped coins were not legal currency.
"Coin which will not weigh the tumbril should be bored.
When offered false coin, return it to the profferer bored or broken in two."

8

Tudors, Stuarts and advancing technology

The smallest coin denominations of the late fifteenth century had virtually no silver in them. Counterfeiters could get away with completely base metal pieces. Most coins of the Tudors, including permitted foreign pieces, were being counterfeited. Particularly favoured were groats, shillings and half-sovereigns. There was a variety of approaches - tin, copper and tin, copper and silver, silver plated copper, silver-plated iron. Counterfeits often underwent a rubbing-down and staining to give them a circulated look. "Multiplying the coin" was an euphemism of the fifteenth and sixteenth centuries for melting down coin to make lightweight or debased counterfeits.

A contemporary forgery of a Henry VII Canterbury mint half groat of 1490-1500, issued under the King and Archbishop Morton jointly. It exhibits several clues; legend error - CA8 for CAN; poor design - letter P touching frame; POSVI lettering uneven; cross out of true, and at 1.36 gm (1.56 gm) it is underweight. 19.5 mm.

Tudor counterfeiters made false dies, casts, used genuine dies, tooled and also gilded genuine coins. Challis[CH] observes that any proficient Tudor goldsmiths could have made minting tools easily and quickly to reproduce hammered coinage. Their great portability would have facilitated safe production and concealment.

A couple of piedforts are known from the reign of Henry VIII. They are two to three times normal thickness, and struck on sovereign dies. These heavy strikings, perhaps made for presentation or die-record purposes, are particularly collectable, and so, inevitably have been faked. A 'piedford' groat of Henry VII that appeared prior to 1856, is actually two genuine groats stuck together.

AN EARLY TUDOR COINER'S MOULD

Carlisle Museum holds a Tudor coiner's 'bivalve' mould[BO], probably made from a single nodule of graphite. It was discovered in April 1865 hidden in a small cairn, by a labourer seeking wall stone. The mould has five coins engraved on it, comprising three types, two of which are imitating Henry VII coins of 1500 or earlier.

The two halves of the mould have peg-holes for registering the designs when the mould was bound together for the insertion of the molten metal. The coins had to be so thin that the metal would not have flowed through without the thicker channel around the designs. This produced a flat metal plate from which the coins were then cut. The excess metal would then presumably have been dropped back into the melting pot. Experiments have shown that the mould must have been pre-heated to have made it work.

RUDDY NOSED RULER

"Sir John Rainsford meeting Parson Brocke, the principal deviser of [Henry VIII's debased silver] coyne, threatened him to breake his head, for that hee had made his Soveraigne Lord, the most beautiful Prince, King Henry, with a redde and copper nose.
"So base and corrupted with copper was his money, as also of King Edward the Sixth, that some of them which was then called Testons, because of the King's head was thereon figured, contained but two pence farthing in silver, and other foure pence halfe penny... (Also) great quantitie of forged and counterfeits were dayly made and brought from beyond seas."

ROYAL PROFITEER

At times, because of sudden rises in the value of gold and silver, merchants sold their bullion abroad rather than take it to the English mints for conversion into coin. One proclamation countering such a situation put it like this: *"every person that wold bring in sylver bolion plate or other wise...whereas aforetime he shall have taken for a pound of sylver but 29 shillings shall now receive clearly of every pound weight of such sylver at his said minte 33 shillings of the same fynesse and alloys." By Henry VIII's time, less than "the same fynesse and alloys" was given in exchange, providing Henry with a profit in excess of £200,000. It wasn't just forgers who coined for their own advantage.*

Boon described the end results coming from this mould as barbarous and poor, requiring a busy market to stand any chance of being passed unspotted, and even then only if mixed in with good coin.

Experiments have revealed a possible modus operandi of hammering genuine coins against the graphite surface, to produce a starting impression that could then be worked to resemble the original. Support for this idea comes from the lettering, some of which is very close to the original and some distinctly not so.

The poor quality of workmanship and the fact that the coins copied were and are still common, points strongly to this being a contemporary forger's efforts, probably very early in the sixteenth century. In 1976 this mould was and may still well be the only one known made from graphite.

Throughout the Tudor period, lead tokens were produced, possibly to function as small change.

Henry VIII's reign (1509-1547) was a continuing time of counterfeiting, clipping, melting down and galley-halfpence. The Henry VIII ryal (10s) was contracted for but is considered not to have been issued. The example at the British Museum is a forgery.

Around the 1520's, English gold coins were better value than continental pieces, and so they 'leaked' to the continent - to such an extent that continental French ecu au soleil were imported to fill the gap. These had a value of 4s 4d each. Also, Flemish and French gold coins of lesser value than the English, were entering the country and so, in 1526, Henry introduced a new issue of gold coins of lower weight and carat to combat this. The financial benefits this produced for him proved irresistible, and so further debasement, of both the gold and silver coinage, followed.

Henry's Testoon (shilling) became so debased that the high spots on his bust, i.e. his cheeks, wore and showed through the coppery core, giving rise to this couplet:

These testons are red; how like you the same?
'Tis a token of grace; they blush for shame!

Three ecclesiastical mints were issuing coins around the 1530's. Henry put a stop to that as part of his general dissolution of church power and property.

In April 1546, William Sharington was appointed under-treasurer at Bristol, with permission to strike gold and silver coinage, including the silver coinage for Ireland, until the Dublin mint opened in 1548. His coins are monogrammed WS. He then lapsed into counterfeit coin production to help Lord Seymour of Sudeley, leading to his imprisonment in the Tower. There he confessed to making light coin, clipping, book falsifying and document burning, for which he was heavily fined but, surprisingly, then set free.

Seven or more young head counterfeit groats of Henry VIII's Second Coinage (1526-1544) were dug up in a cluster from the north bank of the Thames at Southwark Bridge. All appear to have the same source; most likely cast from moulds made from one original genuine coin. The air holes visible in the thickness of a broken example support the casting method.

The Henry VIII Southwark Bridge hoard comprised seven or more coins, dug up in a cluster from the north bank of the Thames at Southwark Bridge. All five examples held by the author are groats of the Second Coinage, 1526-44, and have the same 5 o'clock die-axis and dimple to the left of the hair bulge, strongly suggesting that they were all cast from the same mould.

Groat. Sharp definition. Flaw in shield on the reverse. 25.5 mm.

Groat. Average definition. There is a flaw on the reverse at 10.30. 24.5 mm.

Most Philip and Mary issues (1554-1558) have been forged, the majority in modern times. There are high-grade halfgroat forgeries and Victorian copies of the pennies. The two dates most favoured by forgers are 1554 and 1557.

In Elizabeth I's reign, Edward VI shillings were counterstamped with a portcullis to indicate their reduced value to 4.1/2d. The forged counterstamps, showing the portcullis with chains either side instead of scrolls are probably nineteenth century products[PR]. A report of 1601 refers to an Edward VI shilling gilded to resemble a sovereign.

This Elizabethan time saw the innovation, utilised by forgers, of bismuth as a hardening agent to turn tin into pewter.

There was a spate of forgery in the 1560's. One of the forgers' tricks was to gild the twopence (halfgroat) pieces which could then be passed as Half Crowns. Eventually to circumvent this, the Mint added two pellets to the design (fifth issue - 1582-1600). Another trick was to tool away the rose on the 3/4d, 1.1/2d, 3d. and 6d. coins to make them look like the penny, halfgroat, groat and shilling respectively. Some genuine shillings of 1560-1561 have forged portcullis countermarks with annulets as chains; the genuine marks have lines of which the left one is flawed.

The year 1561 saw the arrival in England of the French technique of milled coin production, courtesy of ex-Paris mintmaster, Eloye Mestrell. He came to England, a Huguenot refugee from France, in 1560. His previous employment at the Moulin des Etuves, the Paris mint, led to him working at the Tower Mint. He left behind debts in France, so his escape may have been more to do with that than with religion. There was also the offer of £25 per annum, a handsome rate for the time. Provided with accommodation to turn out machine-made coins, he produced Britain's first milled money, although the term should really be mill money, as it is derived from the introduction of mill power, supplied by horse or water. Using the term to mean coin edging is incorrect. Graining is the correct term.

By the end of 1561, Mestrell was producing excellent coinage from a horse-operated screw-press. For five years he continued to produce such coinage - the hammered coin workers improving their products as well, in response to the challenge of this new approach. They felt threatened by Eloye, and fought a running battle with him over the next ten years, accusing his equipment and methods of causing every possible problem they could think of. One of the complaints was that his coinage was less accurate metrologically than hand production, a point that seems to have been quite true when his coins are

Genuine 1567 milled sixpence by Eloye Mestrell. V scratch on the obverse. Wgt 2.83 gm. 25 mm.

weighed . The 'Luddite' workers eventually won the day when a traditionalist mint master was appointed in 1572.

This new Warden of the Mint investigated Mestrell's methods for preparing blanks and found them to be slower than hand production and so, in 1572, sacked him, ignoring the fact that he was producing much better quality coins than the hammer workers. Mestrell's subsequent descent into counterfeiting may have been from resentment at this treatment, or just the desperation of the unemployed. It led to him being hanged in 1578.

After Mestrell's mechanical coinage came a return to hand-struck coins that lasted until the arrival of Briot in Charles I's time. Briot used the rocker press for crowns and halfcrowns, and the screw-press and circular cutter for the smaller denominations for both England and Scotland. He sliced blanks off silver rods, a production method used with bronze rods by forgers of the small third and fourth century Romano-British coins,

Traders' farthing tokens in lead, tin and latten proliferated in Elizabeth's reign, filling the need for halfpennies and farthings because her Government could not bring itself to issue base-metal coinage. Lead tokens, dated 1591 or 1598, probably originated in Bristol. Opinions differ regarding their authenticity. The problem in the Bristol area was a plethora of unofficial tokens being issued by all and sundry, most of whom would not then accept them back, claiming that their own products were counterfeit. The solution, taken by the City of Bristol in 1578, was to issue official farthing tokens. A few years later, in order to maintain acceptance of their product, the City had to pay for over twelve and a half thousand counterfeit tokens to be removed from circulation. This illustrates the trouble with most token issues; they could be easily counterfeited but not easily redeemed.

Counterfeiting was not a particularly serious problem in James I's reign (1603-1625), except for the Royal farthings[WE]. From Henry VIII's death, the lack of farthings, exacerbated by rising prices at the beginning of the seventeenth century, led to merchants, particularly in London, producing their own small change in the form of lead tokens. By 1612, thousands of different tokens were circulating, leading to an official reaction in the following year with the grant of a coin issuing monopoly. The existing silver halfpenny was already an inconveniently small coin, so, having made Sir John Stanhope, Baron Harington, James then required the new Baron, as his Treasurer of the Chamber, to mint copper farthings and share the profits. 'Haringtons' were authorised with the instruction that they embody privy marks *"to be altered to occasion, for preventing the falsifying and counterfeiting the same."* So they were tinned, making them look more like silver coins, but mainly as an anti-counterfeiting device. It seems to have worked, as only Lennox farthing counterfeits commonly turn up from James's reign. It is possible that the Harington farthings mostly escaped because there was not a particularly significant circulation.

Renewal of the farthing patent (11th July 1625), specified that *"The making or uttering of any other tokens, whether made or counterfeited within the realm or 'beyond the seas' is forbidden."*

The farthings' monopoly passed from Harington, on his death in 1615, to the Duke of Lennox; then, in 1624, to the Duke's widow, the Duchess of Richmond and finally, in 1634, under Charles I, to Lord Maltravers.

The popularity of these products of Harington and his successors is summed up in the expression "not worth a brass farthing." Some exhibit signs of the distinctive production method, which was to pass metal strips through a rotary press.

Charles I Maltravers type farthing. Off-centre strike. Wgt 0.32 gm. 17 mm.

Richmond and Maltravers farthings, the small change of Charles's reign, were forged in such large numbers that they were as common as the genuine coins. Many came in from the Continent. Richmond farthings (1625-1634) inscribed CARA could be contemporary forgeries. Also there are thought to be no genuine CARO-BRIT pieces. A scissel of Richmond farthings was found at Scarborough. In 1636, the rose farthings, the last in the series, were to have *"a little brass in the middle of the copper to distinguish the true farthings from forgeries."* There are few forgeries of these and they are fairly easy to detect. Because of their low value, all these farthing imitations are likely to have been contemporary.

In 1644, Parliament had to suppress the Royal farthings, because of the failure of the patentees to change them for higher denominations when requested. The Civil War then pushed aside official consideration of this problem.

SILVER COIN SHORTAGE

Due to the plague in 1625 striking down many of the Mint workers, French quarter-ecus were put into circulation in England, at a face value of 19.1/2d each. They were part of Charles I's dowry, and an instance of a foreign coin circulating without a counterstamp. In the same year, following in Mestrell's footsteps, Nicholas Briot arrived, bringing with him the Paris Mint's new coinage methods providing a standardized product. These made it much easier to check coins for counterfeiting, which was prevalent in England and France at that time. With considerable engraving skill and a revised screw press incorporating a collar to prevent metal spread when the flans were struck, Briot turned out some fine coins. But still the need for greater output speed brought back the old methods.

To have parts of two dies appear on one side only, this counterfeit farthing must have been produced in a strip between two badly aligned multiple dies. 16 mm.

Paris finally led the way into the coin machine age, banning hand-production in 1645.

There are many forgeries of Charles I crowns. At least two lead pieces exist of the Simon Crown, showing the obverse side only. They are from the original die in its final stage - cracked and rusting – and are much thicker than normal lead squeezes. They could be trial pieces, or a souvenir creator's efforts.

Royal Farthings

Started by James I and continued by Charles I, copper farthings were issued as a monopoly from which the king got a rake-off without 'tarnishing' his image with an official issue of base metal currency. The different issues have become known by the names of their issuers, starting with 'Haringtons'. Despite their small value, they were extensively - and badly - counterfeited. The harp on the reverse, poorly stringed and misshapen, gives away most copies. Some are full-weight, but many are distinctly lighter.

JAMES I

A *genuine* Harington copper farthing. Type 2, mintmark, cinque-foil on reverse. Wgt 0.58 gm. 15 mm.

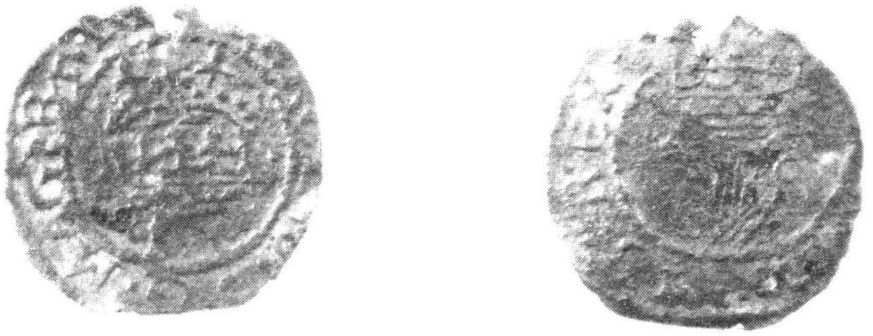

Harington farthing with edge breaks. Seriously underweight at 0.20 gm. 14 mm.

Lennox farthing. Two-stringed harp! Wgt 0.56 gm. 16.5 mm.

Lennox farthing (ex-Mitchiner collection). Wgt 0.35 gm. 15.5 mm.

CHARLES I

Richmond farthing with a squashed harp. Off-struck.
Wgt 0.48 gm. 17 mm.

Richmond farthing with a four-string harp. Off-struck, particularly on the obverse. Bright copper. Slight edge clip.
Wgt 0.42 gm. 17 mm.

Royal farthing. Crude harp with strings descending from right to left.
Wgt 0.29 gm. 15.5 mm.

For in-depth coverage of all these farthings and their forgeries, including Maltravers and Rose-, see *English Copper, Tin & Bronze Coins in the British Museum* by C. Wilson Peck (2nd edition, 1970), pp. 19-82, pl. 1-4.

CONTEMPORARY FORGERIES OF CHARLES I's EQUESTRIAN HALFCROWN

Spiked and split to demonetise it. Plated on brass, with no plating remaining. Wgt 15.12 gm. 33.5 mm.

Plated 1640 type. No plating remaining. Wgt 12.48 gm. 34 mm.

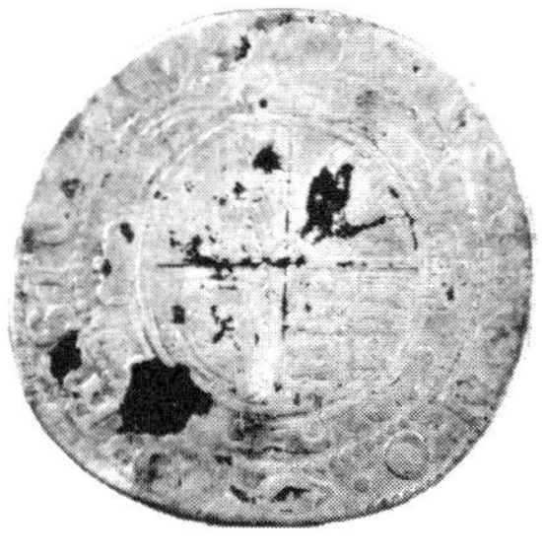

Plated with most of the plating still intact, apart from small breaks on both sides. Full flan. Eye mintmark. Wgt 12.89 gm. 33.5 mm.

Robert Ready, the nineteenth century coin reproducer for the British Museum, made electrotypes of the Oxford mint crown.

A POPULAR CHOICE

Charles halfcrowns have been extensively forged. Base contemporary halfcrown counterfeits, according to Besly, had as little as 44% silver, employing a copper alloy 'silvered' with arsenic, a popular counterfeiting method of the time. The results were very underweight.

Base metal halfcrowns showing a horse with bowed head and the inscription EBOR beneath are contemporary forgeries - with a three figure catalogue value.

A halfcrown with entwined C's mintmark, thought at one time to be from Corfe Castle or Coventry, is now thought to be a forgery. There are three known specimens. One is definitely plated.

An undated Charles I equestrian halfcrown (1644) bearing the legend EBORO under the horse, could be a contemporary forgery. A hoard of cast forgeries was found at the Three Horse Shoes, Eden Street, Kingston-on-Thames, Surrey around 1974. It consisted of eight halfcrowns and the conclusion that they were contemporary rather than modern forgeries was drawn from the fact that they had been made from base metal (pewter).

Tower Mint halfcrowns are known struck on official dies, but plated; official or moonlighters' products? Rough copies of Tower halfcrowns, c.1649, known as Blacksmith's Money, may have been struck in the Welsh Marches. Good examples can reach £1,000! Base metal versions of the 1642-1644 Royal Mint halfcrowns are probably late 18th century forgeries.

The handstruck halfcrown lingered on into the milled coin era, badly worn, clipped, and so much easier to imitate than the new machine-made coinage. Similarly for shillings, where some counterfeits were cast, but most were handstruck.

There are contemporary forgeries of the Tower mint shillings, particularly of the later types, often well worn and showing their base cores through the silver coating. A plated version exists of the Chester shilling, struck from regular dies. The possible explanation for this is that when Chester fell to Cromwell's troops, the mint's dies were 'liberated' and re-used in this way. Many copies of provincial issues are nineteenth century souvenirs sold by museums. Their brightness, lack of tone and neat edges give them away.

CIVIL WAR

In 1642, Thomas Simon**NA** (1618-1665), sometimes called Symonds, engraved a copy of the Great Seal for use by the Parliamentarians during the Civil War. This was considered a forgery by the Royalists.

SIEGE PIECES

Siege pieces could be considered to be tokens of a sort, redeemable when normality was restored, but still having residual value if all went wrong. The Civil War siege pieces fluctuated in weight and were crude in design, making them popular with forgers. Siege money counterfeits are unlikely to be contemporary, given the circumstances of their production. It is theoretically possible that troops, idle through the confined situation of being under siege, might have indulged in counterfeiting the crudely produced emergency coin. But siege conditions would be the worst imaginable to keep secret such clandestine operations, and no siege counterfeit *guaranteed* to be contemporary has yet appeared. There are plenty of "probably contemporary" that should, in the author's view, be "probably not!"

(top) bright, shiny, unreal replica of a Newark 1646 siege halfcrown by Westair Reproductions Ltd (initials WRL stamped on obverse). Sold in a presentation card. The piece below it is from the same cast as this except that the replica maker's initials are missing, and it is less shiny. It has a clear edge join and so would only fool the completely unaware. 40 x 30 mm.

There are three distinct waves of Siege piece forgeries; the Gifford restrikes of the 1780's, nineteenth century and modern, particularly in the 1950's and 1960's.

Early in 1968, the products from forged dies began to pop up at out-of-town auctions. They were Oxford mint silver pounds and half-pounds, and Newark lozenge halfcrowns and Carlisle shillings.

When Charles lost his head, the royal prerogative relating to copper and brass coinage also came to an end, a fact quickly latched on to by many town councils and private traders - and tokens proliferated. There was no official copper coinage during the Commonwealth, so it is not surprising that in just over twenty years from 1649, it is estimated that in excess of ten thousand different *types* were issued. The first wave appeared in 1649 and on to 1653. Then, after a two year lull, a second wave, until they were suppressed again in the Restoration period.

In Rowe's[RO] comprehensive survey of Salisbury's token coinage, he says that farthings were by far the commonest coins issued by the town's traders. There were halfpennies, but never any pennies, although these did appear elsewhere in the country. Sometimes the same tokens would be made in different metals. Also, as a defence against counterfeiters, some would have their tokens made in one metal with a contrasting metal inserted as a central plug. Others made their tokens thick and heavy, presumably to convince people of their 'value' and so keep them circulating, which was the most profitable situation for the traders. The essence of this form of 'coinage' is that the issuers will always redeem their product in regal coinage, if so demanded. Once this fails to happen, the whole system breaks down.

That it was working well in Salisbury is evidenced by the City Council's ire at the loss of potential profit to themselves, causing them to ban it in 1658, describing the practice as *"the great and general abuse...by several persons... presuming (without any authority) to cause certain brass farthings to be stamped...for their several lucre and private gain."* The Council filled the vacuum thus created by issuing £5 worth of its own 'Town' farthings.

The tokens document seventeenth century trade. In his coverage of just Salisbury, Rowe notes issues for apothecaries, book-binders, butchers, clothiers, cooks, drapers, furriers, grocers, haberdashers, innkeepers, ironmongers, pewterers, linen drapers, upholsterers, mercers, milliners, physicians, rat catchers, shoemakers, skinners, and weavers.

These unofficial coins went on until 1672, when legal tender copper halfpennies and farthings appeared. Twelve years later came the tin farthings with the central copper plug - again with the intention of defeating the counterfeiters.

Lead pieces imitating the tin coinage of the late seventeenth century are too crude to be anything other than tokens.

In the 1650's, Blondeau re-introduced mechanised coin production to England, including his secret edge-marking device.

The 'reign' of the Puritans during the Commonwealth (1649-1660), did not halt the sinners, as the contemporary counterfeit halfcrowns illustrated show.

John Tanner, Chief Graver to the Mint from 1741 to 1775, made imitations of Cromwell coinage: sixpence (1658), shilling (1658), crown (1658), half-broad (1656, 1658). There are also poorly crafted Dutch imitations of the crown, c.1700. Both types of imitation are now quite valuable in their own right.

There are cast counterfeits of the 1658 Cromwell shilling.

Cromwell patterns were struck contemporaneously by Thomas Simon. He made puncheons that he does not seem to have used. After he died, some of his puncheons ended up in the Low Countries. There they were used to make false dies, the Dutch version of the Cromwell Crown probably being one of these. The dies for this, however, were not amongst those the Royal Mint bought back from the Dutch, along with puncheons. The Mint appears not to have realised that the dies for the 1658 gold ten shilling and silver shilling and sixpence were false. They made no use of any of the dies until 1738 when a number of pieces were struck. John Tanner produced his efforts at this time, preparing dies for the silver five shilling and gold ten shilling, both dated 1656. The ten shillings (or half-broads) were struck in gold from his dies, c.1738. There are no known originals. It is possible that others may have been struck in the Low Countries prior to 1700. Most are thought to have emanated from the Royal Mint, c.1738, in gold and copper. There are also examples dated 1658.

Charles II came to the throne in 1660. The following year on the 17th May, his Council issued an order for coinage to be thenceforth machine made "in order to prevent clipping and counterfeiting". Exactly a year later, on the 17th May 1662, Blondeau was appointed Engineer of the Mint, with the agreement that the method of his edge-lettering invention would be kept secret. The year 1663 finally saw the end of English hammered coinage, with the arrival of Blondeau's

'Puritan' Products

COMMONWEALTH

A tin-washed contemporary counterfeit of a 1654 Commonwealth halfcrown. There is a test nick in the rim. 6 o/c die-axis. Wgt 11.75 gm. 35 mm.

This imitation of a 1656 Commonwealth halfcrown has been cast on an oval flan from a contemporary counterfeit. The metal has run on part of the obverse. 12 o/c die-axis. At 8.65 gm, a very lightweight effort. 35 mm.

This 1656 Commonwealth halfcrown copy has three small breaks in the plating on the shield frame of the obverse. 4 o/c die-axis. Wgt 13.14 gm. 33 mm.

CROMWELL

Commonwealth shilling of 1653. An unconvincing copy with a cast look and a 'wrong' edge. Wgt 6.71 gm. 30 mm.

A coppery sheen is showing through the silver coating on this 1658 Cromwell shilling. Genuine specimens usually have a die-flaw by the top laurel wreath. Wgt 4.69 gm (6 gm). 27.5 mm (25-26 mm).

The mysterious indentation on this 1658 Cromwell shilling. could be the result of there being insufficient filler in an electrotype 'sand-wich'. Wgt 3.94 gm (6 gm). 26.5 mm (25-26 mm).

machinery for graining or inscribing the edge of coins, which, apart from countering counterfeiting, also defeated 'clippers'. Screw-presses had at last replaced hand production. The next great step forward in coin production took another 150 years to arrive, surprisingly from England, in George III's reign.

Blondeau actually offered Parliament two edge lettering methods to guard against counterfeiting. The first, Virole brisée, was an old method comprising an inscription engraved collar, put round the flan and then machine-struck. The second, Blondeau's secret method, allowed thinner flans to be edge inscribed. The legend DECVS ET TVTAMEN was used, revived on some Elizabeth II pound coin edges.

The gold guinea design was made distinctly different from the silver shilling to discourage gilding. Despite this, gilded shillings can be found with the reverse tooled to resemble the guinea.

There is a noticeable absence of contemporary counterfeits of English silver coinage from c.1663 to 1696. Not so with copper coin, where a wave of counterfeiting led to the introduction in 1684 of the plugged tin farthing, made in this metal to boost the flagging Cornish tin industry. The edges were inscribed NVMMORVM FAMVLVS (Knave of Coins). Although the square central copper plug was intended to act as an anti-counterfeiting device, these farthings were extensively forged, mostly without any attempt to insert or simulate this plug. The edge legend was frequently missed off, and the skill levels ranged from passable to very poor. Forgers started using tin-bismuth pewter, a habit that continued for a while after the regal coinage had changed back to copper. There are also lead copies, but these are so poorly made that they are much more likely to have been tokens rather than forgeries. The government continued to try and discourage the production of private tokens. A law of the time said that token manufacturers must be "chastised with exemplary severity."

These two cast 1663 shillings of Charles II resemble each other much more closely than they do a genuine shilling, suggesting that their source is common, and by the artificial looking patina, modern. Neither is circular or crisp in detail. One has a metal blob on its reverse. Both weigh exactly 4.97 gm (6 gm) and are the correct diameter at 25.5 mm.

The designs on both sides of James II (1685-1688) two guinea pieces were made distinctly different from the silver halfcrowns in order to discourage gilding.

James continued the copper-plugged tin coins introduced in Charles II's reign, by issuing tin halfpennies from 1685. As with the Charles coins, they were extensively counterfeited, again with most omitting the copper plug. Lead copies of the regal tin coinage of James II are as poorly made as those of Charles and so also are more likely to have been tokens rather than forgeries.

Impression in lead taken from a silver crown of James II. This reversed design could be a forger's guide for cutting a counterfeit die.

James's Irish gunmoney pieces have been counterfeited in bronzed white metal. The silver examples known are possibly coins made for his own use rather than fabrications. John White appears to have been the perpetrator of a sequence of gunmoney sixpences dated October 1689 to October 1690. The known genuine sequence is from June to September 1689.

During the reigns of William and Mary (1688-1694) and then William alone (1694-1702), when copper coinage was under private contract, flans were frequently cast, despite the stipulation that they should be rolled and cut.

The copper-plugged tin halfpence and farthings issued from 1689 were extensively counterfeited. Most of the forgeries omit the copper plug. As well as the tin, pewter forgeries of the post-tin coinage were plentiful in the 1690's[MI]. Examples of tin coin forgeries include a pewter cast halfpenny dated 1690, and farthings dated 1690 and 1691 - all lacking plug and edge legend. There is a pewter cast farthing, supposedly of Charles II, dated 1690, which has the copper plug 'suggested' by non-aligned indentations. The edge legend is missing.

Very crudely cast tin farthing with no legends (ex-Mitchiner collection). Wgt 5.34 gm (5.4-6.0 gm). 20.5 mm (22-24 mm).

For a while, the silver hammered coinage still around was allowed to circulate provided it was unclipped and had been officially pierced. It was estimated in 1696/7 that 10% of the broad silver then in circulation, that had been struck prior to 1662, was counterfeit. In Newton's time, (he was Warden of the Mint in 1695, Master of the Mint, 1699) halfcrowns were considered the denomination most liable to be counterfeited.

The 1696 coinage contains many errors - upside-down and back-to-front letters, missing punctuation, shields wrongly positioned, so epigraphy is less useful in distinguishing the genuine article from the fake for this period. Spelling errors occur on genuine coins, e.g. on the sixpence - GVLIEMAS for GVLIELMAS. They abound on the copper coinage towards the end of his reign as standards slumped. These poor regal copper coins stemmed from cheap labour. There are cast halfpennies and farthings, some of which may be genuine.

> *"Some remarkable counterfeit shillings, resembling the coin of K. William, have lately made their appearance. They are well executed, but greatly deficient in weight."*
>
> *The Gentleman's Magazine, 1780.*

Copper forgeries include a 1695 halfpenny that looks die-struck, but could be cliché produced; a well produced 1698 halfpenny and a crude cast.

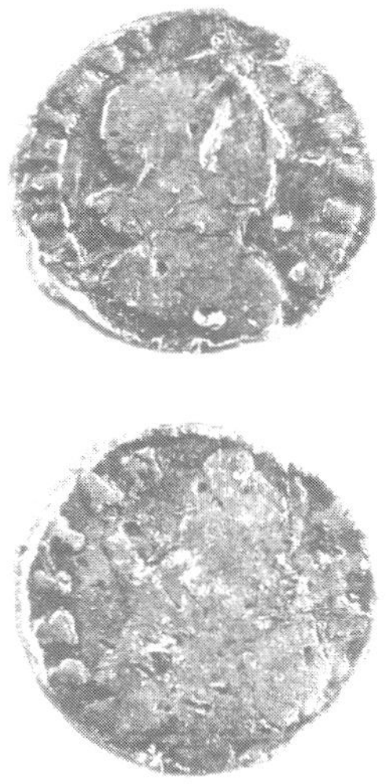

A crudely cast imitation of a William III 1701 halfpenny (ex-Mitchiner collection). Illustrated in the Numismatic Chronicle 1986 - but wrongly recorded there as 1695 to 1698. 5 o/c die axis. Wgt 9.38 gm (8.9-11.5 gm). Correct at 29 mm.

Low weight imitations of the 1694 to 1701 issues, mostly halfpennies, began to appear soon after 1725. The favourite source of metal was melted down current coin.

There is said to have been a practice after 1725 of forging 3/4 weight imitations of the William III copper coins of 1695 to 1701. The Philadelphia hoard found in 1975 in the U.S.A. contained 362 cast copper counterfeits of William III halfpennies dated 1699. The coins are lightweight and sand-cast. Most edges are heavily filed, and some show mould lines or sprues.

Copies of the Tin Coinage of William and Mary

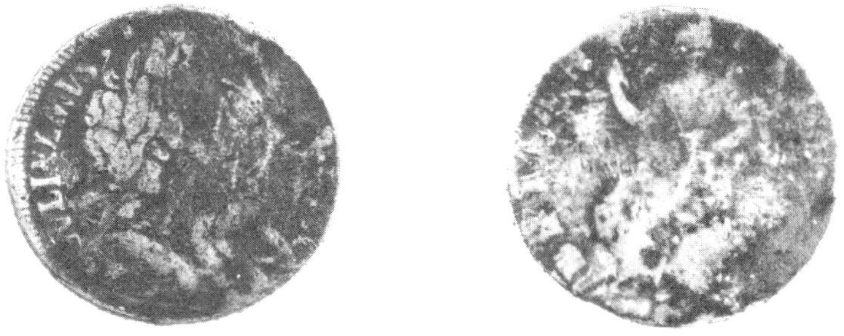

n.d. William and Mary tin halfpenny. Contemporary forgery found at Billingsgate. Silvery and black. Wgt 9.04 gm (10.5-11.7 gm). Correct at 28 mm.

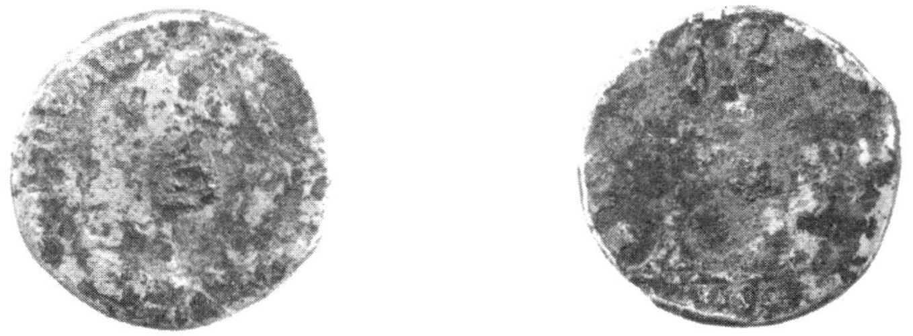

This 1690 William and Mary tin farthing with copper plug is. considerably overweight at 7.88 gm (5.2-5.8 gm). 21.5 mm (22-24 mm). (ex-Mitchiner collection).

1694 William and Mary tin farthing - no plug and in white metal (ex-Mitchiner collection). Illustrated in the *Numismatic Chronicle* 1986 No. 5, p. 181 - where it is erroneously dated 1691. Wgt 5.78 gm (5.2-5.8 gm). Correct at 22.5 mm.

Contemporary forgeries, many cast, and collector targetting pieces, including electrotypes, exist for all the major types of Anne's coinage (1702-1714). The heads on the guinea and the shilling looked so similar that gilding the latter was a popular eighteenth century pastime. The guinea obverses only differed from the shilling in having a lock of hair falling to the right breast. Sixpences were tooled to resemble the half-guinea design and then gilded.

Contemporary cast of a 1714 Anne farthing. Wgt 4.15 gm (4.8-5.8 gm). Correct diameter at 21 mm.

Double-headed halfpennies are probably restrikes. Few halfpennies were counterfeited.

Farthings can be found cast, struck and electrotyped, with 1711 a common date, 1710 unusual. The 1713 farthing was a pattern only. Forgeries of this are usually cast. The 1714 farthing is not particularly rare, yet in 1802, a rumour about its 'extreme rarity' briefly pushed its supposed value up to £500. Not surprising then that they were prolifically counterfeited, but their poor level of design makes them easy to detect.

In Anne's reign, base silver shillings were struck for use in the West Indies. These 'black dogs', made from a lead alloy with a small amount of silver, can easily be mistaken for counterfeits.

Early in George III's reign, quantities of counters**MI** were produced which resembled Anne shillings and sixpences, with dates ranging from 1702 to 1720 (1711 the commonest) and 1761 to 1774 (1761 the commonest); all in the latter group 'exposing' themselves by their impossible dates. The busts are invariably crude and completely unconvincing. The shields on the reverses have two lions where there should be three. Some shields bear four roses in the angles, where genuine pieces show plumes, or alternate roses and plumes or blank angles.

In 1768, workmen pulling down an old house at Norwich, found two dies for coining early eighteenth century coins; one for guineas, the other pistoles. These Portuguese coins were in general circulation in England in Anne's time because of the favourable trade balance with Portugal. Locals recalled that in the year 1710, a bookseller called Samuel Self, who lived in that house, was convicted for forging metal stamps. He must also have been a gold coin counterfeiter, an offence he got away with by concealing these dies.

HOT OFF THE MARK

"Nov. 10, 1696. The last week I took two or three new counterfeit sixpences, butt exquisitly made, and washed with silver, being copper within. Monday was a sommit, they had many sixpences stirring at Hull, with a Y for York on them, tho' they did not begin to coin such sixpences at York till the Wednesday following, so soon is our new monney counterfeited, so that they take new milled money as well as old, onely by weight."

Anne's Counters

Anne shillings, and to a lesser extent sixpences, were profusely copied in the late eighteenth century by Birmingham toymen, for use as gaming counters, although some may have been intended to deceive. The poor style evident in these examples would have made deception difficult. Anne's features range from passable to pitiful. There are many idiosyncratic dates on these pieces, ranging from 1701 (William III) to 1774 (George III).

1702 shilling in pinchbeck. Wgt 3.02 gm (5.9-6.0 gm). 23 mm.

ANNE'S CORRECT PORTRAIT

Genuine 1702 Vigo shilling. Type C, First bust. Wgt 5.99 gm (5.9-6.0 gm). 25 mm.

1761 (George III date) sixpence in bright brass. Wgt 1.99 gm (2.9-3.0 gm). 19.5 mm (21 mm).

1711 sixpence in dull brass. Wgt 2.78 gm (2.9-3.0 gm). 20.5 mm (21 mm).

1761 (George III date) shilling size, copper, crude workmanship. Wgt 3.44 gm (5.9-6.0 gm). 23.5 mm.

1701 (William III date) shilling in pinchbeck. Wgt 3.25 gm (5.9-6.0 gm). 23.5 mm.

1711 pinchbeck shilling. Bizarre portrait. Small cut on rim. Seriously underweight at 2.63 gm (5.9-6.0 gm). 22.5 mm.

Official advice on detecting Queen Anne counterfeits, given in 1741:

" - The Difference between the Gold and Silver Coin of Queen Anne is more difficult to be discover'd after being altered as above mentioned; the Lock of Hair, which proceeds from the Nape of the Neck over the Right Shoulder, and lies on the Right Breast, on the Guinea, being the only Mark by which Persons not well acquainted with Gold and Silver can distinguish the Guinea from the Shilling, which has not that Lock of Hair." - Any Person or Persons that shall be detected in uttering the counterfeit Money before mention'd, or any other counterfeit Money, upon Notice given to the Solicitor of the Mint, such Offenders will be prosecuted at the Government's Expence."

1710 gilt brass guinea with the correct reverse for date, but incorrect 1702-1708 bust. No edge graining. Wgt 4.66 gm (8.3 gm). 26 mm (25 mm).

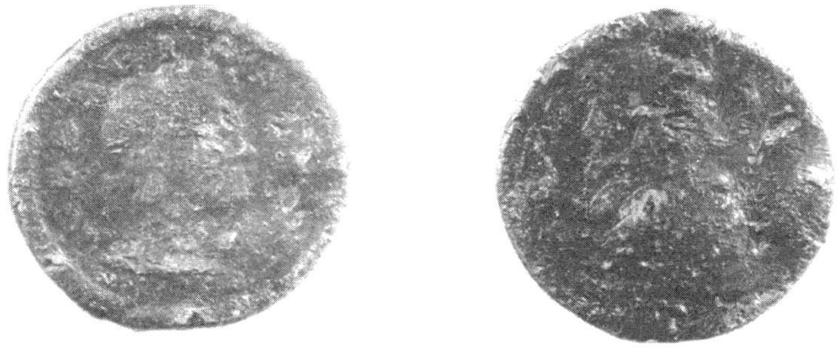

1717-18 George I dump halfpenny copy with high lead content (ex-Mitchiner Collection. Not noted in the Numismatic Chronicle (1986 No. 10, p. 181) as being of the dump series). Wgt 9.68 gm (9.4-10.3 gm). Correct diameter at 26 mm.

1720 George I halfpenny. High-grade contemporary struck copy. 4 o/c die axis. Wgt 8.88 gm (9.4-10.3 gm). Correct diameter at 29 mm.

9

Georgian Epidemics

George I's coinage was less counterfeited at the time than that of the preceding or succeeding reigns. There were two issues of halfpennies and farthings - 1717 to 1718 were 'dumps' on small, thickish flans; 1719 to 1724 were on larger, thinnish flans, still weighing the same. The dumps did not attract much attention, but counterfeiting started to rise again with the latter issue.

EIGHTEENTH CENTURY TRENDS

The main counterfeiting methods of the mid-eighteenth century were false metal imitating gold and silver, low precious metal content or true precious metal clipped, filed or leached from genuine coins. This was melted down, poured into disc-shaped moulds to provide the flans, which were then restruck with counterfeit dies. These were often copies of Portuguese and Spanish coins, which would be less familiar to the general public and so less likely to be detected.

If reduced by clipping or filing, the coin would then need to be rounded off to a perfect circle again, and the edge-graining replaced with a fine file. The leaching method required guineas to be soaked overnight in a vessel filled with aquafortis. When the coin was removed the following morning, a residue of gold would be left behind worth 6d to 9d.

No heavy permanent equipment was the rule, and be unobtrusive was the motto of all coiners. Employ tools that could be claimed to have other, legitimate uses. Even flan moulds could be passed off as button moulds, but the dies were the real giveaways and so required secure hiding places. Coining gangs would buy sets of dies from crooked craftsmen for £3 or more per pair.

Unlike the guineas, half-guineas seem rarely to have been forged during George II's reign (1727-60). But both suffered from being similar in design to shillings and sixpences respectively. The guinea design was changed to differentiate it from a gilded shilling and because of the epidemic of gilded sixpences being passed off as half-guineas, the reverse design of the sixpence became a crowned shield - and the epidemic subsided.

Counterfeit halfpennies and farthings abounded in this reign. The epidemic began in 1725, with the appearance of counterfeits of the 1694 to 1701 copper coinage, particularly halfpennies. The first approach of the counterfeiters was to melt down contemporary coins and restrike copies of the 1694 to 1701 issues on low-weight flans matching the lighter weight William III halfpennies. The forgers then moved on to using low-grade copper to produce imitations of current coins. The copper in a George II halfpenny was worth about half of its face value, so counterfeiters could easily double their outlay on raw material with their lightweight copies. The risk was low, as the counterfeiting of base metal coinage was classed as a misdemeanour only, incurring light penalties. This led to a runaway situation that the Government attempted to slow down by the Act of 1742, making forgers of brass or copper money liable to two years' imprisonment. They also had to produce sureties to guarantee two further years' good behaviour. £10 per conviction was offered to informers and pardons were offered to accomplices betraying their confederates where two or more convictions resulted. Ten years later a proclamation endeavoured to enforce this Act. By the start of 1753, nearly half of circulating copper was estimated to be spurious. Production of George II copper coins ceased in 1755 because of this.

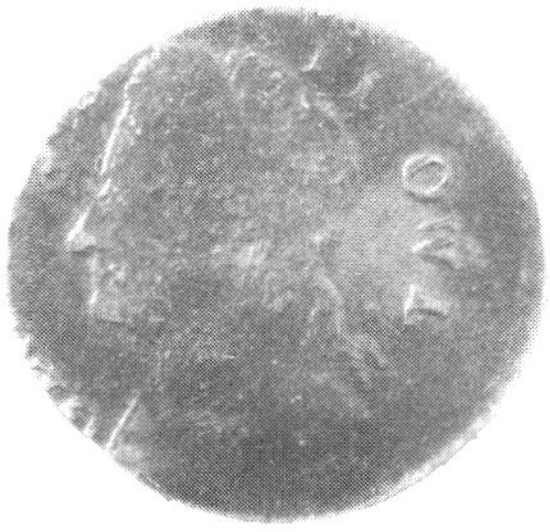

George II farthing with jumbled date. The right-hand legend on the obverse reads OWL instead of REX! The reverse legend is correct. Very thin. Wgt 1.31 gm (4.5-5.3 gm). 21 mm (22-23 mm).

EVASIONS

If coins were "*not an exact similitude*" of the genuine article, a loophole in the law allowed the producers to escape prosecution. Such pieces were dubbed 'evasion coins' and began to appear in diverse quantity, many looking worn because the dies were deliberately made to produce this effect. Anothe trick to get them successfully into circulation was to darken them by frying. A nightly fry-up of the day's output was a regular activity of criminal families.

Contemporary estimates of the false copper in circulation in the mid eighteenth century range from 40 to 98%. Cast copies lessened and die-struck ones increased at this time.

The token factories of Birmingham are high on the list of suspected manufacturing sources of these prolific counterfeit halfpennies. Most fall into the 'adequate' category of design copying. Much rarer are those that are very good or bad. Overweight copies of high quality were early products. George II efforts tended to be more skilfully made than those of George III. Counterfeit English and Irish halfpennies and farthings of both Georges circulated freely in Britain and in the North American colonies. The halfpennies were overvalued in North

THE QUICK AND THE DEAD

October 1733

"The Sessions ended at the Old Bailey, when the following Criminals receiv'd Sentence of Death... Margaret Berry, for Coining... pleaded her Belly, and was found quick with Child".

December 1733

"Elizabeth Wright pleaded her Belly, but was found not quick with Child".

America at 12 to 18 per shilling and so any counterfeits that made their way to the Americas, stayed there.

CONTEMPORARY METHOD OF DETECTION

Cast lead-alloy counterfeits in George II's reign, were exposed by heating them. Depending on the degree of lead in the alloy and the amount of heat applied, they would become pliable, turn white or even melt.

Found on a woman in 1732, 18 guineas plus some broad pieces and 20 Portuguese moidores, showing the extent that foreign coins were in circulation at the time. Not surprising then that forgers took advantage of this, as several of the following warnings show:

1752
YORK
"A tradesman of York was offer'd in payment some £3. 12s. pieces, which upon examination were found debased. They are something thicker than the true coin, weigh from 6 to 8 grains less, and are plated over, the S in the word JOANNES is inverted, and the D for DEI (is reversed). One of them being uncased [i.e. plating removed], the gold weighed about 17s."
The Gentleman's Magazine, 1752.

1752
NEWCASTLE
"There being some cased [i.e. plated] £3. 12s. pieces in this town (Newcastle), supposed to have been made by the same hands that counterfeited the £3. 12s. piece with the letters D and S reversed, the publick are desired to observe, that the letters in the cased £3. 12s. look very coarse; that the T in the words PORT and ET appears something like an ill-made Y; and that the date is 1741."
The Gentleman's Magazine, 1752.

1755
"Several pieces of counterfeit Portugal coin having been discovered in this and several of the neighbouring towns, let it be observed, that most of the 36s. pieces are of the date 1750, the top of the figure 5 scarcely appearing, with the letter B under the head, and the middle of the reverse side smooth, and that they are of a very pale colour. The date of many of the moidores is 1721, and the weight of each is nearly right."
The Scots Magazine, 1755/6.

1755
LEEDS
"James Heely, of Leeds, buckle and button maker, and his wife, were committed to York castle, Oct 29, accused of coining 36s. and 27s. pieces. The following description of the counterfeited pieces was made out by one of the clerks of the mint.
"The 36s. pieces are of two dates: one 1747, without any letter under the head; the other 1750, with B under the head. These have a bad jingle. The top of the head does not come central with the crown on the other side. The letter X in REX is much more distant from the neck of the head than the good ones are.
"The 27s. pieces which are bad, are all of them pale, and have also a bad jingle, different from the good.' The 27s. pieces are said to be dated 1717, 1719, and 1721."
The Scots Magazine, 1755/6.

MINT-OFFICE WARNING

Official advice on detecting counterfeits, given in 1741:

*"Notice given from His Majesty's Mint-Office in the Tower:
"Whereas several evil dispos'd Persons have practis'd the making of Shillings and Sixpences to resemble Guineas and Half Guineas, by putting Scepters upon the Reverse, and guilding them over, to the great Prejudice of his Majesty's Subjects.*

" - To prevent that evil Practice, and the Publick from being impos'd upon for the future, the above impressions are publish'd, that all Persons may know the Difference between the Gold and Silver Coins, which is the same in every King's Coin as the above, viz. the Neck of the Head on the Guinea is without any Robe or Drapery on the Shoulders.

" - As to the Gold Coin of his present Majesty, there are no Scepters on them, but the Arms of Great Britain in a Shield."

Counterfeit of a 1751 halfpenny. 'Loose drapery' (ex-Mitchiner Collection). Wgt 7.94 gm (9.7-10.3 gm). Correct diameter at 28 mm.

1756
"Counterfeit guineas are current in different places. They are dated 1754. The impression of the face is extremely faint, and particularly so under the throat. The figures 1 and 7 are run quite close into one side of the crown, and the 5 into the other side. They weigh in air from one pound to one pound and six pence, but in water, only fourteen shillings."
The Scots Magazine, 1755/6.

1757
"Watkin Morgan was this day committed to the common goal of the county of Caermarthen, for uttering a great number of counterfeit moidores, and 36 shilling pieces. These pieces looked quite fresh, were full weight, but thicker in the middle; the dates of the moidores are all 1722, the 36'es 1747. - Hull's new invented instrument for detecting bad gold will in an instant discover these counterfeit pieces."
The Gentleman's Magazine, 1757.

1757
"Notice was given from the Excise-office, that there are now in circulation counterfeit guineas, dated 1755, which nearly resemble those issued from the mint, and bear their full weight, distinguishable only by a fainter impression of the die on the arms side, a pale reddish colour, and by a more acute tinkling found in sounding them."
The Gentleman's Magazine, 1757.

John Sigismund Tanner came from Saxe-Gorba and worked at the Royal Mint from 1728, engraving new dies as assistant to Croker. He was appointed Chief Graver to the Mint in May 1741, a position he held to 1775. Richard Yeo became in turn his assistant. In 1738, Tanner engraved imitations of Simon's Cromwellian coins under orders from the mintmaster, Richard Arundell.

Sad mad King George III had a very long reign (1760-1820), so more counterfeits would be expected in his reign than in others, all else being equal. But investigations show that all else was not equal and circumstances arose to produce counterfeiting epidemics. There was a silver famine at the start. Even gold coinage was proving inadequate. Then, by the middle of his reign, the Royal Mint's obsolete coining equipment could not cope with the need for small change caused by Britain's industrialisation. Between 1754 and 1797, there was just one official issue of 'copper' coinage (1770-1775). These factors led to the acceptance of foreign coin, its countermarking and overstriking, to the appearance of Bank of England and private token coinage, and to waves of counterfeiting.

GEORGE III GOLD COINAGE
The shortages of Georgian gold invited counterfeiter participation and they duly obliged, leading to frequent warnings to the public:

1762
"A number of counterfeit guineas is now circulating; they are of his present majesty, very well struck off, and made of a high coloured metal, but so very light as to be easily detected, weighing only 12s."

1765
"Several pieces of counterfeit gold coin have lately been discovered at

Birmingham, so nicely finished as hardly to be discovered; they are chiefly 36s. pieces of a pale colour, and the date 1750: The top of the 5 is larger than in the true ones."

"Several counterfeit half guineas are now circulating with great success, which, upon trial, are found to be no more than the thickest and largest six-pences, a little bent, and slightly washed over with a pale gold colour - The new invented patent instrument for detecting counterfeit coin, may be had at St. John's-Gate."

1765

"There are a great number of counterfeit guineas now about town (London). They are of his present Majesty, extremely well struck, in silver, and milled, and so neatly covered with leaf-gold that no eye can discern any difference. The only method of knowing them is by their sound, which is very dull; and to excuse that defect, they have each an artificial small crack, to which their not ringing is attributed. But whenever any person meets with such a guinea, let him rub the edge smartly upon any thing hard, and the leaf-gold, which is very thin, will rub off, and immediately discover the fraud."

Scots Magazine

1766

"There are a number of bad guineas in circulation, which look yellower than the genuine ones, and the sceptres are very imperfect."

"A number of counterfeit moidores and six and thirty's are now in circulation. The moidores are strongly gilt with a pale gold, and a little bent; the composition tin and pewter. The R in the six and thirty's stands too high, date 1750."

1773

"There are at present a number of counterfeit guineas circulating in this kingdom from Holland. They are good gold, but want about three shillings in weight; they are distinguishable only by the u in GeorgiUs; ours are spelt with a v GeorgiVs."

1786

"(A) watchman gave information that he suspected some clandestine business carried on in a court in Chick-lane. In consequence of which, some peace-officers went to search, and found a press, dies, some gold and other metals, with every implement for coining; and some counterfeit guineas, full weight, and executed so well, that they could only be distinguished by being rather thicker in the middle, and brighter than the real ones. It is supposed that many of them are in circulation; and this is inserted as a caution."

"A great number of new counterfeit half-guineas are now in circulation. The head is awkwardly done, the reverse faint; the date 1784; and the weight less than an old six-pence."

Well-gilded copper 1777 guinea, now showing wear on highspots - cheek and nose. Wgt 5.17 gm (8.4 gm). 24.5 mm (24 mm).

FOREIGN COIN FAKES

Counterfeit half Dobras (or Johannes) made of thinly gilded base metal and dated 1746, appeared in 1770. They were lighter, broader and thicker than genuine coins. 1777 saw the appearance of base metal imitations of Spanish milled dollars, halves and quarters. They were of the correct size, but lightweight, looking cast and with hammered instead of grained edges.

The state of affairs in West Yorkshire at this time can be gauged by the advertisement placed in a local paper by the Constable of Halifax offering a reward for the capture of his own Deputy on a little matter

1788 Imitation spade half guinea in good brass. Edge graining is missing. It is unusual in having a cockerel below the bust. The reverse lettering has proceeded too far round, leaving no room at the end for T.E.T.E. Wgt 2.97 gm (4.2 gm). Correct diameter at 20 mm.

This very deceptive gold-plated copper 1791 half guinea, is now revealed by wear on the highspots. It has been crimped as a (cheap-skate) love token. Die-axis is wrong. Wgt 2.56 gm (4.2 gm). Correct diameter at 21 mm.

of gold coin clipping. In Halifax and frequently elsewhere in the late eighteenth century, the two activities of clipping and forging went hand in hand. Forgers made a practice of clipping genuine gold guineas, filing them to restore the rim graining appearance and then 'dropping' them back on the unwary public. The gold clippings were converted into lightweight counterfeits - a popular choice being Portuguese gold coins that, although foreign, were at that time allowed to be used as currency at a recognised value.

One Yorkshire gang of clippers and coiners became so notorious, and locally powerful that their leader was known as 'King' David. *(see THE COINERS OF CRAGG VALE, Chapter 13).*

John Wesley preached in the Halifax area against coiners, and got a hostile reception. Not surprising, in view of the number of coiners in his audience.

SPADE GUINEA FORGERIES AND IMITATIONS

Spade Guineas appeared in 1787 and were extensively forged. There are modern forgeries of the 1798 date. The early 1800's saw the proliferation of die-struck imitations - some to pass as guineas, but mostly for use as brass gaming pieces, as revealed by old dates and by legends such as "In memory of the good old days". Many tradesmen adapted them for use as advertising pieces, by adding their names and messages. According to lawyers of the day, the resultant variations from the original design absolved the producers from prosecution for uttering false coins. There is no doubt, though, that however innocent the tradesmen were who issued them, these tokens, well polished, could be passed off as guineas in busy markets and on dark nights.

1796

"There are now in circulation a number of counterfeit guineas and half-guineas which cannot be detected by weighing them, as they are considerably above the standard. But which upon close examination, though well executed, will be found deficient in the milling .. Larger than the real coin, of a lighter colour, bearing the date 1790."

Scots Magazine

1799

"A counterfeit half guinea, bearing date 1790, is at present in circulation. The circumstances which expose it to detection are, the lines which compose the shield being too small, the head being less prominent, and the edge being thicker than the genuine one for that year. The B, which stands for the word Britannia, is somewhat like a K. It will not bear the test of ringing."

Scots Magazine

In 1817, counterfeit guineas appeared of correct weight, but thicker than genuine, with the head more raised, and made from spurious gold.

THIRD GUINEAS

1802

"The counterfeit Seven-Shilling pieces, of the date of 1800, now in circulation, differ from the good ones in the following particulars: they are paler in colour

Plated Third Guineas

Almost all examples of plated third guinea copies exhibit two give-aways - light weight and wrong die-axis. Also most have a slightly enlarged crown on the reverse. Although there were issues for fourteen different years between 1797 and 1813, three dates dominate the forgeries – 1797, the first year of third guineas, 1798 and 1804, the first year of a revised design. Most copies match the 17 mm diameter of the genuine pieces.

The lettering of this plated 1798 third guinea varies in size and is unevenly positioned and spaced. The reverse has a double dot between Mag..Bri. 10 o/c die-axis. Wgt 1.70 gm (2.8 gm). 16.5 mm.

The gilding has worn off the highspots on this gilt 1798 third guinea. The reverse has a double dot between Mag..Bri. 4 o/c die-axis. Wgt 1.48 gm (2.8 gm). 17 mm.

Plated 1803 third guinea. It has an uneven date (the 8 is taller than the other figures) and is of a paler gold than genuine examples. 11 o/c die-axis. Wgt 1.50 gm (2.8 gm). 17 mm.

1804 third guinea in gold-plated silver, now wearing off. Uneven date figures. Lettering too small. Left end of crown points to letter 'E'. not 'I'. 10 o/c die-axis. Wgt 1.58 gm (2.8 gm). 17 mm.

1804 third guinea. Test mark on each centre. The rim is sliding off the flan. 11 o/c die-axis. Wgt 1.61 gm (2.8 gm). 17 mm.

This shiny gold-plated 1804 third guinea now has a few worn highspots. Die-axis correct. Wgt 1.71 gm (2.8 gm). 17 mm.

---

and they ring more shrill; the milling is more wide, the eye in the head seems swelled, the crown is not so rotund, and appears cut off at the edges; the A's in the inscription want the bar across, and have the appearance, of course, of a V reversed; and the bottoms of most of the letters are more curved: on the whole, they are very well executed, but their weight will detect them at once."

In 1804, forgers were producing third guinea pieces with clumsy and irregular edge graining and with the king's head "torn and lacerated."

MINT COPIES

In 1815, the Royal Mint struck French Louis d'Or for paying British troops on the Continent. To counter them being called forgeries, a letter R was put on the right of the date in place of the Paris mint-marks. Also Tiolier's name was omitted from below the bust and a fleur de lys put on the left of the date.

GEORGE III SILVER COINAGE

George's silver coinage was widely counterfeited. The halfcrowns in silver-coated brass were very convincing but are now old enough to have at least part of the coating worn away, as with the shillings and sixpences. In many cases, there is now no trace at all of the original silvering. This is not surprising, as the thinner the silver coating, the greater the forger's profit - and he only needed to deceive long enough to utter his products successfully.

1765

"A number of counterfeit half crown pieces are now circulating about town, plated over with silver, and extremely well executed; they are found to be a composition of bath metal and copper, and are rather larger than the true ones."

A 1770 Proclamation threatened branding on the cheek with the letter R (for rogue or reprobate?) for clipping or filing.

In 1773, a hoard of Roman silver coinage, found by a farmer digging a drain and said to have weighed a hundredweight, was combined with all the pewter in the area to churn out counterfeits. In the same year the first mention of plated George II shillings appears.

At the end of the eighteenth century, the bulk of silver coinage in circulation was so worn that much of it looked like blank discs. John Cockroft, in 1782, achieved the ultimate in counterfeiting ease, by 'copying' these worn shillings with no visible legend left on either side, thus requiring no counterfeit dies to produce. He just grained the edges and "aged" silver blanks, probably obtained by him quite legitimately from Birmingham, presenting magistrates with the problem of whether such blanks could ever be described as forgeries!

Complete silver-plated example of a contemporary forgery of an 1819 sixpence. Wgt 2.50 gm (2.8 gm). 19.5 mm (19 mm).

A review in 1786 confirmed the poor state of the silver coinage, attributing it to a lack of new issues. Shillings averaged 77% of their issued weight; sixpences 64%. The 1787 issue of shillings, etc., intended to correct this, promptly started disappearing into hoards because of the growing value of the silver content.

1788

"Were apprehended in a garret in Golden-lane, by the officers belonging to the Public-office, Shoreditch, a father, mother, and three sons, in the act of counterfeiting the current coin of this realm called shillings and sixpences. On the officers breaking open the door, they detected two of the sons at work, who immediately threw a quantity of shillings and sixpences into the fire. There were found in the room a great quantity more, with bottles of aqua-fortis, sand-paper, cork, a polishing-board, and implements to finish with, which were secured, and the people committed to Newgate for trial."
The Gentleman's Magazine.

In 1797, counterfeit dollars were being made in both Birmingham and London, costing illicit buyers two shillings each for five pence-worth of metal. At the Royal Mint, John Alston, from Birmingham, was experimenting with his liquid test for the detection of counterfeit silver coins.

1816 is a scarce date and does not appear to have attracted contemporary counterfeits.

1817

"(A) Silver Coinage was formed in 1817, and guarded by a new-invented graining on the edge, but so superior is the activity of wickedness to that of honesty, that counterfeits were delivered without the walls of the Bank, whilst the genuine coins were issuing within..."

SPANISH DOLLARS, COUNTERMARKS
and BANK OF ENGLAND TOKENS

Silver shortage was the reason for the presence of eight and four reales Spanish coins freely circulating in Britain at the end of the eighteenth century. The miniature profile George III countermarks - oval and, later, octagonal on the 8 reales and oval only on the 4 reales - confirmed Government approval of their use. Addington advised that the rate for these countermarked dollars should not be set too high, which would encourage counterfeiting, nor too low, which would encourage melting down for the greater bullion value.

OVAL COUNTERMARKS

In 1797, Pillar and Portrait type Spanish and Latin American dollars (8 reales) were countermarked with a small profile of George III, to function as current coin worth 4s 9d - the silver content being worth 4s 5. 3/4d. The small countermark was easily imitated, and, as its presence raised the value of the dollar, it was extensively counterfeited. The situation worsened in mid 1797 when the value of silver dropped, so the issue was recalled.

The puncheons for the oval countermarking of Spanish 8 reales coins to make them current in England, were those used for marking silver plate. Those held by Goldsmiths' Hall and the provincial assay offices were insufficient and so more had to be made, leading to slight variations, making the detection of counterfeit marks more difficult. The puncheons were around for a long time after their official employment and were used on a variety of foreign coins "for collectors".

OCTAGONAL COUNTERMARKS

In 1804, the easily counterfeited oval was replaced by a larger, octagonal mark, still containing a profile of George III, derived from the Maundy money bust.

The Bank tellers buying in the old overstruck dollars at 5s each, had to decide immediately if they were genuine or not. Whenever an overstrike only was considered counterfeit, they would not buy the dollar and the owner had to go to Binns & Wood, who would pay 4s 8d for it. What the public did not know was that Binns & Wood then sold them all on to the Bank for 4s 8.1/4d each. This ploy stopped the public from thinking that the Bank was diddling them out of 4d by

Countermarked Dollars and Bank of England Tokens

1792 Mexican 8 Reales of Carlos IV of Spain countermarked with George III bust in an oval frame. The strike has removed the plating from the corresponding part of the reverse. The plating has also gone from the tip of George's nose and from parts of the bust perimeter. There is a wedge-shaped test cut on the edge. Wgt 28.31 gm (27.07 gm). 41 mm (38-40 mm).

1792 Mexican 8 Reales of Carlos IV countermarked with George III bust in an oval frame. Lighter and smaller than the preceding example. Wgt 26.42 gm (27.07 gm). Correct diameter at 39 mm.

This counterfeit 1792 Mexican 8 Reales of Carlos IV with a false octagonal countermark was copying the genuine Spanish coins, which official overstamping was converting into British dollars. There is now no trace of the silver-coating. Wgt 24.11 gm (27.07 gm). Correct diameter at 39 mm.

Plated 1804 Bank of England Dollar. Silvering off nose and chin. Obverse 1 (Coincraft). On the reverse, the K below the shield is missing. 11 o/c die-axis. Wgt 24.67 gm (25 to 28 gm). Correct diameter at 40 mm.

This example of an 1811 3 shilling Bank Token is quite exceptional in still having its full silvering on the copper core. Two small test cuts on the reverse edge show that someone still detected that it was a 'wrong-un'. 11 o/c die-axis. Wgt 14.29 gm (15 gm). 34 mm.

This 1s 6d Bank Token, dated 1816 is silver-plated on copper alloy. Wgt 6.04 (7.4 gm). 27 mm.

Plated forgery of an 1812 three shillings Bank Token. Two holes have been bored through it to convert it into a button. Highspot outlining is the only trace left of the original silverplating. Wgt 14.45 gm (15 gm). 35 mm.

claiming to recognise a counterfeit overstrike.

18th April, 1804
"Two individuals had passed 20 dollars with false stamps and had in their possession 30 more; the Bank wanted to know how to prosecute them. The case put to Piggott (Sir Arthur Piggott, the Bank's counsel) was that dollars worth from 4s 3d to 4s 9d each were circulated "for the accommodation of the public" at 5s each with the promise of redemption at the latter price. The difference was sufficient to tempt people to forge the stamp on the coins and pass them off as being issued from the Bank. Now the Bank admitted that the issue was one of Public convenience, not supported by any Act of Parliament or Proclamation, but they claimed that, whether or no they were issued with authority, the imitation of them was a cheat and punishable at Common Law, as individuals would accept them thinking that the security of a 'public body' guaranteed their genuineness." Piggott said the Bank had no more rights than any other individuals, so a bill was hurriedly put forward and became law on the 10th July and an announcement was issued to the public two weeks' later saying "In future any one who shall make, coin or counterfeit, or cause or procure to be made with intent to resemble or look like dollars would be judged guilty of a Felony and be transported for up to seven years." Importing such pieces was made an equal offence.

From 1804 to 1811, despite the official hope, counterfeiting continued with the octagonal countermarks. Also, almost as much as for the oval marks, the puncheons for the octagonal marks were being used 'unofficially' for many years' afterwards. They were also used on foreign coins other than Spanish or Spanish Colonial, to provide 'varieties' for collectors. Opinions differ on the Spanish 4 reales with an octagonal countermark. Some say all such are forgeries.

Throughout this period, the Government did its best to discourage the forgers, as the Bath Chronicle reminded its readers on the 15th August, 1811:
"Bank Tokens. Counterfeiters are liable to seven years' transportation; Utterers, first time, six months' imprisonment; second time, two years' imprisonment; third time, fourteen years' imprisonment."

If forgers were 'exported' to the Colonies, then so were their skills, which was tough luck on the Colonies! One Bank token forger escaped prosecution because if found guilty he would only face imprisonment and he was already a French prisoner of war in Portchester Castle!

COUNTERFEIT COUNTERMARKS
Some counterfeit 8 reales coins can be found with genuinet countermarks. Others with counterfeit ones. If a coin looked doubtful, it could be checked by using a silver penny such as the Maundy, as a touchstone. Countermarked halved and quartered dollars have been regarded with suspicion by numismatists, but may well be legitimate Mint strikings, as they had no precedent to bar such, nor to countermarking other foreign coins.

Oval marks appear on 8 reales of Mexico, Bolivia, Guatemala, Chile, Peru and of Spain from Madrid and Seville; of France (1792 Ecu). Octagonal marks appear on 8 reales of Mexico, Guatemala, Chile and, very rarely, on U.S. dollars. One is illustrated on page 29 of the January 1996 issue of *Coin News*.

Genuine countermarks on copper coins and tokens may not be due to master punches straying into the wrong hands, but to Mint trials or simply curiosities produced by Mint staff. Coins exist which are believed never to have circulated as countermarked pieces and yet have been overstruck with genuine dies. Some pieces have been falsely countermarked for collectors. N. Du Quesne Bird points out that disused countermark punches may have been around to be misused for most of the nineteenth century. He adds that Goldsmiths' Hall records a number of prosecutions against goldsmiths for owning false punches.

OVERSTRUCK OR 'REGENERATED' DOLLARS

Boulton proposed to take Spanish 8 reales and overstrike them completely with an English design, terming the result 'regenerated dollars'. In reference to the Bank of England overstrikes, Boulton commented on the ease with which they could be counterfeited. Also, if his method was applied so that some of the original design still showed through, this would make counterfeiting even more difficult. His idea was accepted and these dollars, all dated 1804, were issued at 5s each by the Bank of England from 1804 to 1811 (possibly longer).

1804

"Dollars were delivered to the Bank on May 16th and *The St James's Chronicle* of June 2d reported that they already had been counterfeited.

"A great number of counterfeit dollars (have) found their way into circulation... The Spanish dollars entrusted to Mr Boulton to re-coin, amounted to £2,500,000; these were of different sizes in their original state, some... a quarter of an inch in diameter larger than the others.

"In re-coining these Mr Boulton judged it expedient to have them struck in a steel collar; in consequence of which all the pieces ... were perfectly round when re-coined, and precisely of the same diameter.

"Previous to this process, the Spanish dollars, though of various sizes, were nearly of a weight; those of a larger diameter were of course thinner than the small diameter. From the great difference in their sizes, it was thought necessary to assort them into three classes, namely, No's. 1, 2 and 3, for the purpose of distinguishing the true from the bad.

"Mr Boulton then directed a gage-plate to be made, the dimentions of which perfectly fit either No. 1, 2, or 3. The manner in which the dollars are measured by this plate, is either horizontally or vertically. The plate measures the circumference, the thickness and the diameter. The publick may be able to judge of the difference between the counterfeit dollars, of which there are two sorts, and the good one, by the following standard of weight: The good dollar, re-coined by

Mr. Boulton, upon the average weighs 416 grains; while the thickest of the counterfeits only weighs 375 grains; and the thinnest not more than 310...
"It may be necessary further to observe, that the edges of the true dollars are perfectly flat; while those of the false and counterfeit ones are not so, having a rim down the middle of the edge, which may be plainly distinguished by a glass.
"The publick are certainly much indebted to Mr Boulton for his intended 'gauge plate' for the detection of counterfeit dollars. I hope the same will soon be to be procured, and that some method will be adopted that they may not be forged also."

Because the second striking, in 1810, still carried the date 1804, instances occur of the underlying Spanish coin showing a later date, such as 1808. The silver Bank Tokens of 1811, also still dated 1804, prompted private issues, leading to the Bil that was passed in 1812, prohibiting them. The next issue did not appear until 1816.

As Boulton's Bank dollars overstruck on Spanish coins, required heavy steam powered machines not available to forgers, many then resorted to base metal counterfeits. Brass counterfeits, die-struck and silver-coated, are common, and of good quality, except that the silver wearing off has exposed most to present-day detection.

The forgers of 1816 could take silver dollars worth around 4s and turn them into redeemable Bank Dollars worth 5s 6d, hence the existence of good silver forgeries.

Aimed at alleviating the shortage in silver coinage around their value, 3s and 1s 6d Bank of England tokens were issued for each year from 1811 to 1816.

The 3s tokens were being forged by September 1811 in thinly plated copper pieces, described in the Press of the day as having a fainter king's bust, thicker letters and a wreath that rose too high and was poorly designed. The reverse had an almost illegible date and a similarly obscure letter O in the word Token. Also the figure 3 was larger than normal. A dull ring when dropped, plus a whiter appearance added to the ways in which the public then could spot these duds. The 8 in the date on the forgeries is too small and fine, making it appear to be in two parts. Most were made in Birmingham.

Genuine tokens dated 1811 to 1815 are catalogued in F condition at £12 each. 1816 at £150, which probably explains why there seem to be no counterfeit examples for this date.

July 1812, a bill was drafted to double the penalty for uttering forged 3s Bank Tokens from six months to twelve, making it the same as for forged sixpences.

The Bank was on weaker legal ground with token forgers compared to dollar forgers, so it indemnified its Birmingham Agent, Payne, against breaking in on suspected forgers and finding no evidence of

Three Shilling Bank Tokens Survey

An analysis by the author of 26 randomly obtained forged tokens, revealed the following:

1 All were silver-plated brass, with one only retaining the full silver-plating. However, this is probably an incorrect picture as fully-plated pieces may still be deceiving.

2 Twelve had an incorrect medallion die-axis, and so could be queried on that aspect alone. They varied between the 11 o/c and 11.30 positions.

3 All were under the correct weight of 15 gm, falling between 11.3 and 14.4 gm. 23 were more than a gram underweight.

4 Just three were the correct diameter of 35 mm, with 14 lower and nine higher. The lowest was 34.3 mm and the highest, 35.4. An odd feature was that all the 1811 dated tokens were correct or higher, whereas all other dates were, with two correct exceptions, lower.

5 The genuine tokens were issued from 1811 to 1816. Although the sample is small, this graph showing their distribution over these dates, does seem to suggest a trend:

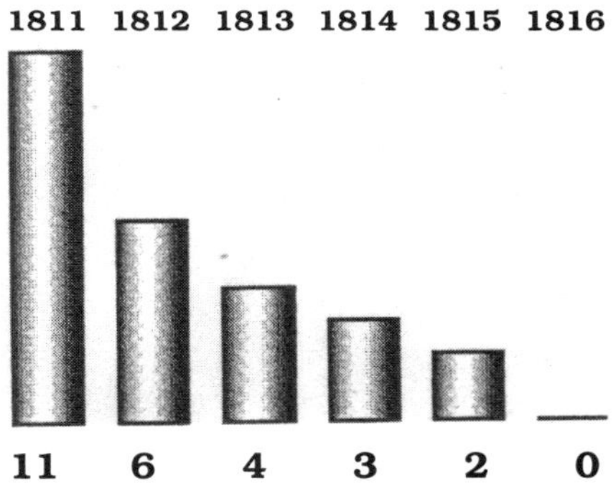

their efforts. When doing so, he was to ensure that he had a fully motivated team to catch the perpetrators off-guard and, hopefully, in the act of coining or forgery. Birmingham was notoriously the centre of such illegal operations at that time.

1s 6d tokens were counterfeited in quantity for the years 1811 to 1815. Brass counterfeits, die-struck and silver-coated, are common and of good quality, except that the silver wearing off has exposed most to present-day detection. Without this giveaway, many would have required close and careful study. They are often lightweight, smaller and have a bad ring. Hair ribbons behind the head are close to the neck on the forgeries, but point away from the neck on genuine pieces.

In 1956, a hoard of 65 1s 6d tokens, all dated 1811, was found near Birmingham[SHE]. The tokens had all been struck from one pair of well engraved dies on underweight flans of a tin-alloy plated copper. The find-site was half a mile from the farm of William Booth, who was sentenced to death in 1812 for counterfeiting, including 1s 6d, 3s and dollar Bank Tokens. On his premises were found coining tools, dies and presses. Unearthed were £3,000 of genuine banknotes, 200 gold guineas, and around £600 in 'bad silver'.

When coining at the Soho Mint was completed, the Bank wanted to claim the dies, but Boulton held out for them to remain his, for their scrap value, subject to their destruction being witnessed. If this had been properly carried out, the ensuing plague of restrikes would not have occurred. Boulton's son, Matthew Robinson Boulton, contracted to make dies for 5s 6d piece tokens "containing the Inscription & Devices mentioned in the Act of Parliament of the Session of Parliament for preventing the Counterfeiting of Tokens intended to be used and circulated by the Bank." Patterns were made, but no tokens were ever issued.

Private silver tokens of the early nineteenth century were extensively counterfeited, some so skilfully that they have been included in works of reference as genuine.

The spate of silver Bank Token forgeries around the period 1811 to 1814, was followed by the vast majority of forgeries of George III silver coin, in just the last four years of his reign - 1817 to 1820.

Example of a George III halfpenny evasion..
1775 CLAUDUIS ROMANUS/PAX PLA CID. 26.5 mm (29-30 mm).

GEORGIAN COPPER

Epidemic level counterfeiting occurred with George III copper coinage; in particular the halfpence.

'If any person after the 24th of June 1771, shall buy, sell, take, receive, pay, or put off any counterfeit copper coin, not melted down or cut in pieces, at or for a lower rate or value than the same by its denomination imports, or was counterfeited for, he shall be adjudged guilty of felony.' *Statute II George III*

Some were notably barbarous. These poorly made counterfeits were purchasable at a considerable discount in the 1754 to 1797 period, although supplanted to an extent by illegal token coinage in the last decade of that period.

As soon as the copper coins of the 1770's appeared, they were being melted down and the metal used to make lightweight counterfeits. The first counterfeits of the copper halfpence of 1770-5, were of quite high quality, and were marginally underweight. All the details of the genuine design were reproduced. As the shortage of change got worse, counterfeiters got bolder - weight, usually 30% or more below standard, and quality went into decline. They were always struck from false dies. By 1773, the quantity of counterfeit and underweight coinage in circulation led to a spate of pocket balance advertisements. By 1779, many people were regularly counterfeiting copper coins.

The Royal Mint took a random sample of halfpennies in 1787, and

found this dire situation:
80% forgeries, 12% blanks and 8% possibly genuine.

A Hoard of around 325 forged halfpence was found in central London in 1981[SHA]. All had been defaced by cutting into two or more pieces. Some were not completely cut through, leaving the segments still joined together. They comprised mostly first issue George III halfpennies, die-struck and ranging in diameter from 26 to 29 mm. There were also blanks, and some very worn copies of William III, George I and II halfpence, plus one or two Irish George II and III halfpennies. The precision of the cutting suggests official defacement. An unusual event if so, as it is known that Customs officials were the only keen pursuers of counterfeit copper coins in the eighteenth century. The Mint appears to have decided to turn a blind eye to the situation.

Evasion. 1771. GRAGORY. II. PON/ BRITAIN. RULES. The wrong date exposes this as a counterfeit George II farthing. 20.5 mm (22-23 mm).

Although counterfeiting copper coins continued to be regarded by the authorities as a minor offence, there were still those who preferred no risk to even a small one. As in the previous reign, they produced 'evasions', which at first glance appeared to be ordinary coins of the realm, but on closer inspection could be seen to carry incorrect legends and/or designs. This difference meant that, by the technicality of not being exact copies of coins of the Realm, they evaded the law introduced in 1771.

Where a genuine coin said GEORGIVS III REX, these came up with colourful and varied legends such as ALFRED THE GREAT, CLAUDUIS ROMANUS, BRUTUS SEXTUS, GUGLIELMUS SHAKESPEARE plus reverse legends replacing BRITANNIA with MUSIC CHARMS/ PAX PLACID/ BATERSEA/ GLORIUS PELLEW and many others.

Evasion depicting a mechanised Britannia 1790 SHAKESPEARE/ HALFPENNY. 27.5 mm (28-30 mm).

Some evasions were satirical, others political. Most were made in Birmingham and many are undated. Those with dates span 1686 to 1798, with the majority later than 1770, yet it now seems certain from die-linking evidence, that all were produced over the period 1796 to 1798, so the dates can be as fictitious as the rest of the coins. The bulk of these probably emanated from just one or two token manufacturers, who sold them in bulk at varying discounts. William Lutwyche, who was striking genuine trade tokens from well-made dies, is shown by die-links to have used the same dies for producing evasions. The Colonel Kirk evasion was by Lutwyche. Many other minor producers, particularly in and around Birmingham, churned out much lower grade pieces. Peter Kempson has been mooted as another manufacturer engaged in evasive production, but hard evidence seems to be lacking. John Gimblett imitated one of Kempson's designs, and also produced pieces with the legends CAPTAIN PELLEW and CLAUDUIS ROMANUS.

These evasions, also known as medleys, imitation regals, and, in America, as 'bungs' or 'Bungtown coppers', flourished up to 1800, many ending up in Canada.

The vast majority of evasions were halfpennies, with some farthings bearing similar legends, such as GEORGE SUS-SEX. A silver striking of an evasion farthing bears the legends GEORGE RULES/ BRITANNIAs ISLES. Its dies were also used to strike copper pieces.

PROVINCIAL TOKEN PRODUCTION

The term 'Provincial' referred to the tokens being different from Regal currency, not to any geographical aspect, and so it encompassed tokens emanating from London as well as from the provinces. The years 1787 to 1798 were the great first Provincial token period.

As a consequence of the small change crisis in 1787, token money (local 'coinage'), was started by the Anglesey Copper Mining Co., the owners of the Parys Mine in Anglesey, and quickly spread all over Britain. It didn't take long for forgeries to start appearing, including copies of Parys Mines' famous Druid design[DA]. All dated 1784 and 1792 are forgeries.

"New Anglesay Coin. "(See our Plate, fig. 1) This Copper Token, as it may be called, in imitation of those struck in the last century, for the like purpose, (one of which, issued at Holyhead ... is here copied, fig. 3) [HVGH DAVIS 1666 / IN HOLY HEAD around HIS 1D; BW Wales 41] is coined in Birmingham for the use of the great copper mine in the Isle of Anglesea, called Paris Mountain, they not being able to procure good halfpence for the payment of their labourers...
"This token was scarcely issued, when it was thought worthwhile to counterfeit it; which has been done by some able artist, as may be seen by an inspection of our plate, fig. 2... In the reverse the 1 D. is omitted, and the date placed at the top instead of the bottom. The whole reverse is also turned, in the counterfeit, the opposite way to the genuine one.

"There is also a second counterfeit, nearly resembling the former ... dot placed over the second figure of the date instead of the third.."
The Gentleman's Magazine, 1788.

So-called 'North-Wales' tokens are Birmingham copies of the Druid tokens. Their inscribed promise to redeem the tokens for pence of the realm was an empty one as they did not show any issuer's name. The Welsh expression "not worth a red harp halfpenny" came from this, echoing the English "not worth a brass farthing". It seems likely that the American saying "not worth a red cent" had a similar origin.

A Shropshire ironmaster, John Wilkinson, was the next to start issuing tokens. Then the floodgates opened and businesses and tradespeople joined in, often adding sales messages to the tokens. Political emissions included medalets, which may also have been used as currency. English and Irish tokens were counterfeited contemporaneously, prompting the genuine issuers to take advertisements in their local papers warning of imitations.

Coin dealers started providing bulk supplies of tokens to all and sundry at prices nicely below the face values ascribed to them, having in some cases, commissioned dies from Mint engravers. It became fashionable to collect these tokens, and so dealers had special collectables designed showing off the die-sinkers' artistic skills. Their face value was less than the cost of production, so collectors were clearly prepared to pay over the odds for them. Some collectors even started having their own issues struck, to swap with other collectors! Then, inevitably, the fakers got in on the act, striking tokens apparently issued by tradesmen who either lived far enough away not to discover the misuse of their names, or by completely fictitious people. Then came the 'rare errors' combining one tradesman's obverse with another's reverse (mules), or with 'faulty' edge readings, to encourage collectors to pay over the odds. It was reported in 1995 that a forger had sold postage stamps with "unique printing errors" to gullible philatelists to the tune of £100,000, showing that the only change in two hundred years is the profit potential!

For a long while, tokens served a useful purpose, but eventually, in the last years of the eighteenth century, *so many* forgers had realised that real tokens did not have the protection of the law and were making their fortunes by issuing light imitations of the best-accepted ones that the country became swamped with them. A 1797 report spoke of a rolling mill in London supplying coiners with flans to any required sizes.

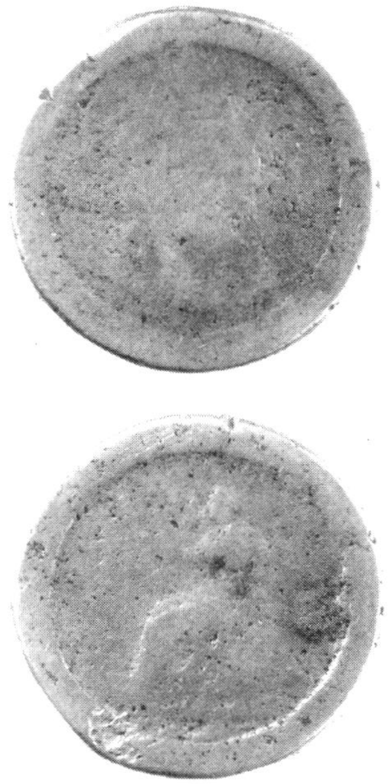

1797 Cartwheel penny copy, cast in copper. Poor detail, but may have been made that way. It is not completely round and has a bump by a flaw. Wgt 27.29 gm. (28.3 gm when issued but less worn genuine coins can drop to 26.8 gm). 35.5 mm (36 mm).

The circulating small change was by then a fantastic jumble of forgeries, tokens and advertising tickets often outnumbering the worn, barely discernible regal coins. The Government had to act, and, in 1797, stepped in to pronounce *all* tokens illegal, at the same time introducing the famous cartwheel pence to take their place.

These were manufactured at the Soho Works of Boulton and Watt in Birmingham. They comprised a one ounce penny and a two ounce twopence. Patterns were made of a halfpenny and a farthing, but neither was issued. Instead, in 1799, Soho halfpennies and farthings arrived and nearly all token coinage disappeared. But the Government had not learnt its lesson, for the same drastic shortage of small change as in 1787 recurred in 1810. There was a difference though. The price of copper had risen so much that it paid people to melt down the old copper coinage and even the good quality tokens for their scrap value.

Tinned 1797 Cartwheel penny. Wgt 26.38 gm (28.3 gm). Correct diameter at 36 mm.

By 1811, groups all over the country were considering once more issuing tokens, with the difference that they were now nearly all city councils, business syndicates and large industrial outfits, rather than the enterprising individuals of the eighteenth century. Their tokens differed in being practical mass-produced products of the Industrial Revolution, rather than the previous hand-struck efforts of artist-craftsmen. From 1811 to 1817, copper tokens were tolerated by the Government.

NECESARY CHAING

Tokens can be divided into four groups - official, unofficial, forged official and forged unofficial - and in various categories. Firstly the bona fide traders' tokens, the general, unnamed tokens, ad tokens, 'collectables', and collectors' private tokens specifying their particular interests.

Many forgeries and fictional traders' tokens appeared until Parliament in the following reign intervened once again, declaring tokens illegal (except from a couple of workhouses) and issuing a large quantity of copper farthings, from 1821 to 1826, halfpennies and pennies from 1825 to 1830 and a plentiful supply has been around ever since, killing off at last the need for token coinage.

THE CARTWHEEL COINAGE CONCEPT

Matthew Boulton, whose partner James Watt was rapidly advancing the steam engine in many new spheres, saw the need for a new copper coinage that would defeat the forgers who were then flooding the country with copies of the 1770's copper coins. One estimate puts the percentage of forged copper coins circulating in the last quarter of the eighteenth century at 60%. It may have been even worse, for the Royal Mint took a random sample of halfpennies in 1787 and found 92% bearing poor impressions of the king's portrait. In 1797, just before the cartwheel coinage eradication of counterfeits, their 'value' to counterfeiters was estimated to be around £300,000 a year.

Matthew Boulton, 1787.

In 1788, Boulton reckoned that he could produce halfpennies at half the Mint's costs. He latched on to a good point to emphasise in his attempts to win a Government contract for coin production. In an application of 1789, he observed "I receive upon an average two thirds counterfeit halfpence for change at tollgates, etc., and I believe the evil is daily increasing as the spurious money is carried into circulation by the lowest class of manufacturers who pay with it the principal part of the wages of the poor people they employ. They purchase from the subterranean coiners thirty six shillings' worth of copper (in nominal value) for twenty shillings, so that the profit derived from the cheating is very large."

Boulton's ideas:

1. Coins with their intrinsic value of metal less only the manufacturing cost.
2. Use of a retaining collar to give the coins a constant diameter.
3. Broad, raised rim, embodying incuse lettering.

1792

"We are happy to inform our readers, that Mr Bolton has succeeded in his application of the steam-engine to coining. The effects of his machine are such as to produce a beautiful impression, not imitable perhaps by any other means; and, though a considerable saving will accrue from its use, the difficulty of its construction, which is too great for a common artist, and its expensiveness, render it improbable that it should ever be employed by those who counterfeit coin.

"Its advantages over the common machines are various. It works much more quickly: It cuts out the blanks: It stamps the milling, the face, and the reverse of the piece, at once: the ground receives a fine polish from its pressure alone; all the pieces are exactly of the same diameter: its force may be regulated in an instant, and continues invariably the same: It may be worked by boys, and its use requires no practice. Mr Droz, who has assisted in improving this invention, has already begun to use the machine in making coins for the East India Company."

The Gentleman's Magazine

1795
"The copper money might be greatly and easily reformed by dies of superior workmanship; and, had Mr Bolton's coinage taken place, as the publick was led to expect, from the very beautiful specimen of his pattern-halfpenny, it would soon have put a stop to the prolific exertions of the other Birmingham manufacturers."

MASS PRODUCTION AT BOULTON'S SOHO MINT
He got nowhere until 1797, when the Government finally accepted his recommendations and gave him the contract to produce what became known as Cartwheel pence. Thus Boulton and Watt and steam-powered mass production ushered coin-making into the nineteenth century. There were also the first elements of automation in Boulton's machines. Such was their success that they were sold around the world - despite the vibrations of each strike being of an instant headache level!

The Bank noted the destruction of Soho coin dies, "according to contract", yet a number carried on being used there, after their legitimate use had ceased, turning out 'fun' coins and creating problems for future coin collectors. Another example of Boulton's free-wheeling approach was that, despite decrying their existence, he produced tokens for others and then for himself.

Few contemporary counterfeits of the 1797 Cartwheel Coinage are known, but lightweight Cartwheel pennies began appearing around 1812. They were struck from genuine Soho works' dies, but on flans 2 mm thick, instead of the genuine 3 mm. The dies may have been used clandestinely in the works, or have been sold or stolen. The pieces have noticeably rounder rims than the genuine cartwheels. They arose again later, mostly from the misuse of Soho dies, including muling, by Young, Taylor and Till. Taylor was using Soho dies and punches to produce restrikes and fantasies from the late 1860's. He switched obverses and reverses around, polished and reworked the dies to produce 'interesting' products for collectors and was still doing this until at least 1880. For a while, the restrikes were recognised as such. Now, confusion reigns, with many sales catalogues not specifying one way or the other.

Dies used for restrikes long after their original, official use, usually suffered from rust. This can leave clues on restrikes, such as rust pimples. If the dies have been tooled to remove the rust, there is a loss of fine detail.

The next great step in the evolution of coin production was Uhlhorn's lever-action knuckle-press, patented in 1817. This dominated coin production until modern times, with over 500 produced, many by Ralph Heaton & Co of Birmingham.

PROFIT SOURCES
Debased copper, thin flans and reduced diameter gave the forger his profit. Cast specimens are extremely rare, which is not surprising as casting does not lend itself to mass production - the pre-requisite of profit-making for small value items such as these. Brass rather than

copper was used for casting. The Georgian forgers using dies, frequently muled them, i.e. mixed obverses and reverses, thus making more varieties without more effort.

The two main centres of counterfeit production in late Georgian times were London and Birmingham. Makers would charge distributors about 10 shillings for 21 shillings' face value of counterfeits, who in turn would charge utterers and unscrupulous traders about 21 shillings for 28 shillings' face-value. A 1797 report spoke of a rolling mill in London supplying coiners with flans to required sizes.

Birmingham's prolific illegal output in the late eighteenth and early nineteenth centuries led to 'Birmingham halfpence' and 'Brummagen' becoming popular names for counterfeits. Brummagens were darkened to look circulated by pan-frying in batches. 'Worn' dies were employed for the same reason. Huge quantities of halfpenny sized flans were legally made in Birmingham and passed via distributors to coiners to put to illegal use.

PREVENTATIVE MEASURES
The Act of 1742 threatening two years' imprisonment for copper coin counterfeiting, was not fully enforced. In 1771, a new Act made it a felony. Warrants could then be issued for premises to be searched for coining equipment. This seems to have been as ineffectual as the previous Act, for copper coin counterfeiting from 1770 to the end of the century was worse than ever. Generally, the Act was not enforced. A Parliamentary bill was introduced in July 1811 for the prevention of token forgery.

1817 saw a great reduction in the counterfeits in circulation as old coin was exchanged for new.

DRIFT TO AMERICA
Many counterfeit George III halfpennies found their way to colonial and Independent late eighteenth century America.

GEORGE IV
George IV's silver coinage was counterfeited to a lesser degree than George III's, due possibly to design changes in the regal coinage. But the sixpences were popular with forgers, who gave them a gold wash and then passed them off as half-sovereigns. This was not countered until William IV's reign, when the half-sovereign of 1831 was reduced in size to 18 mm diameter. The public objected and eventually, in 1834, it went back up again to 19 mm! A design change eventually solved this problem.

Unofficial farthings**BE** were the same size as George IV regal farthings, but, to circumvent the 1817/18 legislation, they carried no value and clearly advertised the issuer. From 1821, with the availability of small change, counterfeit farthings and halfpennies ceased to be a problem.

THE WATCH-CHAIN FASHION

There was a brief fashion in the late nineteenth century that saw brass imitations of George IV £2 pieces dated 1823 ranging from passable to crude, being made specifically for fixing to one's watch-chain. Some had loops attached for this purpose.

1823 two pounds with all the gilding gone. The letter X has a missing serif on the left base of the right stem. Correct diameter at 28 mm.

1823 two pounds. As the preced ing piece, except for a loop at the top. 27.5 mm (28 mm).

Good, Bad and Ugly copies of George IV Coinage

1825 half sovereign struck from well-made original dies, but with uneven lettering. The plating is still almost complete. 7 o/c die-axis. Wgt 2.74 gm (4 gm). 19.5 mm (19 mm).

1825 gilt half sovereign made from crude, hand engraved dies. Oversized letter 'U'. Gilding almost intact. 1 o/c die-axis. Wgt 2.42 gm (4 gm). 19.5 mm (19 mm).

1826 sixpence in copper. Edge join is visible on this unusual welded cast. Wgt 3.19 gm (2.8 gm). Correct diameter at 19 mm.

William IV

Counterfeits of high value coins during William IV's reign (1820-1830) led to the renewed use of coin weights.

William IV 1836 halfcrown copy in hard white metal. It has good detail, let down by a dull silver appearance. Wgt 10.32 gm (14.1 gm). 31.5 mm (32 mm).

10

Modern Times

Victoria reigned over a country where counterfeiting hardly touched the 'upper classes'. According to the Royal Mint, there was very little counterfeiting of British gold coins in the nineteenth century. Between 1860 and 1870, no more than five cases were dealt with by the Treasury Solicitor's Department.

Although Victorian counterfeiting had lessened generally from the Georgian levels, it had not by any means disappeared, as a report on the final takings at the 1851 Great Exhibition shows, noting £90 in bad silver, mostly halfcrowns. "There is good reason to believe that there is at present a considerable number of spurious halfcrowns in circulation in Great Britain, for which we are indebted, it is said, to German enterprise. These coins ... are equal in quality to the halfcrowns issued from Her Majesty's Mint. They are not cast, but stamped in proper coining machinery from excellent dies. They are of full weight, indeed, the only difference between them and the English coin is a minute fraction of an inch larger in diameter and slightly thinner.." - *The Engineer.*

Some, presumably through a lack of numismatic knowledge, forged halfcrowns dated 1861, 1866, 1868 and 1871, dates never officially produced.

The reverse of the specially designed 1887 Jubilee sixpence made it look too much like a half-sovereign when gilded, so this was changed to a simple value word surrounded by a wreath. The farthings of 1897 to 1917 were blackened at the mint so they could not be 'passed' as sovereigns. The reverse of the half-farthing bore the legend HALF FARTHING beneath a crown, to guard against it being silvered and passed off as a groat.

This 1887 half sovereign is in fact a gilded sixpence, illustrating why they were quickly withdrawn and replaced with the preceding type of reverse design bearing the legend SIX PENCE! The diameter of both coins is 19 mm. Wgt 2.88 gm (4 gm).

Bi-metallic coins were suggested - and adopted 150 years later! The small model pennies that Moore produced in November 1847 to promote this idea, are still plentiful.

By the 1850's, bronze coinage was known to be more difficult to counterfeit, and so, from 1860, it replaced copper.

THE COUNTERFEIT CAPITAL

By 1890, Birmingham had become the undisputed counterfeit coin

Victorian 'enterprise'

1863 sovereign in platinum. Wgt (holed) 8.01 gm (8 gm). Correct diameter at 22 mm.

This is a deceptive gilt white metal copy of an 1880 half sovereign. It has a nick out of the rim. At 1.70 gm (4 gm), it is seriously underweight, but still has the correct diameter of 19 mm.

Silvered 1837 'To Hanover' medallion, possibly to pass as a shilling. 23 mm.

With this silvery 1845 crown, the raised flaw across the face, the bump over the eye, and similar bump on the harp on the reverse, all say cast. The edge inscription may have been stamped in after casting. Wgt 28.23 gm (28.3 gm). 38.5 mm (39 mm).

Gilt 1887 £5, wearing off on the reverse only. Tail less rounded. Thick. Die-axis incorrect. Wgt 28.31 gm (40 gm). Correct 37 mm diameter.

Gilt 1887 £5, struck from superior false dies. Thin. Wgt 20.85 gm (40 gm). 36.5 mm (37 mm).

Gilt 1887 £5. Patches of gilt worn off. An edge-mount has been removed. Wgt 28.21 gm (40 gm). Correct diameter at 37 mm.

Genuine 1889 five shilling, heavily gilded to pass as a Jubilee 1887 £5 piece. Wgt 27.89 gm (5s - 28.3 gm; £5 - 40 gm). 38.5 mm (5s - 39 mm; £5 - 37 mm).

capital of Britain. Favourite targets were shillings and sixpences. The occasional half-sovereign and sovereign were cast in bell metal (brass/pewter alloy) and gold-plated.

Report in the London Gazette of 1848:

"Nothing could be purchased without a dispute. Over every counter there was a wrangling from morning till night. On a fair day or a market day, the clam ours, the reproaches, the taunts, the curses, were incessant, and it was well if no booth was over turned and no heads broken. No merchant could contract to deliv er goods without making some stipulation about the quality of the coin in which he was paid."

So counterfeiting still called for specific responses from the authorities.

A contemporary description of a typical counterfeiter's modus operandi sees him renting a small house for no more than a week, before he moves on - always a step or two ahead of the Police. In these 'safe' houses he casts his 'soft' products, impressing an oil-coated genuine coin into plaster on hot sand to make a half-mould. The plaster is allowed to harden, the coin drops out. Then the plaster is coated with oil, the coin also recoated, replaced and molten plaster poured on to the top. When this sets it is separated and the coin, or coins if a multiple mould, removed. Flow channels are impressed into the half-moulds which are then fixed together and a molten mixture, usually of pewter and zinc, poured in through the channels. The coins are then silver-plated. The apparatus for this comprises two stone-jars with copper wire bent round in the silver solution jar to hold the pieces for plating. Acids in one jar are connected to the other jar by copper wires, thus forming a crude electric battery. Having been silver-coated, the coins are rubbed with blacking to remove their freshness.

A VICTORIAN TWO-MAN UTTERING TEAM

The 'swag' carrier had the stock of counterfeit coins, a basket and a large bottle. The utterer, with a supply of genuine coins and *just one false coin*, would go into a shop or public house and order something well below the value of the false coin proffered. The change from the transaction would then create a 'return' of good coin, plus the product purchased. The utterer then left, met up with the swag carrier, decanted the surplus cash and product - into the basket if solid, the bottle if liquid, received his next bad coin and repeated the performance at a fresh establishment. If a suspicious shopkeeper or barman queried the coin, the utterer would express surprise and change it immediately for a good coin. If the police were fetched, he would vigorously protest his innocence, as evidenced by the presence on him of all good coin bar the one in question. Clearly a neat tactic that experience evolved. Court cases show that uttering was the only counterfeiting crime where Victorian women often got involved. The favourite coin to be passed was a halfcrown, which on the usual small purchase, would provide over two shillings' worth of genuine change.

MUGS AWAY

Sources of raw material for the Victorian counterfeiter included pewter mugs stolen from ale houses, Britannia metal spoons and 'acquired' scrap-metal.

By the end of the century, copy quality had risen considerably from the earlier, thinly silvered brass efforts mimicking George III and IV denominations. Because of the drop in value of silver at that time, it became profitable to strike or cast full silver copies. To increase acceptance, they were given a built-in worn look.

TO HANOVER

The 'To Hanover' brass medalets were known to have been passed off as sovereigns at crowded venues such as race-courses, prize-fights, pubs, etc. These became more deceptive in the 1870's, probably deliberately, with the change of the reverse design from a crowned horseman attacking a three-headed dragon, to the Pistrucci type

St. George and the Dragon, as on the standard sovereign. They were mostly dated 1837, which kept them within the law, as no genuine sovereigns combined that date and design.

Impressive shiny gold 1904 sovereign, but of the wrong weight, thickness and size.

After a comparative lull following the end of the George III epidemic, counterfeiting seems to have started an upsurge again in the latter part of Victoria's reign that has lasted right up to the present day. Most of Edward VII's higher value coinage has received the coiners' attention. In his reign (1901-1910), the reducing machine, devised by a French engraver, Frederic Janvier, was introduced to improve coin design procedures.

The debased silver coins, issued in 1920, took on a coppery sheen when they began to wear. This led to the appearance of many poor quality counterfeits, mostly of halfcrowns and florins. By 1928, halfcrowns were the commonest counterfeits. Lead impressions exist of defaced George V crown pattern dies. With a value of £15,000+ for a genuine 1933 penny, it is not surprising that 1935 pennies turn up tooled to look like this date.

George V halfcrowns were popular counterfeiting targets.This example dated 1920, has a worn bust surrounded by oddly fresh looking lettering. Test digs on both sides. Die-axis - 1 o/c. Wgt 10.6 gm (14.1 gm). Correct diameter at 32 mm.

FIGURE IT OUT!

An official, taking the number of counterfeits being spotted at Post Office counters around the country in 1932, produced a projected figure of just £163 worth of counterfeits, out of a total of fifty million poundsworth of halfcrowns, florins, shillings and sixpences then in circulation! The author's research collection contains £37 worth of these denominations up to 1932, which, if the above figure were correct, would represent 22% of all then thought to be in circulation!

The few proof coins that exist from Edward VIII's brief reign mean that any attempt at a counterfeit would receive such rigorous inspection as to discourage almost anyone from even contemplating the idea. However, one unofficial pattern crown did appear in Britain soon after the Second World War. It is said to have come from the USA. At least three types of fantasy crown exist: silver EDWARD VIII KING AND EMPEROR/George and Dragon; silver with double florin design reverse; bronze with wreath crown.

1940 counterfeit florin with test scratches on bust. Wgt 11.00 gm (11.3 gm). 27.5 mm (28.5 mm).

'IMPROVING' SOVEREIGNS

After 1945, the popularity of Britain's gold sovereign around the Mediterranean pushed its value sufficiently above the gold content value to make full metal value counterfeiting worthwhile. Lebanese forgeries of British sovereigns, made in the 1940's to early 1950's replaced the copper in the alloy with silver, whilst maintaining the gold level, thus offering better value than the official coin. Their colour differs slightly from the official sovereigns - a shade less red and lighter toned. Another source started in Greece in 1946, with crude cast efforts. But sovereign counterfeiting became a significant problem from the 1950's with the opening of factories in Italy and Syria. From these, sovereign fakes were distributed to parts of Africa and the Middle and Far East. The problem was eventually eradicated by legitimate mass production and by the European Courts finally accepting them as legal tender subject to counterfeiting laws.

Postwar London saw a mini-upsurge in counterfeiting. Convincing fake halfcrowns, made in an antimony alloy, were circulating there in 1947. In 1948, five-shilling coins were being gilded to pass as £5 pieces.

As soon as Elizabeth II coins began to appear, forgers followed in the footsteps of their predecessors and produced copies in considerable quantities. The principle, as ever, was that the public, being initially unfamiliar with the new coinage, would be more easily fooled. Coins leading to decimalisation offered a further 'unfamiliarity' opportunity, with the large 50p coin being a popular target – over-demonstrated by the two chemists, whose story appears opposite! This denomination was most forged when first issued, so 1969 is a common date. Its appearance produced a spate of florins filed to the 50p shape. 10p's have been flattened out to 50p size. A 10p has been wrapped in silver paper to pass as a 50p. In one instance, where labour costs could not have been fully assessed, a halfcrown had been carefully filed to 50p shape. In another, a crude lead effort had been made by impressing a genuine coin into the lead, resulting in a reverse image. This was found in the Thames, folded in two.

Copies of the 50p have been made by lead casting and by striking plated zinc and tinned brass flans. Blank flans turn up, presumably made for slot machine use. The British Museum has a set of aluminium moulds in its Black Museum.

Counterfeiting of 50p coins has since evaporated. The author has not yet encountered any examples of the later, smaller version of this denomination.

DECIMAL TRICKS

Pound coins have been sliced in half, and makeweight metal stuck to the cut sides to make two for the price of one. One £1 coin attempt was anomalously dated 1971 because it has been 'made' by joining two 1p coins with a lead band. As the portcullis design on a 1p would be a complete giveaway, both sides show the Queen's head. Some old pennies have been cut down to resemble 2p size. On the outer edges of counterfeiting are the foreign coins, objects, counters, discs, etc., which, whilst remaining unaltered, are passed as current coins. For example, the author's sister was given a handful of pound coins as change, but discovered later that one presumed pound was an old threepenny bit.

It probably costs forgers more to produce current coinage than the Mint, but because the metal cost is so much lower than the coin value, they can still make a profit. An even better profit comes from a new type of forgery, now becoming more prevalent - discs designed solely to fit into vending machines, with no attempt to mimic the designs on the real coins.

PRESENT DAY PIRATES

Pound coin counterfeiting is still going strong - cast, die-struck and pressed. A 1996 Bank of England estimate put the total 'value' then

THE 1961 HALFPENNY

The 'unique' Elizabeth II halfpenny of 1961 has to be a date altered by tooling because no tools or dies were made at the Royal Mint for a halfpenny for that year.

THE 1965 GOLD HALFPENNY

In 1969 a 22ct gold halfpenny, up for auction, was seized by the police and declared a counterfeit by a Birmingham court because it had not been legally or accidentally struck by the Royal Mint, and was false and resembled a coin of the realm. It went into the Royal Mint museum.

Silver-coated copper-alloy 50p, with the silver wearing off the high-spots. Wgt 13.24 gm (13.05 gm).

1973 lead alloy 50p. Wgt 16.01 gm (13.05 gm).

in circulation at around 20 million pounds, with the rider that they were probably still on the increase. The Royal Mint says that the main metals used are types of nickel-brass for the rarer good quality pieces and a lead alloy for the poor majority. The latter, known to The Royal Mint as 'garden shed' efforts, almost always have correctly paired obverses and reverses and edge inscriptions. They are mostly of poor execution, with a 'wholesale' price of around 10p each. The better copies are near, but not quite the correct nickel brass of the genuine ones. It would need a spectrometer to spot this difference. The puzzle with the better efforts is how often they have wrongly paired obverses and reverses and/or edge inscriptions. There may be some idea on the part of the perpetrators that they could get away with them not being exact copies, as with the Georgian era evasions. The Royal Mint says that this ploy would fail if tried, as one side only resembling a coin of the realm is sufficient for a conviction. Sources of distribution of counterfeit pound coins are initially detectable, but soon become too diffuse to track down.

The £2 coin was made bi-metallic as a deterrent to counterfeiting. Examples are already revealing this to be a vain hope.

The police estimate that there are between fifteen and twenty forgers' workshops currently operating in the U.K. The Story never ends...

"I THOUGHT THAT WAS YOUR JOB!"

As the news item below reveals, possible distribution problems did not seem to have been fully considered by the two chemists said to have been the makers.

*"**Forgers Caught**. Police and officials from the Mint were today removing further heavy equipment, including two electric furnaces, from the purpose-built coin counterfeiting factory discovered in West London. Detectives who discovered nearly **four tons** of fake 50p pieces at the factory in Woodstock Road, Chiswick, have made urgent inquiries throughout the country, and now believe they succeeded in preventing any distribution of the £135,000 worth of newly minted coinage. They have been told that the counterfeit racket was a highly professional long-term plan which could have flooded the country with 'perfect' fake coins over a long period.*

"The gang had poured a large investment into equipping the Woodstock Road building with machinery specifically designed to offer long-term production. Detectives from 'X' Division have travelled to various towns in the south-east and Midlands to check on the planned coin distribution network. But they are confident that they swooped on the coin factory in time. Two men who have been helping police inquiries at Southall police station since the factory was found three days ago are expected to be charged later today."

Evening Standard
3rd June, *1976.*

Check Your Change

Comparison with this crisply detailed genuine £1 coin shows up the lack of fine detail in most counterfeits. Almost all of the latter are the correct diameter of 22.5 mm, but the wrong weight. Thicknesses can vary.

This 1996 £1 with Welsh dragon and edge legend, should be the Northern Ireland design for this year. It is made from a hard metal of varying thickness; has an erratic edge legend and is a deeper colour than normal. Both die-axis and weight are correct.

A most deceptive forgery of a 1992 £1, except for a slight loss of detail differing from that which usage removes on genuine pieces, and for being too thick, ranging from 3.29 to 3.32 mm, compared to the 3.20 mm of genuine coins.

This 1963 penny has been cut down to pass as a 2p.

A poor cast of a 1982 20p. Wgt 5.05 gm (5 gm).

'DIRECT' TESTING

This varied selection of 'exposed' counterfeit £1 coins shows that the public is still employing destructive methods of checking as from the earliest days of coinage:

Nipper-clenched.

Nipper-snapped.

Dug.

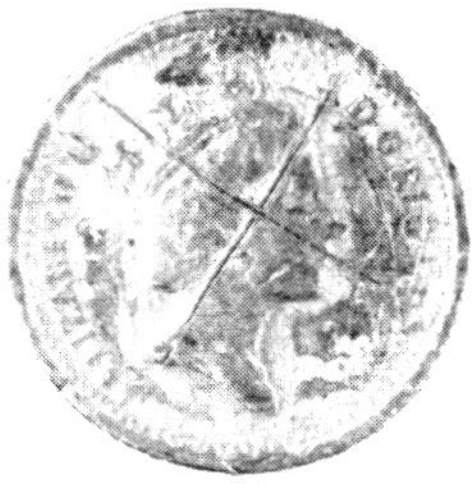

Scratched.

EDGE CHECKS

The edge inscription on this hard metal 1996 fake (top) is too large and too italicised, as comparison with the genuine one beneath it shows. Also it has a Dragon reverse instead of the Celtic Cross.

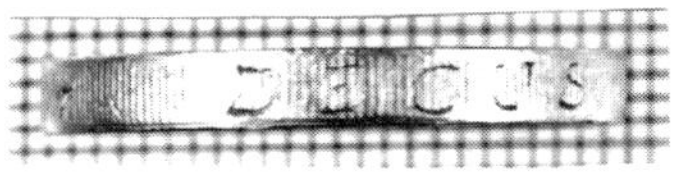

The graining of this cast of a 1992 coin has not made it to the edges.

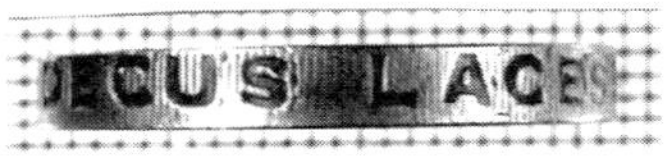

This hard metal, good weight 1990 £1 has the Flax reverse, instead of Leek, and a hybrid legend - DECUS LACESSIT TUTAMEN. There are two directly opposing 'marker' indentations in the edge-graining. The die-axis is at 2 o/c instead of being upright.

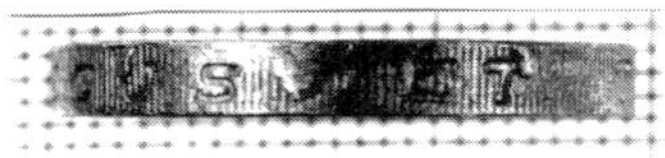

This 1996 lead alloy copy has casting blobs on the edge.

TWO EASY PIECES

Part of the plating has broken away.

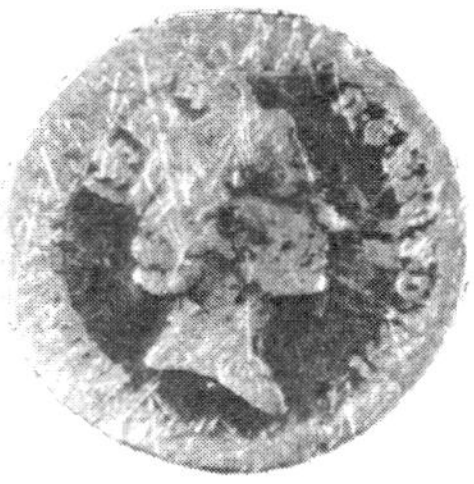

'Gutter' coin. The coating has been removed by traffic wear.

It seems that where most lead alloy fakes have correct combinations of date, legend and design, the hard metal copies often mismatch. This is a prime example - a 1995 dated £1 coin, with a 1994 reverse design and a 1996 edge inscription.

(left) a genuine £2 coin. (right) a counterfeit with dulled detail, and test scratches in front of the face.

The centre of the counterfeit is loose and has swivelled round so that the design and the rim lettering no longer align correctly on either side.

11

Scotland

Scotland's first coinage, that of David I, appearing in the first half of the twelfth century, can look forged, as it copied the English coinage of the time, but with a tendency to blunder legends. That some are retrograde suggests direct die-copying from English examples. Others have well-formed letters, but in random order. The meaningless legends, frequently blundered and retrograde, also made his fourth issue coinage (1153-) look like counterfeits.

In the thirteenth century, Scottish coin, *of equal standard*, was accepted in England. Alexander III second coinage sterlings (c.1280-) have two standards of imitation - poor, probably homegrown, and superior, probably Continental Sterling. Continental Sterling copies of Scottish pennies are investigated in a 1998 article by Ferguson and Jones[FE].

Scotland's fourteenth century turney, a base imitation of the Gros Tournois, was banned in England by Edward III but allowed in Ireland. Groats, half groats, pennies and halfpennies were all being crudely made around 1403.

The first documented evidence of base coin forgery in Scotland comes in James II's reign, in the Act of 1451, which refers to "false cun-yeouris". Very few examples are known. Copies of post-Act groats are more frequent. Continental imitations of 'Iacobus' coins occurred in the mid-fifteenth century.

The Act of 1485 recalled all the latest struck placks, because of "greit quantities of fals countirfatit money plakkis" made in Scotland and beyond, so well as to be impossible to tell counterfeit from genuine. Either the recall was comprehensive or the problem exaggerated, because few counterfeits now exist.

Misspelt legends occur with James II's second coinage (1451-1460). Add to this the debasement of Scottish silver coinage of the fifteenth and sixteenth centuries, reaching a low of 0.04 fine, and one can see how easily pieces could be mistaken for counterfeits. James III's 'black money' farthings (c.1466) lacked any silver content. There were crude contemporary counterfeits of his billon placks and also penny counterfeits. They also exist for James IV's billon pennies.

GLASGOW MINT

A contemporary base metal forgery of a silver penny of probable fourteenth century date, which is inscribed VILLA DE GLASGOU, is the only evidence that there had ever been a medieval Glasgow mint.

Contemporary counterfeits of the James V bawbee are very rare. His quarter bawbee was probably a pattern. Early sixteenth century plack counterfeiting was sufficient to deter people from accepting any placks - until the 1517 Act invoked the death penalty for refusal. It also instituted widespread searches for counterfeits.

Scotland's base metal coinage in the sixteenth century was of a low skill level, making the task of counterfeiters that much easier, and detection that much more difficult. So draconian punishments were introduced - hanging being the least terrible. Drawing and quartering and burning were possibilities for the convicted. A frequent way of minimising some of the risk was to have the pieces made abroad, with Flanders a popular manufacturing centre of the time.

Forgeries exist of the Ryal (£3) of Mary Stuart, Queen of Scots (1542-1567). Bawbees (1542-1548) were counterfeited in quantity[HO]. A 1543 Mary period I gold 20 shilling coin thought to be by Jons, a nineteenth century Dunfermline forger, is described and illustrated in *SCBI 35, pl. 116, 1826.* There are copper-cored contemporary counterfeits of the 1555 testoon. No contemporary forgeries are known of the groat.

By the 1550 Act, clipped French coins were outlawed. Death and total goods confiscation awaited anyone caught flouting this law. The natural reaction to this dire threat led to a second Law in the following month making it a capital offence to refuse *unclipped* French coins! Official measuring rings were the arbiters, but are thought not to have been generally available.

Counterfeit coinage of the Marians in Edinburgh Castle in 1572 has been investigated by Murray and Rampling[MU/RA]. So many counterfeit billon placks and copper lions of James VI and earlier were in circulation by then, that for two and a half years, placks and lions were banned. Then, in 1575, they were all called into the mint for inspection. The poor counterfeits were weeded out and the genuine pieces countermarked with a star enclosed in a heart and re-issued. The countermarking on the AE Penny of 1575 is only genuine if it is a heart and star. In the recall of 1580, counterfeits were to be cut and returned to their owners.

James VI (1583-1590) billon eightpenny groat. Foreshortened shield round an emaciated lion. Missing 'I' at end of EDINBVRGI and shrunken thistle on the reverse. Wgt is correct at 1.8 gm.

CULROSS HOARD

A counterfeit hoard of James VI billon placks (1583-1590) was discovered in 1996 at Culross in Fife[HO1]. All 121 pieces appear to be from the same forging workshop. Examination suggests that flans were cast in a brass alloy, struck, and then lightly coated with tin to give them a silvery appearance.

The similarity of the designs of the twopenny plack and eightpenny groat led to cheating and so to design change.

Mintmaster James Acheson's report to the king in 1597, spoke of all the false twopences and pennies in circulation, which he attributed to the ease with which the poor base coinage could be imitated. His improved minting method produced a better quality coin. Then came machine-made coins produced by Nicholas Briot and his son-in-law, John Falconer for Charles I. Copper turners were the first machine-made coins of Scotland. The American Numismatic Society has a Charles I turner for which a 1627 Louis XIII double turnois was used as a flan.

HALFGROATS OR FARTHINGS

The Earl of Stirling's 'Turners' or 'Bodles' were a token halfgroat coinage which also circulated in England, but there as farthings. Contemporary counterfeits reveal themselves by their extremely poor lettering and bad striking. Any that have lion or lis mintmarks are counterfeits. They were worth counterfeiting because the genuine pieces were valued too highly for the metal content.

Counterfeits imported from England were a problem of the seventeenth century. The Proclamation of 1661 condemned them as being a third lighter than genuine coins. It also drew attention to the legends usually found on them - NOMEN DOMINI SIT BENEDICT and DEVS PROTECTOR NOSTER.

The British Museum holds a pair of defaced dies for the James VII 60 shilling pieces of 1686 that were never used at the time. Matthew Young had acquired them from the Roettier estate c.1827. He presented the dies to the museum, but only *after* he had used them to strike sixty silver and three gold pieces.

GENUINE FORGERIES

The Act of October 1696 decreed that an express warrant from the King (William III) was required for all copper coining. If the amounts laid down by previous Acts were exceeded, *the coins were to be classified as forgeries* and the makers punished accordingly.

Suspicion of forgery could be serious, even without conviction, as two soldiers found in December 1696, being deported and banned from returning.

In 1828, Matthew Young restruck pattern crowns and guineas of 'James VIII' of Scotland on Norbert Roettiers' original 1709 and 1716 dies in bronze, white metal, silver and gold. The dies were then defaced. Modern reproductions exist.

An investigation into the state of the Scottish coinage in 1789, gave rise to the following report:

"We have frequently seen advertisements in the papers of goods to be sold for counterfeit halfpence. These halfpence, it seems, were circulated in Scotland; where, or for what reason, cannot well be accounted for; the common people would not receive the halfpence of King George the Third... The Magistrates have been at the pains of ascertaining the value of the counterfeits, and found that nearly seven of them was worth one sterling penny. They pass current in Scotland 24 for a shilling."

DUTCH TREATS

"For some years back a number of what is called doits, a copper coin, current in Shetland only *for 1-8th of a penny, have been brought into Shetland by the Dutch herring fishers... (A)t the year's end, the whole of these doits centre in the hands of the kirk-treasurers and shopkeepers, who lately have found a very profitable outway for them, which is, by sending them to Leith and Edinburgh ... (to) pass them there for farthings...*

"The value of copper in a doit is not quite 1-16th part of a penny Sterling; so that, by this little cheat, those who take them in at Leith and Edinburgh receive one fourth value of the price of the goods they give in exchange. These doits have been coined in the different provinces in Holland."

Scots Magazine, 1790.

The coinage of Scotland and England became one in the eighteenth century, bringing to an end Scotland's comparatively brief history of counterfeiting. This did not stop Scots from copying Sassenach coinage however, as evidenced in modern times by an 80 year old Edinburgh man who, in 1965, produced over 14,000 counterfeit 1954 and 1955 florins. A Royal Mint assayer described them as 'of excellent quality'.

12

Ireland

The story of counterfeiting in Ireland is of local forgeries, Scottish 'imports' and Low Countries' copies.

The Irish Sea area made use of Anglo-Saxon and foreign coins from c.800 A.D. Then after nearly two centuries, King Sihtric III (Silkenbeard), a Viking ruler in Dublin, gave his Hiberno-Norsemen their own coinage - probably around 995. For the first quarter of a century it was imitative, being direct copies of the silver pennies current in England at that time - firstly of Æthelred II (978-1016), then of Cnut (1016-1035). Some even bear English moneyers' names. From then on, distinctive designs were issued. The extensive research into the English die-cutting centres of this period, enables the imitations to be separated from the originals by style alone. One complication is that dies are known to have moved from England to Scandinavia and Ireland; from Ireland to Scandinavia and even to England. It is probable that late tenth, early eleventh century England was at that time the best at die-production and so attracted 'export orders' for its high-grade carbon steel products with their hardened steel caps securely forged on to the softer metal shanks.

This Hiberno-Norse coinage ran from 995 to 1150, but long before the end of this period, the quality had deteriorated so much that many are now almost unrecognisable. Around 1110, they became so thin that only one side could be struck. These pieces are called bracteates.

Design and weight continued to decline, so that, by Norman times, the English silver penny was being copied on flans too light to be acceptable outside Ireland. By the second quarter of the twelfth century, the Ostmen silver coins were so debased with copper as to be acceptable in limited areas only of Ireland.

Contemporary counterfeit halfpennies imitating the Dominus coinage (1190-1199) have blundered legends. Around 1197, dies began to be engraved outside Dublin. The consistency of the variants that then began to occur, almost certainly rules out blundering. By 1200, farthings were being produced locally, technically infringeing King John's prerogatives, but not enough to justify the wrath they invoked. Contemporary counterfeits have blundered legends.

In 1204/5, new coinage was struck in Dublin, comprising pennies to the same weight and fineness as the English pennies of the time, plus halfpennies and farthings. Triangular frames appeared in the designs and continued for over a hundred years. The pennies spread into England and the continent where they turn up in hoards.

All Dublin pennies that have oval pellets are now considered to be continental imitations.

Henry III voided long cross counterfeit penny mule - Ireland/London. NICOLE ON LVND. A rarity from the Brussels Hoard of 1903. Wgt (split and holed)1.45 gm. 18.5 mm.

In the time of Henry III, there are imitations of 'Crux' Watchet coinage in the Hiberno-Norse series[BL]. Some long-cross pennies have an Irish obverse with a London reverse.

English coinage was reformed in 1247; Irish not until 1251. Late thirteenth, early fourteenth century sterling imitations divide into crude forgeries of suspected local origin, and those struck from good-quality dies of probable continental manufacture. Henry III's Irish coinage was copied on the Continent.

At the start of the fourteenth century, the continental copies of Edwardian sterling, crockards, pollards, etc., found their way to Ireland, including in smaller quantities, copies of Irish prototypes of John, Henry III and Edward I pennies. Pennies with blundered legends are most likely contemporary counterfeits. Those with variant legends are continental sterling. English/Irish and Irish/English mules are imitative, as examples with unrelated issue dates of the impersonated obverse and reverse designs make clear.

Edward II clipped groats were counterfeited by the cliché process (silver foil pressed against a genuine coin and filled with lead, or soldered to base metal cores). These were known as Oraylly, Raillyes or O'Reilly's money and circulated in Ireland in the fifteenth century.

The denier tournois of Philip IV of France (1285-1314) must have circulated in Ireland, as it was being forged there during Edward III's reign in the 1330's. These coins became known as turneys, or black money. In 1338 they led to a ban on the circulation of inferior continental pennies, not to be enforced however until the new Irish coins were available for circulation!

Quantities of cliché forgeries (with lead-solder cores), were a feature of the start of the fifteenth century. They were clipped which, by masking the giveaway edges made them more deceptive. By the middle of the century, clipping of genuine coins was general. An anti-counterfeiting device of secret marks called 'privy' marks was introduced on Edward IV's later Irish coinage.

The brass 'farthing' in the National Museum of Ireland, with a facing bust and cross and pellets on the reverse, with strokes for legend, is probably a forgery of an English halfpenny of Henry VII or VIII.

The 1470-1473 and 1473-1478 coinages attracted contemporary counterfeits in fairly crude style and poor metal. Irish indicators are often missing. A crudely produced Wexford minting is considered to have been unofficial.

Lambert Simnel, the false Earl of Warwick, had Irish type groats and pennies struck on being crowned Edward VI in Dublin Cathedral in 1487. They bear the legend EDWARDVS ANGLIE FRANCIE, royal arms shield/ET REX HYBERNIE, cross and three crowns.

In 1552, shillings were issued that were identical to the English shillings except for a harp mintmark. Crude contemporary brass (and some copper) imitations, struck in Ireland, were known as 'bungals'. They circulated in Connacht at a penny each. Spink now value them at considerably more! Quantities of silvered copper or lead forgeries exist, with a variety of deviations from the true design. A source in York was striking base English pennies for use in Ireland at this time.

Mary Tudor first and second issue shillings, groats, half-groats and pennies have been counterfeited. Victorian copies were made of the groat and penny. Groats bearing dates (local dies dated MDLIII and MDLIV) are suspect. The halfgroat attracted superior counterfeits. English base coins were shipped to Ireland in Elizabeth I's time. They too became known as bungals.

INCHIQUIN MONEY
Gold and silver pieces of certified weight, but without legal tender status, were issued by the Lord Justices of Ireland in the seventeenth century. The term 'Inchiquin money' was attached to them as they were thought to have been struck by Lord Inchiquin during Charles I's reign. In the early nineteenth century (prior to 1817), counterfeit Inchiquin coins were known - of the crown, halfcrown, shilling, sixpence and fourpence, but not of the ninepence. In 1860, Aquilla Smith blamed these forgeries on a Dublin silversmith who was thought to have made them on the instructions of a mysterious collector. Smith acquired examples from the silversmith's estate of all the forgeries, plus some silver flans ready for stamping. They had all been artificially patinated with burning sulphur fumes, giving them a black appearance. The Ulster Museum has four examples (ex-Carlyon-Britton collection). False examples of three different values (shilling, sixpence and groat) were sold by Sotheby's in 1857. Spink's catalogue carries a warning about modern counterfeits of most of these coins, but adds that there are variations as well.

Halfcrowns were produced c.1642 either in Kilkenny or, as some think, in the Welsh Marches. Because of the crudeness of their design and manufacture, they were dubbed Blacksmith's halfcrowns. An example is described and illustrated on page 331 of Volume 2 of *The British Numismatic Journal.*

ORMONDE MONEY
As with Inchiquin money, Ormonde money was issued by the Lord Justices of Ireland in 1643 and was legal tender in England. Ormonde crowns of 1643-1644 were forged. Undated silver crowns, silver-plated on copper cores are contemporary fakes. Over-precise

EDWARD VI
Examples of contemporary brass imitations of Edward VI shillings of 1552 (harp mintmark). They were known as 'bungals'. Any silvering they might have had has gone.

Shilling with a brown patina. Wgt 4.48 gm. 28.5 mm.

Shilling found in the Thames. Wgt (broken edge) 3.17 gm. 29.5 mm.

Charles I Cork Siege piece farthing, 1643-4. This forgery is probably a nineteenth century product. It has a flat flan compared to the indent-ed circle on a square of the original. The size is correct (may be thinner). The castle is larger than on the illustrated Seaby's example - S.6562A.

nineteenth century copies exist. A plated crown, that is possibly an eighteenth century effort, was valued recently at £275. It was thought that the BM had a couple of examples of the gold fakes, but, despite a thorough search in 1973, including the coin weight and counterfeit coin cabinets, no trace could be found.

ORMONDE PISTOLES

Ormonde Pistoles and Double Pistoles of 1646 are described by Seaby and Brady**SE** as authorized but non-regal gold coins. There are modern counterfeits, made in the U.S.A. Three are illustrated in *The British Numismatic Journal* for 1973. They first became known in 1971, via American photographs sent to Baldwin's. These were of two pistole coins, clearly struck from the same die-set. They failed on three different counts:

1 Hammered plate, instead of crucible gold.
2 One had a pierced metal bulge.
3 Both resembled a mid-nineteenth century book illustration more than actual coins.

Of a similar copy that turned up later in the 1970's, Patrick Finn surmised that it had been made by a plaster cast technique. He suspected a Californian die-engraver of being the forger. It became something of a cause célèbre when the American Numismatic Association Certification Service 'authenticated' it, despite it being made from inapplicably near-pure gold. A review led to the Certificate being withdrawn and to mention of at least eleven other known false pistoles. The Association added that it had a strong idea of the perpetrator's identity.

If there *are* early counterfeits, they might have been copied from the two genuine Ormondes that were in the Earl of Ellesmere's collection. It seems unlikely that a cast could have been obtained, because there is a serif type on the counterfeits that is not present on the Earl's coins.

CONFEDERATE CATHOLICS' ISSUES

Confederate Catholics' crowns and halfcrowns imitated the Ormonde coins. There are some modern forgeries of the 1643-1644 silver shilling and sixpenny Cork issues of the Southern 'Cities of Refuge' of the Confederate Catholics. Silver shillings with the word CORK encircling the date 1647 on the obverse are modern cast counterfeits.

Contemporary forgeries of the crudely produced bronze Kilkenny halfpennies and farthing issues of the Confederate Catholics, 1642-1643 are common. They have blundered legends and crude style.

FARTHINGS

Harington farthings had a tinned surface to deter counterfeiters and also to give the coins a silvery, more valuable appearance. Duchess of Richmond farthings were counterfeited in quantity. Crown and harp were poorly designed, legends blundered, flans irregularly shaped and often oversize, leaving space outside the legends.

St Patrick's halfpennies and farthings appeared, c.1674, with anti-counterfeiting brass plugs in their centres.

James II made Gunmoney counterfeiting high treason and informers were rewarded. Halfcrowns dated September 1690 are probably all tooled August coins. Shillings dated August 1690 are probably all tooled August 1689 coins. Sixpences dated March 1689, March 1690 and October 1689 to October 1690 are probably all counterfeit. John White is suspected *(see Chapter 13)*. Shillings and sixpences in gold, dated respectively February 1689 and June 1690, are later strikings.

In 1690, pewter coins were issued with brass plugged centres, apparently to distinguish them from lead cast counterfeits.

Bizarrely, if the counterfeit gold and silver pieces being made in Ireland in William III's time, were cut through the centre or defaced in some way to show they were not genuine, they could be tendered!

The year after the 1696 halfpenny appeared, counterfeits, known as 'raps', poured into Northern Ireland from Scotland and Europe until there were more of them than genuine coins in circulation. In an endeavour to stem this tide, a proclamation was issued threatening imprisonment for those importing false money.

England's Great Recoinage of 1698 led to an epidemic of forging, producing harsher penalties for forgers, which led many of them to seek the safer shores of Ireland to continue their nefarious activities.

WOOD'S IRISH REJECTS

George I's mistress, given the right to coin money, sold this right in 1722 to William Wood, an ironmaster from Wolverhampton, who proceeded to produce halfpennies and farthings for use in Ireland. Dean Jonathan Swift, for political reasons, accused him of using poor metal and of making undersized coins, neither of which seems to have been true. Despite this, Swift succeeded in stirring Irish feelings, so that the coins were rejected and finally ended up being used in the British Colonies in America, alongside Wood's Rosa Americana coinage. On one example of Wood's halfpenny coinage, the harp has been tooled off to create a variety. Harp string variations on the regal coinage are thought to be mint codes.

By 1722, poor counterfeits, or 'raps', were everywhere. This situation continued to the end of the century. As the 1800's started, a copper mine owner called Cammac had produced counterfeit halfpennies in such quantities that they were called 'cammacs' after him. Because they filled a need, they were accepted at Government offices and even used by the army to pay the troops. Not until 1804, when the Post Office announced its rejection of them was there any official repudiation. In the same year, The Bank of Ireland took in counterfeit silver in bulk and paid a bullion rate for it.

Lack of good silver in the late eighteenth century led to worn silver shillings and sixpences being kept in circulation by being counter-

WASTE DISPOSAL

In 1652, some Londoners dumped quantities of counterfeit and clipped English coin and base 'Peru-pieces' in Ireland. Several were caught and executed. Their counterfeit halfcrowns were said to contain no more than 2d worth of silver.

William & Mary 1693 halfpenny, cast in iron. Harp strings crooked. Wgt 7.65 gm. 25.5 mm (28 to 31 mm).

This 30d Irish Bank Token of 1808 still has most of its silvering. A flaw on the token's reverse has almost completely removed the letter N from BANK. 31.5 mm (32 mm).

1805 10d Irish Bank Token in base silver. 22.5 mm (23 mm).

marked with Traders' names and initials and used as token coinage, known as slap tokens.

A 1760's shortage of copper coinage led to the Dublin toymaker and army button-maker, John Roche[MI], issuing his own 'coins' - VOCE POPULI farthings and halfpence. There were other, less successful issuers. Lightweight counterfeit coppers, mostly minted in Birmingham, flooded into Ireland in the latter part of the eighteenth century. In the nineteenth century, contemporary counterfeits became more obvious because of the engrailed edge and crisp strike of the genuine pieces. Erratic graining is a frequent giveaway.

BANK TOKENS

George III Bank of Ireland coinage, 1804-13, with values of Six Shillings, Thirty Pence, Ten Pence and Five Pence have been faked in quantity, with Birmingham the chief suspect source. They were made by silvering base metal. Some contemporary counterfeits of the six shilling bank tokens were made by 'skinning' genuine pieces and sticking the two wafer-thin surfaces to a brass core, adding a silver collar to conceal the brass edge. Pieces now tend to have brass showing through the silver at various places on the surface. There are cast base metal counterfeits of the thirty pence tokens, including some in lead. When cast base metal counterfeits of the ten and five pence tokens started turning up in quantity, the law on counterfeiting had to be extended to cover them. The contract for the 1806 ten pence tokens stipulated that they should all be dated 1805.

Amongst the prolific, and sometimes good quality counterfeits of the 'London Coinage' halfpennies are some with completely false dates. The following dates are known: 1775, 1776, 1781, 1782, 1783. The counterfeits usually show poor crown-tops on the Harp reverse. Some were made to look worn. An 1805 Soho halfpenny copy is a rarity. It is usually given away by missing double pips on the base of the harp.

HIBERNIA EVASIONS

Most Irish evasions have similar legends to their English equivalents. One distinctly Irish evasion penny shows a bust of Daniel O'Connell instead of George IV and IRELANDS ADVOCATE/MAY OUR FRIENDS PROSPER.

The British Museum has a tray of notably inept George IV Irish penny counterfeits. Contemporary counterfeits of the 1822/3 penny are common.

An official survey in 1852 reported that the copper coinage was worn and mixed with private tokens, counterfeits and foreign coins. The halfpennies and farthings were the domestic Irish coins. The pennies tended to leave the country. Unofficial farthings were issued in Belfast, Cork, Killarney and Waterford.

Hibernia Evasions

An undated evasion halfpenny - ALFRED THE GREAT /MUSIC CHARMS. 27 mm (29 mm).

An undated evasion halfpenny - LOUIS THE SIXTEENTH /MUSIC CHARMS. 27 mm (29 mm).

This undated evasion penny, c.1822/23, depicts Daniel O'Connell instead of George IV. The obverse reads IRELANDS ADVOCATE; the reverse, MAY OUR FRIENDS PROSPER. Bronze on lead or white metal core. Cupped. It has been referred to as a token. 34 mm (35 mm).

This rare contemporary forgery of a Soho halfpenny was originally thought to be a proof. It is a very good copy with slight differences only - e.g. no double pips on the harp base. 27 mm (29 to 30 mm).

Unusual contemporary halfpenny with both sides having a harp reverse - of 1766 (type 1) and 1769. The dies have been made with a deliberately worn look, to produce apparently well-circulated coins. 27.5 mm (29 to 30 mm).

IRISH EXPORTS

"Forgeries. were manufactured some years ago by a silversmith in Dublin, under the direction of an obscure collector, who usually disposed of his rare coins in England. When the remnant of his collection was sold after his death, I purchased a complete set of these forgeries, and, at the same time, a few small blank pieces of silver, cut into a polygonal form, and filed preparatory to stamping them."

1860 report by Aquilla Smith.

ISLE OF MAN

Isle of Man coinage started about 1020 by being struck from a set of Dublin dies, followed by very crude copies of these dies.

Little is known of the intervening years, but by the mid seventeenth century there were many counterfeits in circulation prompting the Act of Tynwald of 1646 - *"to falsify, forge and counterfeit, clipp and diminish any kind of current coin is treasonable."* This was more comprehensive than in England at the time, where base metal coinage was not covered.

The 1709 pennies and halfpennies are unusual in having been cast. There is a modern forgery of the 1709 halfpenny, cast in lead. By 1733, the Isle of Man was swamped with counterfeits. All coins issued to that time were made illegal and new pennies and halfpennies issued. These too were counterfeited. Some genuine 1733 pennies were made in Bath metal (from cannon). The 1733 penny with two O's in the legend instead of Q's is possibly an Irish counterfeit.

LUNDY ISLAND

Lundy coins (Puffin pennies and halfpennies - the halfpenny Puffin shows the top half of a Puffin!) are in a sense real but not genuine currency, having been issued illegally in 1929 by the island owner, M.C Harman. Until disabused by mainland authority, he thought he was sufficiently independent to have a right to issue his own coinage.

In 1965, Harman's dies were acquired by Modern World Coins, who issued a double set commemorating the 40th anniversary of Harman's purchase of Lundy. They were struck in bronze, nickel-silver and gold. They have no numismatic standing and are recognisable by their plain edges. The originals have the edge inscription LUNDY LIGHTS AND LEADS.

Euro-trash

It will be interesting to see how counterfeits of the Euro coin occur in the unique situation of a dozen countries sharing a modern coin made by the identical method and partly to the same design. When these inevitable counterfeits accumulate, they could reveal which countries have the biggest problems with forgers. Also, who are the most skilful, assuming that their products are detectable! The first counterfeits to appear of Ireland's Euro coins were certainly detectable. They had a clue that even the unfamiliarity of the new design could not disguise. The 'O' had been missed off the word 'EURO'.

13

The Coiners

Nobody knows who invented coin counterfeiting, but whoever he may have been, he was undoubtedly one of the great, unsung villains of history. It was clearly like letting a genie out of the bottle, for the idea was adopted as enthusiastically as coinage itself and has been around ever since, right up to the present day, with its dud one and two pound coins. Ever since banknotes appeared, they have had a parallel history, but with the advantage over coins of greater unit value - a fact clearly appreciated by a £20 and £50 counterfeiting gang jailed on the 20th of January 2000. They are said to have produced two-thirds of all fake currency circulating in Britain from 1993 to 1998. The coin-to-note value difference is graphically illustrated by the coin counterfeiting factory found in West London. It had been set up to flood Britain with fake 50p's, and contained heavy equipment, included two electric furnaces and a stockpile of half a million faked coins weighing nearly four tons!

A notorious 19th century coiner.

The vast majority of counterfeiters are unknown as are their individual reasons for engaging in this activity. Occasionally, one leaves behind a hint, as did he with a predilection for imperial ladies, especially of the Severan period. Another coiner confessed all in a mid nineteenth century booklet, entitled Beware of Base Coin, describing how drink was his downfall, leading him into the company of passers of bad coin. Having succumbed to the tempting profits of passing bad money, he started trying, at first very unsuccessfully, to produce his own counterfeits.

Women rarely figure in the records as creators of counterfeits, although many in the eighteenth century suffered severe punishment for passing dud coins. In the mid 1960's, a Police authority said that there was "no trace of women forgers."

GREED, NEED, VANITY and DESPAIR

Greed has always been the main motivation for counterfeiting. There are other motives such as Need - the lack of regal small change creating a vacuum inevitably filled with imitations. Vanity - as shown by Renaissance artists such as Cavino and Cesati, who produced their own 'Roman' coins, some completely fanciful flights of imagination. Despair - in our present times, it is difficult to appreciate what being poor meant in the past. If a man could not feed his family, desperation could easily drive him to risk the frightening penalties detailed in the next Chapter. Then there are those whose motives fall into none of these categories, represented by the young man who counterfeited banknotes to give to his heart's desire in order to impress her with his affluence. He lost his life for love - at Tyburn.

Quasi-official coin production has sprung up wherever the central authorities were not exerting firm control. Mints would be started at local, civil and religious power centres. Responsibility would usually be delegated to a mintmaster, who could become the scapegoat if problems arose with the central power. It was also usual to reduce the precious metal content to enhance the profit. Some copied the popular coins of the day, adding their names to the designs. Others went for more direct copying, with the clear intention of fooling the public.

COUNTERFEITING FOR COLLECTORS

In the 1650's to 1750's, responding to that era's enthusiasm for ancient coins, counterfeiting centres in Venice, Madrid and Stuttgart churned out thousands of copies of silver Roman coins. They usually have a thin, flat look to them. The Bombay and Calcutta mints have struck coins to order and have issued many restrikes, mostly of proof brilliance. These lapse quickly into a tarnished and nasty greasy look. Tiny pimples, caused by corrosion pits on the dies, can also give them away. Gold restrikes tend to be of a deeper shade. The Middle East and Italy are two prolific sources of pressure-cast fakes.

> FAKE VALUES!
>
> Several of the past masters in the 'art' of coin counterfeiting, such as Becker, Cavino and the Paduans are now collected in their own right, or should it be in their own wrong!
>
> An attractive 'Becker' can fetch £100 or more.

Over recent centuries, these countries have surfaced as the main sources of counterfeits - Greece, Italy, Lebanon, India, Yugoslavia, Iran, Thailand, Germany, Hong Kong, Morocco, Singapore, Malaysia, Afghanistan, Bulgaria, Spain, Syria, the UK and the USA. Italy has been a centre of forging from medieval times to the present day. In 1964, it was rumoured that very high quality forgeries were emanating from a new group of mainly Italian based forgers. Their products were thought to be contaminating both private and public collections.

This was a mid nineteenth century opinion on the main sources of counterfeits at the time:

"The best imitations of Greek coins seem to be made in the Greek Islands and in India. The latter are generally cast, but the former are struck from false dies. The best forgeries of English coins were made by Emery: a man named Singleton is also said to have been similarly employed."

The eighteenth and nineteenth century forgeries of British coins were mostly limited to significant Anglo-Saxon and later hammered coins[LA]. The modern, pressure-cast forgeries concentrate on the gold coins. Forgers have imitated the majority of European gold coins, the most counterfeited of all being the British gold sovereign, with estimates of up to 40% in circulation being forged. Some end up in the jewellery trade stamped 'F' for forgery. In the Near and Middle East, the sovereign is a trusted unit of value. In consequence, pieces from Victoria's time on have been extensively counterfeited, particularly in the Lebanon, where the copies have slightly more gold in them than the genuine article. This 'generosity' by the forgers is only made possible because of the mark-up on the coins over their gold content value. After a period in which such counterfeiters escaped conviction because their copies were of 'obsolete' coinage, the British Government re-introduced sovereigns in quantity to close this legal gap.

POPULAR CHOICES

Up to the end of the nineteenth century, the popular counterfeiting choices aimed at collectors have been Greek decadrachms, Roman Aes grave, rare types of medieval gold coins, Renaissance gold, silver bracteates, Thalers, Siege pieces and countermarked coins.

In the twentieth century, many less rare Greek and Roman coins have been targeted. The ten years up to the mid 1960's saw an escalation in modern forgeries, including more copies of common coins. There have been skilful cast forgeries of Elizabeth I gold sovereigns, Charles I half-pound coins and Newark Siege pieces.

The late 1960's saw superior forgeries of ancient Greek and Roman coins coming from the Middle East. Forgeries also turn up of Indo-Greek, Visigothic, Transylvanian, German, Anglo-Saxon, English, Italian and other continental medieval coins.

In the 1980's, low-mintage gold coins of the nineteenth and twentieth centuries were the forgers' main targets. A 1980 report said that forgeries *containing the correct gold content* are not known for Krugerrands, Austrian 4 Ducats, Austrian 100 Coronas, Hungarian 100 Coronas, Mexican 20 and 50 Pesos. Plated or gilded forgeries exist of the Krugerrands, Austrian and Hungarian Coronas.

THE ROGUES' ROLL-CALL

First comes someone who could be thought of as Aristotle Nonimas, (or A.Nonymous), the Greek who invented coin counterfeiting, and, in so doing, started this world-wide cottage industry - still around after two and a half thousand years.

The earliest namable counterfeiter was Polykrates, the tyrant of Samos. The Greek historian, Herodotus, wrote that Polykrates bought off the besieging Spartans in 525/4 B.C. with counterfeit Samian coins. Some of these fakes still exist and are described in Spink's coin catalogue as *counterfeit staters in lead, originally plated with electrum* - worth £2,500 each!

For 1,800 years, from the seventh century B.C. to the twelfth century A.D., the names of individual counterfeiters were clearly not considered worth recording. Then, occasional references start occurring, increasing with time.

13th Century

In the late thirteenth century, one captured counterfeiter said that he belonged to "the society of false moneyers."

A town burgess, a hospital chaplain, and people of similar standing were indulging in the practice of counterfeiting at the end of this century. The first convicted forger, whose name has come through from medieval times is John le HAVEKERE. Records show that, in 1279, he was hanged for forgery.

14th Century

A Nottingham counterfeiter, and member of the Coterel outlaw gang, William de USTON was counterfeiting at Radmanthwaite, north of Mansfield from 1327/8 to 1331/2. The Da SESTO brothers struck imitations of Roman coins at the Venetian mint - late fourteenth to early fifteenth century.

15th Century

A report of 1443 records a group in the town of Speyer, who were 'skimming' gold and silver to coat obsolete foreign coins which were then sold to gullible countryfolk as the actual coins given to Judas.

William BURNLEY and brother John, from Halifax, West Yorkshire, are recorded as having claimed sanctuary in December 1499 to escape charges of coining; an early instance of the enthusiasm for counterfeiting in that part of Britain.

16th Century

This was the Golden Age of forgery, according to the eighteenth century writer (and forger), John Pinkerton. Pirro LIGORIO (1493-1580) was an author, turned counterfeiter, described by his friend Antonio Agustin as a producer of estimable products 'inspired' by antiquity. This bishop-antiquary considered elegance and accuracy to justify such pieces.

Jacobus WATTERHOUSE and Laurence HAULESWORTH were coiners of Sowerby, West Yorkshire in 1530 - further early examples of the popularity of this activity in Yorkshire.

Tudor coiners came from all walks of life - including, not surprisingly, goldsmiths with their skills, equipment and appropriate metals readily to hand, and soldiers, used to taking risks.

Sir William SHARINGTON (fl.1546-1550)
In April 1546, Sharington was appointed under-treasurer at Bristol, with permission to strike gold and silver coinage at the Bristol Mint, including the silver coinage for Ireland until the Dublin mint opened in 1548 (his coins are monogrammed WS). By then he had lapsed into counterfeit coin production, buying a quantity of church plate and minting it into underweight testoons, which gave him huge profits, running into thousands of pounds. He became a fellow-conspirator of

Thomas Seymour to gain his protection, but Seymour's plots and Sharington's frauds were discovered. In December 1548 he was dismissed from his post and in January 1549, arrested and taken to the Tower where he confessed all - making light coin, clipping, book falsifying and document burning. He was convicted of counterfeiting £12,000 worth of testoons and heavily fined. Surprisingly, by the end of the year he had been pardoned, and even more surprisingly, in April 1550, he was trusted to go to France on a money-collecting mission for the King.

In the same year as Sharington's conviction, French moneyers employed at Durham House were charged with counterfeiting.

SAID CELLINI TO THE POPE *"I could but I wouldn't and I didn't"*

In 1529, Benvenuto CELLINI (1500-1571) was appointed engraver at Rome's mint where he designed and made dies for the Pope for crown-pieces, 'Vos Electionis' and St. Paul's bust, using a series of small punches for the separate parts of the designs.

He got into trouble with the Pope when false coins struck with his dies started appearing in Rome. In his Memoirs he recounts this conversation:
Pope - *Benvenuto, do you think you could find it in your heart to make counterfeit money?*
Cellini - *I am much better able to counterfeit coins than the low fellows that are generally guilty of this crime... When I make the dies for the Mint, I every day before dinner gain at least three crowns... without resorting to the infamous and less profitable trade of false coining.*

Gold Scudo of Pope Paul III, designed and engraved by Cellini in 1534. It shows why the Pope was so concerned that a skill like this might be applied to counterfeiting. 26mm.

Two Mint workers were eventually found to be the real culprits. The main perpetrator was hanged and his accomplice sent to the galleys.

In 1558 in Florence, Cellini wrote about both hammer and screw methods of coining. He tried unsuccessfully to persuade the King of France to let him strike all French coins using the new, mechanised methods. His volatile temperament led to him being imprisoned several times. During one of his stays in prison, he taught a fellow-inmate how to counterfeit keys.

CAVINO and the Paduans

Sixteenth century Padua housed a school of engravers, turning out copies and fantasies of ancient Greek and Roman coins. Pieces by them are now known as 'Paduans'. The practice seems to have started much earlier, with medals copying bronze coins of Galba and Vitellius being issued in 1390. Paduan coins were the inevitable response to demands arising from the Renaissance fashion for Italian princes and grandees to have cabinets of ancient coins, particularly Greek and Roman. Gaps were filled with copies. Gentlemen on the Grand tour would be offered Paduans as souvenirs of their trip.

The best-known Paduan is Giovanni da CAVINO (*also referred to as John Cauvin or Cavinus*). His reputation has lasted because of the quality and quantity of his work and because most of his dies still exist (in Paris). Cavino, a contemporary of Benvenuto Cellini, is thought to have been born in Padua in 1499 or 1500. He died there in 1570, having left behind a series of remarkably good copies of Roman coins.

A goldsmith like his father, he was a skilful engraver who, c.1540, teamed up with a historian friend, Alessandro Bassanio, to create a range of pseudo-Roman coins, some inspired by originals, others by statuary, etc. He also produced medallions depicting local notables of the time, but only his large-brass Roman forgeries are of interest here. He claimed not to have designed them as such (a claim also made by Becker), and to have been upset that they were used to deceive the collectors of the time. So did he and fellow Paduans such as Camellio (Vettor Gambello) and Cesati (Alessandro Greco) produce fakes or innocent imitations? The answer is probably both. Some were artistic impressions of the originals or complete creations of the artist's imagination - almost artists' exercises.

Large-brass sestertius of Vitellius. Cavino Paduan No. 28. Slightly worn. A.VITELLIVS. GERMAN. IMP.AVG.P.M.TR. Laureate bust of Vitellius. The reverse shows a helmeted Mars carrying a spear and a trophy over his shoulder. It imitates a genuine coin with a similar inscription on the obverse.

Cavino used a genuine Roman bronze sestertius as the coin flan on which to strike this 'sestertius' of Claudius. Some of the undertype still shows through.

But the use of genuine Roman sestertii for overstriking with the Paduans' freshly cut dies, points to deceit, as do the pieces including artificial damage, ageing and patina. They were *never* signed. Cavino used some imitative reverse dies for his 'notables' medallions that could be seen as evidence of his intention not to deceive, but his choice of rarities and concocted 'rarities' of obvious attraction to collectors is strong evidence to the contrary.

The fantasies of this time may have been intended only to show off the engraver's artistry.

This supposed silver coin of Caracalla is one of Cavino's fantasies.

Some pieces can be identified as Cavino's because of his style preference when tackling Empresses. The Romans emphasised their breasts, Cavino their stomachs!. He is considered not to have cast any pieces. Struck examples are collectables, cast are generally not, as they were made much later from struck Paduans with the consequent loss of detail, making them visibly inferior products. They arose when demand continued but the Renaissance artists' dies were no longer available for striking pieces. More of these casts now exist than the original Paduans. Most of these fakes of fakes are considered to have been made after the sixteenth century, although the Paduan tradition of copying lingered on there until the eighteenth century. Late casts, most probably nineteenth century casts of casts, have even greater loss of detail, and are often under-sized because of shrinkage.

Enea Vico, writing in 1555, mentions Giovanni and "his young son" Vincenzo, cutting excellent iron dies. Vincenzo may have continued to strike imitations from his father's dies after 1570. Another son, Antonio, may also have helped, but the third son practised law.

CAMELLIO (Vettor Gambella or Vittore Gambello) (c.1455-1537) is another of the Paduan 'school' of counterfeiters of ancient Roman coins. He is known for a very plain Cleopatra.

Famous historic figures such as Helen of Troy, Alcibiades and Hannibal were 'awarded' coins and medallions in silver, bronze and lead by Paduan fantasy fabricators, including Jean Barrin, Camellio, Cavino and Cesati.

VENI VIDI VICI

Klawans[KL] considers it possible that the most famous Cavino fantasy, with the VENI VIDI VICI reverse, may not in fact be by him, but by someone weaker in portraiture than Cavino.

Its mention in a 1592 coin book confirms its Renaissance origin. It may have been a product of one of the following - Carteron (Holland); Congornier (Lyons, France); Michael Dervieu (Florence, Italy); Galli and Laroche (Grenoble, Switzerland); Novello and Sesto (Cararra, Italy).

MARMITA of Padua was a painter who switched to coin and medal counterfeiting. Ludovico, his son, was said by Vasari to produce extremely proficient counterfeits.

Probably at the start of the nineteenth century, a Dutch counterfeiter called Carteron was producing some fine Roman copies, including serrati Numi, that can be mistaken for Paduans.

A Renaissance goldsmith and gem engraver, Valerio Vincentino BELLI, (1468-1546) counterfeited Greek and Roman gold coins for his own collection. Vasari[VA] refers to Belli's medals of the twelve Caesars. He was a contemporary of Cavino, but much less skilful, producing only fair imitations of the originals. To the modern eye, his busts on coins of ancient figures do not look classical. Two of his efforts are of Aeneas and Lysander[JO].

Antinous sestertius, "Antinoon". Greek coins exist bearing his name, e.g. Ae drachm, Alexandria, Egypt, but no known Roman. He was Hadrian's 'favourite'. The poor detail suggests that this is a nineteenth century cast of a Paduan.

CESATI

In 1549, Alessandro CESATI, nicknamed El Greco, was Master of the Papal Mint. He is now rated as an inferior artist to his contemporary, Cavino, being considered not to have grasped the ancient style of the coins he was copying. Jones[JO] illustrates two examples of Cesati's Greek 'coins'; a gilded Mithradates VI fantasy bronze based on a silver tetradrachm and a bronze copy of an Alexander the Great gold stater showing four elephants pulling Alexander's regal dais.

In another imaginative piece, he created a coin of Priam, King of Troy on which he depicted a view of Troy itself. To encompass a genuine coin of Priam, who reigned in the twelfth century B.C., the history of coinage would have to be pushed back 500 years.

In his 1555 book, as well as his reference to Cavino, mentioned above, Enea Vico[VI] discussed Cavino's fellow Paduans. The best of those named by him as making deceptive new iron dies in his time, was Giovan-Iacopo of Padua. His brother, Federico Bonzagna, was also mentioned, together with Cesati (Alessandro Greco), Cellini, Camellio (Vettor Gambello), Leone Leoni (Leone Aretino) and Jacopo da Trezzo. Except for Cavino and Cesati, little is now known about most of these or their 'creations'.

Otho used only gold or silver on his coinage, revealing this cast bronze as a fantasy Paduan.

COUNTERFEITERS IN SCOTLAND
Bruntoun, an Englishman, is recorded in the sixteenth century as having taught three Edinburgh women how to make chalk moulds for counterfeiting. The women were caught, tried, condemned, strangled and burned. Dundee merchant, Robert JACKE, was hanged and quartered in the 1560's for importing counterfeit hardheads from Flanders. Thomas PEEBLES, an Edinburgh goldsmith, struck counterfeit nonsunts (twelve penny groats), Lyon hardheads, silver testoons and half-testoons. A woman, one of his 'passers', caught with some of his "Lyonis, callit Hard-heidis" in the market, named him as the supplier, and dies and counterfeits were found in his house when the Bailis searched. His property was forfeited and he was condemned to death by hanging and executed in 1563.

Eloye (Eloi) MESTRELL(E) (*Menestrell, Menstrell(e), Minstrell, Ministrelle, Mistrell or Elloye the Frenchman)* (? - 1578) – *father of England's first machine-made coinage.*
In 1560 Mestrell came to England, a Huguenot refugee from France. He left behind substantial debts, so his escape may have been more to do with this, than with religious persecution. His previous employment at the Moulin des Étuves, the Paris Mint, led to him working at the Tower Mint, where he introduced the French semi-mechanised methods of coin production, first used in France ten years' before. This *"new manner of coyning devised by Elloye the Frenchman"* brought him the handsome salary of £25 per annum. The Calendar of Patent Rolls of 24th March, 1561, cleared the decks for this innovator with a *"Pardon for Eloy Mistrell, born at Paris in France, for all treasons, felonies and offences committed before 1st March, 1. Eliz. in respect of clipping or counterfeiting Coin."*

By the end of 1561, he was producing excellent coinage from a horse-operated screw-press. His lis-marked gold coins with their serrated security edges were struck up to September 1568, when he was accused of complicity in forgery. In 1569, he was convicted in London of helping Philip Mestrell (his father or brother?) to forge four Burgundian crowns. Presumably because of his usefulness at the Mint, he was then pardoned, but not Philip, who was hanged at Tyburn for the offence. The two Englishmen who were hanged with him for clipping silver coins and casting tin shillings, were not then quartered, which was Philip's fate for having forged *gold* coins. Eloye was reinstated in 1570. When a traditionalist mint master called Martin was appointed in 1572, he held a trial which appeared to confirm that the hammer workers were right in claiming Mestrell's method of producing flans to be too slow. Mestrell was fired, and is next heard of five years later, being convicted in Norwich for stamping counterfeit shillings. He kept himself alive for a while by implicating his accomplices, Drury, Browning and Goodwin, but in the end, in 1578, all were hanged. It was a sad end for an innovator, whose coinage was clearly superior to that of his hammer-striking contemporaries at the Mint.

In 1580, a London mint official - an Engraver and Assay-master called John BULL - was accused of coining false Angels.

Not content with being just a counterfeiter, Elizabethan rogue, Edward KELLEY, was also an alchemist, medium, necromancer and fraudster. He met a violent end on the Continent in 1597, trying to escape from prison, where his patron had put him, having decided that his 'ability' to turn base metal into gold depended upon him being provided with the gold in the first place!

THE NOTORIOUS MIRANDOLA MINT
The little Italian town of Mirandola which lies north of Modena was famous in the Renaissance for the superb coins produced at the town mint[BE] - and infamous for its other output - of counterfeits of foreign coins. Santo di Bochali was put to death in 1524 for striking forged dupioni and ducati. Ninety years' later, the infection had spread to Modena, a town which had often banned the influx of Mirandola 'products'. There the mintmaster was convicted of counterfeiting and the mint closed for a while. Back in Mirandola, under mintmaster Rivarola, who by then (1623), also controlled the Tresana and Corregio mints, counterfeit coins were being mass-produced to foist on to the German markets. Imperial reactions to this onslaught damped down production for a few years, but it was up and running again by 1630, imitating other states' coins to the end of the century. Mirandola lost its independence in 1711.

17th Century

John NOTT and his partner, Robert PRICKTRE, were condemned to death in 1601 for counterfeiting the low-grade Irish silver coinage - "some five or six pounds thereof." The metal they used was described by Nott as making "a very fair counterfeiture" of good silver using just copper, tin and the mysterious ingredient, "tinglass - a black kind of metal."

Sir John BROCKETT (fl. January 1601-1603)
He was appointed commandant of Duncannon Fort in southern Ireland, in June 1601. By January 1602/3 he was in the Tower of London charged with coining, having been informed on by Richard Milne (or Meillin), a Scotsman he had confided in.

Back in Ireland, Brockett's sons, John junior, lieutenant of the fort, and Thomas were also imprisoned, together with the informer Milne, who however was given "some better libertie least he should be discomforted in his information."

If the prosecution is to be believed, Brockett's desk was loaded with evidence of counterfeiting: "som quantitie both of Spaynishe and of our mixt moneys counterfeited, and in one of the crucibles found there are two coyned peces in the bignes of our three pence found fastned to the little panne."

The full inventory of the contents of Sir John's desk, when searched on the 9th of March 1602, gives a vivid impression of what a cast coin counterfeiter needed at that time:

"One Tinckers mowld.
Three peeces of brasse and a pese of Ordinance detayned from Sir Georg Bowchier Kt., whereof one pece was wrought and beaten owt.
Five crusabells whereof one groat, and another with newe pennee not fully wrought sticking to the bottom.
Two boxes contayning quicksilver.
A payre of Tinckers pynsors.
A small instrument to sawe.
A file.
A goldsmithes hammer.
A pax contayning bone ashes with two small peeces melted.
A goldsmithes brushe and a haresfote.
A gilding pynn.
A scrach brush.
Six stones of rock allome.
A pax contayning Sandyver (*Sain de Vare)* and saltpeter.
A small bagg contayning refined clay.
A tuch stone, a silver spone and a sledge.
There is left in the forte a brasse pott full of charcoale with a proporcon of charcoale in the chymney, and an old copp kettell."

Faced with this mountain of evidence it is not surprising that he eventually confessed, saying any coin could be counterfeited in a pair of wood, iron or clay moulds with the middle cut out and filled with sand, chalk or ashes. A coin would then be pressed between to make the mould shape for the metal.

Sir John's defence was that he was only going to make coins of England's enemies, and pass them abroad! His arrest curtailed an operation that was clearly going to expand, as a shed was already constructed for the purpose, by deep water - a handy dumping point for incriminating evidence.

Daniel GOFFIN was a French die-cutter who operated c.1615-1630, at Sedan. Towards the end of that period, at a La Vanette mint, he cut dies to imitate German, Italian and Spanish coins.

A warning from the Surveyor of the Melting-house in his Highnesse Mint, carried in the *Publick Intelligencer* of 22-8/10/1655, stated that "Abraham Stapley is a false Coiner of Money, for in his house at Deptford were found several false Coining Irons for half crowns, and false half crowns with the date 1655, and this is to give notice to all persons whatsoever, that shall receive any of the said money of Stapleys, dated 1655, there being none of that date in his Highness Mint coined to this day the 26. of October." Freedman considers that genuine pieces of this date do exist[FR] which, if correct, would make this a rare instance of a forger anticipating a Mint production.

Richard OLIVER, convicted of coining halfcrowns and shillings in 1662, claimed to have bought the stamps for this purpose from an under-graver of the Royal Mint called Hill.

The reverend Edmund ROBINSON lived at the appropriately named

Bank End near Holmsfirth in West Yorkshire and was hanged at York in 1688 for coining. His cellar activities were aided by his son, who not only was let off, but later worked for the Mint, presumably on the basis that if you can't beat 'em, employ 'em.

William CHALLONER was the poacher who tried to turn gamekeeper. He was already well known as a skilled counterfeiter of English coins when, in 1696, he offered his services to Sir Isaac Newton, then Master of the Royal Mint, for the prevention of counterfeiting. He proposed, for a modest sum, to increase the power of the Mint's presses to enable them to turn out coinage with such high relief that counterfeiters could not reproduce them. Another of his ideas was to defeat counterfeiters making casts by having a channel around the edge of the coins. After checking out his ideas, the Royal Mint said they were unworkable, and - oh, by the way, you're imprisoned for counterfeiting. He talked his way out of Newgate, but was again imprisoned and received his final comeuppance in 1699. It is said that fellow counterfeiters applauded the execution of this enemy within their ranks.

Postscript. Two and a half centuries later, the Royal Mint adopted some of his ideas.

Yet another Yorkshireman, a Leeds' silversmith called Arthur MONJOY, was executed for counterfeiting Charles II coins.

James ROETTIER, Tower Mint coin engraver, was found guilty at a 1697 Mint Enquiry of smuggling James II and Charles II coinage dies out of the Mint to France and was immediately dismissed. Norbert, his brother, a Jacobite sympathiser and the centre of 'a scandal', had fled to France two years' earlier. Another member of this skilful family, John Roettier, engraved hardened steel dies and puncheons to produce Mint medals. Strangely, these dies remained the property of his family, not of the Mint[HO].

18th Century

This century contained one of the great epidemics of counterfeiting, which combined with a greater recording of affairs to produce more information about offenders than in all the preceding centuries.

SHABBY BUTTON MAKERS

"Take you in the mood, what e'er base metal come.

You coin as fast as groats at Brominghum "- so said Dryden (Spanish Prior prologue), and a 1696 commentator referred to the *"shabby dishonest button makers in the dark lanes of Birmingham."*

THE BIRMINGHAM FORGERS
Birmingham was one of the main centres of counterfeiting in the late seventeenth and eighteenth centuries. Hammered groats are known to have been forged there around 1676.

By the mid eighteenth century, Birmingham and the surrounding manufacturing towns in the Black Country, such as Bilston, Wednesbury and Wolverhampton, had become notorious as the main sources of fake and 'evasive' copper coin. At this time, Birmingham toymakers got heavily involved in copper coin forgery, the first being arrested in 1744.

Lightweight counterfeit coppers, mostly minted in Birmingham, came flooding into Ireland in the latter part of the eighteenth century. This was also a peak time in Birmingham counterfeit production of silver coinage, brought on by the invention of a way of rolling out sheets of metal with a core of copper and two thin outer layers of silver. These sheets had flans stamped out and struck into many different types of British and foreign copies. In the 1790's, Spanish dollars were popular targets, much of the output going to the east. The forgers claimed patriotic motives. To complaints about this practice, from Boulton and other concerned citizens of Birmingham, the Government turned a deaf ear. Also occurring at that time was the forging of French money, with some forgers receiving Government payments.

From the time in 1787 when Thomas Williams moved the production of his Parys Mines tokens to Birmingham, that city became the centre for their production - and for their counterfeiting. 'Birmingham Company' tokens were contemporary imitations of the Birmingham Mining and Copper Co's tokens of 1791-3, which were also widely counterfeited.

A known counterfeiter in late eighteenth century Birmingham was William LUTWYCHE. Die-link chains connect his legitimate advertising and Condor tokens to evasions to straight counterfeits of Georgian copper. Epitomising the point of the evasions is the case of James Groves and John Randell, acquitted at Warwick as their pieces were "not to the likeness of the current copper money of the Realm."

ABINGDON REJECTS

From the Oxford Gazette, printed at Reading, *"Last week was a general meeting of the tradesmen at Abingdon, who came to a resolution to take no more Birmingham halfpence, and hope the tradesmen of other towns will follow their examples."*

Matthew Boulton, innovative coin producer and master of the Soho Mint in Birmingham, was a vigorous pursuer of forgers at this time. One Birmingham forger of Soho pennies, caught red-handed by Boulton and members of his staff, was Richard Barber. The Royal Mint, jealous of Boulton's success in coin manufacture, deliberately let him down at Barber's trial, and Barber went free. The Birmingham Museum and Art Gallery holds the Barber counterfeit penny exhibited at his trial. His obverse die shows a weak nose and forehead on the bust.

Boulton's proud boast was that *"I never struck an unlawfull piece of Money in my Life."* He certainly devised methods to frustrate others

BIRMINGHAM 1745

"About seven years ago, the town of Birmingham was visited by the solicitor of the mint, upon an information that several persons were employ'd in making counterfeit halfpence: when several offenders were taken into custody and brought to justice, being try'd at the county assizes and order'd to suffer two years imprisonment: whether the persons who suffered were the only, or capital offenders, I shall not determine. However time has shewn that the punishment of two or three was not sufficient to deter others from the like practices: on the contrary, the last winter and the preceding one, these counterfeit halfpence abounded more than ever, inso much that few payments were made without a large proportion of them.

"Several advertisements were published, offering a reward for apprehending the makers, but without success. This was followed by a general refusal of them, and their circulation in that form ceased; but soon after (viz.) the beginning of last spring; these authors publish'd their works in a new edition: the practice of making counterfeit halfpence was revived with this improvement, that whereas they were before cast in sand, they are now made in a stamp or press.

"The way of uttering them is to send large quantities to different parts of the kingdom, where tradesmen who employ a number of low hands, and can stoop to low practices for gain, oblige their workmen to take them as wages..."
The Gentleman's Magazine, 1752.

less scrupulous, such as the oblique edge graining \\\\ which sand-casting could not cope with. Sunken lettering was another trick to foil the forgers. Prussian coins were being counterfeited in Birmingham, according to Boulton.

Boulton's validating oval and octagonal countermarks (1797 and 1804) on imported coinage were easy for forgers to replicate. This was not the case with his complete dollar countermarking.

THIRSTY WORK

The members of a Birmingham coining gang based in Fish Street Hill were caught by their urgent thirsts. They sent one of their children for beer with coins still hot from manufacture - as the little girl patiently explained to the inquisitive barman.

31st March 1774.

Lightweight 1797 Cartwheel pennies began appearing around 1812. They were struck from genuine Soho works' dies, but on flans 2 mm thick, instead of the genuine 3 mm. The dies may have been used clandestinely in the works, or have been sold or stolen. The pieces have noticeably rounder rims than the genuine cartwheels.

Counterfeits, including silver shillings of Elizabeth I (second issue, mintmark martlet - S.2555), emanated from Birmingham in the early 1980's, showing that old habits die hard.

In America, in 1720, Edmund HUNT (U.S.), a goldsmith by trade, was hanged for counterfeiting Spanish silver coins. His wife, Martha, was fined £500. In 1721, in the City of London, Barbara SPENCER was convicted of coining what she claimed was just a few shillings. Unlikely as she employed women to pass her products. Two of her 'passers' were also apprehended but later, surprisingly, acquitted. She was strangled and burned at Tyburn.

Many coiners became "The felons of Botany Bay", deportation to Australia being a common punishment for their crime. Some of these expert rejects from England were known to sand-cast forgeries of the early eighteenth century 'dump' coins of the Australian colony of New South Wales. The engraver of the genuine dies was an ex-convict, himself suspected of coining false dumps.

An American conviction for counterfeiting and passing Pistoles, was handed out to Duncan CAMPBELL in 1731. His punishment was to stand in the Pillory for two hours and receive 39 lashes "at the Carts Tail", followed a few days later by a further 31!

John Sigismund TANNER (-1775)
Tanner came from Saxe-Gorba and worked at the Royal Mint from 1728, engraving new dies as assistant to Croker. Richard Yeo became in turn his assistant. Tanner engraved imitations of old coins, tackling, in 1738, Thomas Simon's Cromwellian coin patterns and the 1656 halfcrowns which may originally have circulated to some extent, judging by the wear on a number of them. Following Simon's death, some of his puncheons found their way to the Netherlands and were used to produce copies of Cromwellian pattern coins. The Dutch imitation of the Crown was poorly crafted. In 1700 the Mint bought back the puncheons, plus the false dies made with them. Thirty eight years later, strikings were made from all but the cracked crown dies. Tanner cut new crown dies and also, using Simon's puncheons, dies for a half broad.

CROMWELL CROWN of 1658

Genuine

Tanner copy

John LEONARD (fl. 1750) was an Exeter man who mimicked guineas and half guineas by tooling sceptres on to shillings and sixpences which he then gilded. William LIDDELL (fl. 1751), was a Rochdale cloth dealer, who was charged in Durham with distributing 2,000 counterfeit halfpennies.

John WHITE (fl. mid 1700's -1788)
In Dolley's article[DO] on Two 'Unique' Plantagenet Pennies from Midlands Mints, he investigated a suspicious short-cross penny of Henry III which, bearing the word OXENE, was attributed to the Oxford mint, making it unique. He considered that it had been tooled from a common London mint coin to produce this 'rare' mint name, with convincing evidence as to the validity of this contention, e.g. the existence of a London (LVNDE) coin with an obverse struck from the same die. As this actual coin has been known of since the eighteenth century, was there a forger of that time with such tooling skill as to fool experts for nearly two hundred years? Apparently there was, and his name was John White, a hatter with a shop in Newgate Street in the City of London, who tooled coins to enhance his coin-dealing sideline.

> In the second half of the eighteenth century, citizens of London, Birmingham, Halifax and Hull had particularly to be on their guard against coin counterfeiters.

Not all experts were fooled, even back in his day, as this 1784 report shows: *"..the two English pennies of Richard I prove to be spurious... These pennies are thought to be the fabrications of a certain collector, notorious in this way, and who must suppose that to embarrass the path of any science with forgery and futility implies no infamy............*

WHAT FRIENDS ARE FOR

The Vienna Cabinet ended up with the false dies cut by the Lorrainer, Claude Augustin de SAINT-URBAIN. One of his pieces, a variant on an aureus of Philip II (A.D. 244-246), may have no genuine counterpart. His royal friend, the Emperor Francis I imprisoned him for a period on bread and water, on learning that he had been counterfeiting ancient and modern coins and then passing them.

Saint Urbain was a most skilful forger, an exception to the rule that forgers' techniques are simpler than those of official producers.

....The crime is certainly greater than that which leads the common coiner to the gallows, inasmuch as it is committed with more ease, and the profit is incomparably larger. The person above hinted at may therefore rest assured that, when his death shall have rendered the mention of his name safe and free from cruelty, not all his good qualities will prevent its being delivered to posterity with perpetual contempt and obloquy."

This forecast referring to White's posthumous reputation proved remarkably accurate. His obituary was kind: 17 Nov 1787 *"Mr John White, hatter, of Newgate-street, an eminent medallist and collector died."* But just a year later an encyclopaedic entry referred to him as *"John White (d. 1787), a notorious coin forger. (He) also had important genuine coins, although his reputation cast suspicions on everything he touched. His collection and library were sold by Gerard's a year after his death (Ency. I, 1788.4, .6)."* Also described by Haigh as *"the notorious forger"*, and by Sainthill as the man *"who imposed spurious coins of Richard I on the unsuspecting honesty of Snelling."*

He was a fabricator of extremely rare and 'new' types. Many of his 'products' ended up in the British Museum and the Hunterian Museum, Glasgow. An example from the former is a sequence of James II gunmoney sixpences dated October 1689 to October 1690. The known genuine sequence is June to September 1689.

Adept at providing 'background' to his pieces, e.g. "found on the coffin of Hardicanute," in 1756 White appears to have instigated the publication of a book supposedly intended to help young coin collectors. It was entitled *Twelve Plates of English Silver Coins* (authors R. Withy & I. Ryall) and included drawings of some of his forgeries and fantasies, an excellent device for 'authenticating' them. Spink recently sold a copy inscribed on the title page "The Gift of Mr John White to James Deane, Colchester."

Joseph WOOD (fl. 1750's)
In the eighteenth century, clipping was a capital offence. Apart from reducing the value of the coins, the clippings thus gleaned were often then used to make counterfeits. Wood was a clipper, as this 1757 record reveals -
"Three persons were taken into custody by means of an information to Justice Fielding, for clipping, filing, and otherwise diminishing the gold coin of this kingdom: and on searching their houses and lodgings, a great quantity of clippings, filings, diminished coins, sheers, files, crucibles, and moulds for casting ingots, were found.

"The three principal persons concerned, who are now in custody, are Joseph Wood, and Jemima Wilcox, who lived in Charles Square, Hoxton; and Wm Wright, who lodged at the sign of the Castle near Moorgate, and had also a lodging ... in Silver-street, near Aldersgate. It appears that the above-mentioned persons have circulated a great quantity of filed and diminished guineas and moidores, and have also sold quantities of gold in ingots and filings to several refiners in different parts of the town."

"Joseph Wood, otherwise James Collins, had formerly been a carpenter in Birmingham of considerable business, but had failed; on which he and one White, an agent of his in town, commenced money-filers; they were furnished with money by means of bills from the country, and by one Lambley, called in the sessions paper, a Money-taker in Smithfield; and in receiving, exchanging, and putting of(f) their money, one Jemima Wilcox, a single woman, was their principle instrument.
"This woman by her frequent appearance at the bank began to be taken notice of, and one of the tellers, remarking the late prodigious increase of light money, began to entertain a suspicion that she must be connected with persons concern'd in diminishing it. An accident, however, of one of his brother tellers paying her £100, for £90, hastened the detection; and by dodging her to Wood's lodgings, the whole scene of villany was found out."

Wood and his confederates were sentenced to death at the Old Bailey in December 1757.

Joseph STELL was hanged at York in the 1760's for forging golden guineas which were said to be so poor and light as to be worth only half a real one.

COINERS' CUNNING
Coiners bought coining irons from crooked craftsmen at £3 upwards per pair. No heavy permanent equipment was the rule, and be unobtrusive was the motto of all coiners. Employ tools that could be claimed to have other, legitimate uses. Even flan moulds could be passed off as button moulds, but the dies were the real giveaways and so required secure hiding places. A complete set of forgers' dies was found hidden in a house wall, near Hebden Bridge, West Yorkshire, on 9th March 1835. It was for making counterfeit Portuguese coins, as was a part set found in old cottages at Cragg Vale around the same time. They ended up in the local museum. In 1906 a book was published that linked these finds to a notorious local gang of the eighteenth century, the Cragg Vale coiners.

HARTLEY and THE CRAGG VALE COINERS (fl. 1760's-1770's)
The Cragg Vale coiners were a gang of bullyboys, ruling the roost in their part of Yorkshire. The founder of the gang was an iron worker who moved his family to this remote area, where he could not have expected to get legitimate work. He and his sons got to know of others already engaged in the 'business' in the area and recruited them into what became a gang of scores with many more on the fringes. Their modus operandi was to approach likely candidates, get them to 'lend' the gang a couple of guineas, or silver coins, which would be clipped, 'restored' and returned to the lender with half the clippings as recompense. Local innkeepers were one regular source.

The gang became so notorious and locally powerful that their leader David Hartley was dubbed 'King' David. He was the hammerman and leader. Strike too fiercely and the flan would split or break. Strike too softly and a weak impression would result. A skilled touch was needed which the 'King' had, and used to impress both coins and people.

The Coiners of Cragg Vale

In eighteenth century Yorkshire, a gang of coiners became so notorious, and locally powerful that their leader was known as 'King' David. They clipped and passed guineas, and melted down the gold clippings to make into coin flans that they then struck into lightweight counterfeits of Portuguese Moidores. At that time Moidores were accepted as legal tender in Britain. A government man got on their trail, despite the den where the forgeries were struck being at the top of a high hill in the middle of deserted countryside. David's gang planned and murdered the poor government man, a tactical error as he hadn't the power to arrest any of them, and their action only succeeded in bringing the full weight of the law down on them.

The Dusty Miller - a popular pub for coiners, not far from the steep sided valley known as Cragg Vale. It was in this pub that murder was plotted.

The track leading up to the coiners' den.

Bell House, the coiners' den.

Forgers sought remote areas, or the exact opposite - crowded town centres, in which to carry out their operations. Too far to be heard, or too surrounded by other noise. Hartley chose remoteness - at the top of a high, steep hill, as the author can vouchsafe, having laboured up it to take this photograph. Standing at his front door, one looks down over a great sweep of countryside, where anyone approaching can be seen from a long way off and where no one could see or hear what they were up to.

Replica of a Portuguese Moidore counterfeit in a commemorative plaque on the quayside wall at the local town.

Display of Hartley's coining dies in the local museum

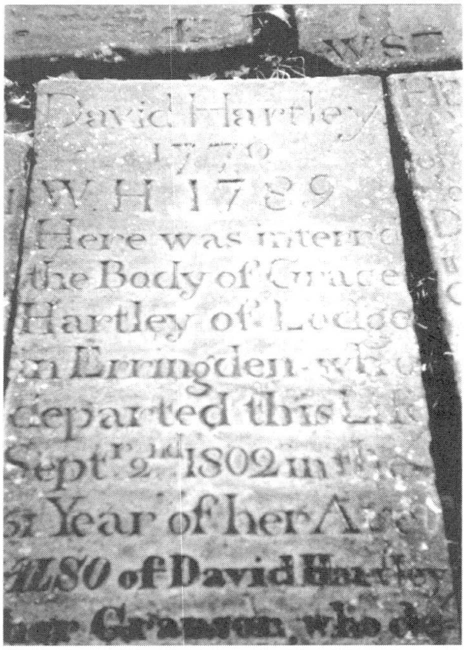

David Hartley's gravestone in old Heptonstall Church.

The nucleus of the gang comprised his father William, his younger brother William, known as *the Duke of Edinburgh* and brother Isaac, *the Duke of York*. It was Isaac who caused the ultimate downfall of the gang when he offered £100 to anyone 'disposing' of an investigating Government Man. He even tried raising funds for the murder from other Northern coining gangs.

James Jagger, Thomas Spencer, Thomas *round-shouldered* Clayton, *foul* Peter Barker, *handsome* John Tatham and John *thick lips* Parker were other known members of this most notorious of all coining gangs. Clayton was arrested some four years after leaving the gang, for counterfeiting shillings.

The occasional contemporary copies of guineas and half-guineas suggest that there were some skilled engravers around. Lightouler was the coining iron engraver used by David Hartley. Amongst the other known Yorkshire engravers of the time were Joseph Shaw of Bradford and Thomas Sunderland of Halifax, who also coined.

Top preference at this time for coins to counterfeit were the Portuguese Moidores and their fractions - half and quarter moidores. They were accepted currency throughout most of the 1700's, and were valued at 27s 6d per Moidore from 1714 until the end of the century when they were finally demonetised. The engravers chose these coins because the designs were less familiar to the public and the engravers' relatively low levels of skill would therefore be less noticed. This may have been wishful thinking, as comparisons between fake and real pieces show the former to have been so crude that anyone half awake would have spotted them. An eccentric crown was a feature of the poorly designed moidores struck by the Cragg Vale coiners. Covering such deficiencies to some extent was the fact that by the 1760's, Moidores had been circulating for forty years, none having been officially struck since 1722. Their other great advantage was the lack of a head on either side to tax the skill of the engraver. These were the main coins struck by the Hartley gang.

THE FATAL STEP

William Deighton (or Dighton, as his name is spelt on his tombstone) was a Supervisor of Excise, which meant that he could not officially arrest coiners for what was a non-Revenue offence. Despite this, his investigations alarmed the gang leaders and they put out a contract on him. Matthew Normanton (later Normington) and Robert Thomas (later Tommis) were the two 'hit-men' brought in by the gang on promise of £100 to murder Dighton, which they did on the 10th of November 1769, near his home in Halifax. He was shot through the head, possibly with the blunderbuss that turned up at the home of yet another coiner some years later. This was Thomas Murgatroyde, in the wall of whose home, dies for striking half guineas were found.

Clipping and coining had been going on in the Halifax, Huddersfield and Bradford areas for some years with impunity before this rash crime finally stirred the authorities to decisive action. The Mint Records note many prosecuted for clipping and coining. Often these were due to paid informers, some of whom were just as unscrupulous in 'finding' coiners (innocent people), as the real villains were in coining. Hartley's isolated home on a hill, Bell House, was far from such 'nuisances' who could be spotted long before they reached it. Any incriminating evidence could be concealed - a smith's furnace for instance could swallow up coin clipping shears. So it is not surprising that the gang's downfall came via a judas in their midst, James Broadbent, who was tempted by a £100 reward. His evidence led to David Hartley's arrest. When the local Merchants topped up the Government reward for finding Dighton's murderers to £200, Broadbent implicated Thomas and Normanton in this crime. He was luckier than Abraham Ingham who rather foolishly announced at Heptonstall that he was going to inform on the murderers and was promptly murdered himself.

David Hartley was hanged, not for the murder, but for coining, and is buried in Heptonstall churchyard. The two murderers of the Excise man were acquitted, but some years later they were both hanged for lesser offences, so justice did finally catch up with them. Another of the Cragg Vale coiners, Thomas Greenwood, had his premises searched after he was caught with two clipped guineas on him. The searchers found Portuguese Johannes, coining implements, files, shears and arsenic. Despite all this, he was released after his trial. Six years later, in 1779, he was again before a jury, charged with high treason and sentenced to death, later commuted to transportation to Africa.

In the little museum behind the old church in Heptonstall, there is a display case devoted to the Cragg Vale coiners. It includes a set of their coin dies for striking Portuguese gold Moidores. Moidore = moeda d'oura = money of gold.

Cragg Vale also harboured the Turvin Gang of Coiners. There were thought to be up to ten gangs in the Halifax area at that time, so it is not so surprising that when John Wesley preached there against coiners, he got a hostile reception due to the number of them in his audience!

Robert IREDALE was yet another Yorkshireman (Southowram, Beacon Hill) to pay the supreme penalty for counterfeiting (1776). In 1777, the Reverend William DODD too was hanged for forgery. He asked the hangman to pull on his legs to hasten his end. His last, unexplained, words were "Come to me."

Birmingham button-makers were notoriously involved in counterfeiting. One such was John GIMBLETT, jnr. (107 Snow Hill), a producer of Georgian copper evasions, some of which show the initials I.G.

Dr. Andrew GIFFORD acquired a castle punch, c.1780, and is then believed to have produced false Scarborough siege pieces inscribed CAROLI(J) FORTUNA RESURGAM. These oblong, octagonal and round silver pieces are heavier and thicker than genuine pieces. Some do not have the castle impression showing through on the reverse.

In 1782, John COCKCROFT achieved the ultimate in counterfeiting ease, by mimicking worn shillings with no visible legend left on either side, thus requiring no counterfeit dies to produce. He just grained the edges and 'aged' silver blanks, probably obtained by him quite legitimately from Birmingham.

A 1787 Machin halfpenny. Slightly undersize.

Captain Thomas MACHIN & Machin's Mills
In 1784, he had a Mill built on land he owned, just outside Newburgh, New York, USA. There, from 1787, he and his confederates struck illegal copper coinage, including lightweight, counterfeit George III halfpennies dated 1747, 1771, 1772, 1774, 1775, 1776, 1778, 1787 and 1788. Their crude die-work and single (unfimbriated) instead of double line (fimbriated) crosses on Britannia's shield separate them from the genuine coins and also other American and English counterfeits. The Machin gang was very successful, with two results. It was engaged to cut dies for the legitimate Vermont Mint, and halfpennies became so plentiful that their value dropped and with it the profit in counterfeiting them. So around 1790 the Mill closed.

Assorted fake Spanish pieces, found in the pockets of Zachariah Field (U.S.) in 1730 were made of base metal and were "of very ordinary Workmanship." He got life imprisonment. An associate, Joseph Watt had his ears cropped.

John MILTON[MIa] (1759-1805) was a young designer/die-engraver at the Royal Mint, responsible for the 1788 Barbados penny. He worked at the Mint for ten years, achieving a salary of £80 per year by 1795, as "die-sinker and Assistant Medallist". He lived in Rolls Buildings, Fetter Lane. Then, in October 1796, he was found to be making dies for counterfeiting French Louis d'Ors and Portuguese gold Johannes. Dismissed the following year, he turned to the production of fine quality limited edition and collector specified tokens. He also made dies for such as Matthew Young. When Milton passed away, Young purchased his dies, made restrikes, and then sold the dies to W.J. Taylor who made yet more restrikes.

Thomas SPENCE[TH] (1750-1814) was a poor Newcastle-upon-Tyne schoolmaster, who came down to London to set up in High Holborn as a bookseller. He made, distributed and sold tokens to promote his unconventional political ideas. He published a book about eighteenth century tokens, *The Coin Collector's Companion*, in 1795. He actually advertised his willingness to create mules and may have been the first perpetrator of intentional muling. His pieces fell out of favour once the token collecting mania of 1795 died down. When he became bankrupt, Spence sold his dies (probably made to his instructions rather than by him) to Peter Skidmore, who put them to less high-minded use.

Peter SKIDMORE a Clerkenwell (and Holborn) ironmonger and specious token maker made some dies and acquired others. He took over the bankrupt Spence's dies and bought others from Kempson, whom he also imitated. He mixed dies to create 'collectable' mules. He was probably the main producer of counterfeit Georgian farthings.

William LUTWYCHE[MIb] was a late eighteenth century, Birmingham-based maker of advertising and Condor tokens. These pieces have been connected by die-link chains to evasions and Georgian copper counterfeits. Another token maker in Birmingham in the late 1780's, and, in the 1790's in London, was Charles JAMES. Apart from dies he cut for himself, he also supplied dies to Lutwyche, Skidmore, Spence and Williams.

John WESTWOOD (1774-1850) was mostly Birmingham based, but ended up in London, via Sheffield and Lichfield. He was the son and nephew respectively of Obadiah and John Westwood, two noted eighteenth century engravers. The latter was known to Matthew Boulton as an associate of counterfeiters of coin and engraved Glasgow banknotes and his brother, Obadiah had a reputation for dubious token production, so John was clearly following in the family footsteps when he produced copies of the Southampton *St Bevois* halfpenny, and the Anglesey *Monogram* penny. He also catered for the late eighteenth century token collecting mania by producing specious half-halfpennies, halfpennies and pennies bearing designs derived from real tokens.

The evasions inscribed GOD SAVE THE QUEEN/BE AS YOU SEEM TO BE and dated 1796, were probably produced by William WILLIAMS, a London token manufacturer. He definitely produced those inscribed PAYABLE AT W. WILLIAMS/NORTH WALES.

Late eighteenth century U.S. mintmaster Samuel BROOME, diverted many tons of state copper into making lightweight (and thus more profitable) Connecticut coppers. When this enterprise came to an end, he sold his minting machinery to Captain Thomas Machin (q.v.). Broome had an associate, Abel BUEL whose branded forehead and cropped ears showed his previous involvement with coining.

Peter KEMPSON was yet another Birmingham button manufacturer suspected of illegal manufacturing in the late eighteenth century. Die-link chains connect his legitimate advertising and Condor tokens to evasions and to straight counterfeits of Georgian copper. So far, no links have been detected between the evasions and the counterfeits. He is also known as a fictional token maker, aiming his pieces, such as a series of London Buildings, at token collectors, and as a legitimate token manufacturer, particularly during the 1811 silver coin famine.

19th Century

Matthew YOUNG (1771-c.1837)
He was an English coin dealer who has been described as the dominant London dealer of the later eighteenth and early nineteenth centuries, working initially from 46 High Holborn and then from 41 Tavistock Street, Covent Garden. In 1828 he appears to have acquired the original dies for the 1688 Florida Token. The denomination of this tin coin, also known as The American (or James II)

RUINED

"About 35 years since, a person, nicknamed 'Castle' Jacobs, concealed himself in one of the apartments among the ruins of Dudley Castle, and for some time carried on the business of coining; but being at last suspected, a number of persons set off with a determined resolution of taking him.

One of the windows commanded the Castle hill, and he observing their appearance set fire to his apartments. On their arrival the place was in flames, and the man was never heard of from that time until about a week since, when some of Lord Dudley's people, pulling down the ruins, discovered a perfect skeleton, and four crucibles, with a great number of pieces of base coin."

The Gentleman's Magazine, 1783

Matthew Young - the only known likeness (unfortunately).

Plantation token, was 1/24th real. From other original dies, he struck 60-shilling coins dated 1686 and a crown dated 1716, for James VII (the Pretender) and James VIII of Scotland respectively.

He obtained the dies that had been made by John Milton for 1788 and 1792 Barbados tokens after Milton's death, and restruck them in proof condition. He muled Boulton's Soho coinage, as did Till and Taylor, two other acquirers of ex-Soho Mint dies.

Young's restrikes are better looking than the originals and are now collectables in their own right.

William BOOTH (-1812)
The forgery of Banknotes, presumably because of their higher value, appears to have been regarded as more heinous than coin counterfeiting. In the early nineteenth century it was still a capital offence, a fact clearly not lost on Booth, a Staffordshire farmer turned forger of both coins and notes. He transformed his farmhouse into a mini-fortress complete with trapdoors for quick escape. He also created an elaborate cover for this non-farming activity by producing penny tokens dated 1811 and inscribed PAYABLE BY Wm. BOOTH PERRY BAR. Perry Bar is some five miles north of Birmingham. He and his gang, possibly as many as eleven men, forged 1s 6d, 3s and 5s Bank Tokens, gold third guineas, William III halfcrowns and Anne shillings, £1, £5 and £10 Bank of England banknotes and local banknotes. The minor gang members were paid a regular wage - of 25s per week, about twice what they could expect in a legitimate job of the time. His profits may have reached £25,000 a year.

One specialist dealer in low denomination counterfeits, in Newcastle-under-Lyme, confessed to getting his supplies from Booth, leading to a raid on Booth's fortified premises that did not withstand the onslaught. Found there were £3000 in good notes, and £2000 worth of gold coins. In 1812, he was tried and publicly hanged at Stafford. Not without difficulty, for the hangman's trap failed twice. Examples of his token counterfeits and a banknote plate are held in Birmingham City Museum. His penny tokens, which are extremely rare, were reproduced late in the nineteenth century. The originals can be identified by the presence of square dots under the *m* of his abbreviated forename. A hoard comprising 63 of Booth's forged 1811 1s 6d tokens was dug up from a garden in Great Barr in 1956. The British Museum displayed some in its August 2000 Illegal Tender Exhibition. A copper plate for printing Dudley Old Bank £5 notes, ploughed up on Booth's land in 1865, was on display at The Money Show that was held from July to September 2000 at the Birmingham Museum.

Henry MORGAN (fl. March 1811 to 1813)
There are many instances of contemporary forgeries of nineteenth century trade tokens. Notices placed in local newspapers by the issuers of the genuine tokens warned the public of false pieces. But perpetrators could also place notices. Henry Morgan advertised in the *Star Newspaper* and in the *Evening Star* his silver tokens, on which

he offered to engrave any design and despatch to anywhere in Britain - by coach. Clearly an express service. What he did not inform the readers was that he supplied underweight tokens. Also, if he did not get their contracts, he was liable to forge their tokens anyway. He was most active in this respect with Bristol tokens. An 1812 issue of the Bath Chronicle drew attention to the "infamous deception" re the Twelve-Penny and Sixpenny Tokens perpetrated by "the well-known Mr. H. Morgan" and his "Resident Agent in Bristol". His versions of these Birmingham made Bristol tokens can easily be identified from genuine Garratt tokens by the variations in the legend. In the following examples the correct spelling is followed by Morgan's version in brackets: *Payable By Messrs Fras. (Frans) Garratt (Garrett) Wm. Terrell (Wr. Terrail) Edwd. (Edmd) Bird Lant. (Lamt.) Beck & Frans. (Frann) H Grigg (Gregg).*

The token denominations he supplied legitimately were sixpences, shillings and one shilling and sixpences. Initially he was providing a necessary service, but his greed and that of his customers led to an ever-decreasing token weight. Eventually, an indifferent Parliament had to respond and an Act prohibiting all tokens, except for some workhouses' emissions, appeared on 1st January 1818. It is considered that without Morgan's prolific output, Parliament may well have ignored the problem for even longer than it did.

Morgan was a slippery customer and no one ever located his factory - his advertised address of 12 Rathbone Place, Oxford Street, London being just a *poste restante*. It is thought that he may have been an agent for some Birmingham companies such as Thomason or Halliday.

The HEWORTH Forger.
In 1812, a pot containing 23 coins of Ecgfrith was discovered at Heworth in Durham. For many years they were the only coins known of this ruler, until metal analysis showed an exact match with the alloy used in George III's copper coinage. Once more there were no known coins of this ruler. It appears to have been a hoax aimed at the local historian, John Hodgson.

Samuel & James INGLEY were Bank Token forgers, whose premises in Lower Priory, Birmingham were raided by the police in July 1814. They were caught die-stamping 3 shilling flans. Their products were described as very well executed, ringing well and shrill. Another account attributes their arrest to a forged 1804 Bank of England Britannia dollar with the counterfeit countermark WZ. One of their counterfeits exists with the added inscription S. INGLEY'S COUNTERFEIT. Similarly, a flan of theirs, with a nicked edge, revealing the base metal core, has one side punched A COUNTERFEIT BLANK/OF/S. and S.J. INGLEY'S/WHO WERE TRIED AT/WARWICK ASSIZES, 1814:/AND TRANSPORTED/FOR 14 YEARS[GU]. Their sentence was actually for twelve years.

Also known at times as Mr James and Dr. James Edwards, James SINGLETON (fl. c.1825-1843) produced mostly cast forgeries. These included coins of Eadwald, Eanbald, Regnald and Wigmund. Some of the pieces illustrated by Lawrence may be his.

1839 SINGLETON WARNING
"*Forgeries of Ancient Coins. I.Y. informs us, that a fellow is going the round of the provincial towns [presumably James? Singleton], and has lately paid a visit to London, where he has disposed of false coins to the unwary. He has a stock of forgeries of the rarest Anglo-Saxon pennies, and of several uncommon Greek coins, among them some of Heliocles.*"

"*Caution to Coin Collectors. The Cork Constitution paper, and the Hampshire Independent, caution ... against a person who has lately been in Ireland vending with great success a large quantity of forged Roman, Greek, British, and Saxon, and Anglo-Gallic coins. It is presumed this is the same individual who was some months since in London engaged in the same trade. He is described as a Scotchman, thin, genteelly dressed, and about sixty years of age.*"

A Sotheby's catalogue of 1849 describes a Cromwell shilling in gold as "*a Cast from the Shilling, by an old Forger named Singleton.*"

Dr. Frank Smith EDWARDS (?-1865) was an American maker of die-struck copies of U.S. 1796 'with pole' half-cents. His dies were hand cut and are said to have an oversized design, larger letters and a different head from the genuine coins. He died in October 1865, and his dies are believed to have been destroyed.

Carl Wilhelm BECKER (1772-1830)

Modern forgeries are, to a greater or lesser degree, mechanically made, usually providing quite clear evidence of this when one knows what to look for. The biggest threat to being fooled is from the gifted freehand die-cutter. So far, the most notorious of these has been Carl Wilhelm Becker, who is widely regarded as one of the most skilful forgers of all time.

He was born at Speyer in Germany on the 28th of June 1772. A contemporary description of the adult Becker refers to his blue eyes, dark brown hair, healthy complexion and to being just under five foot six inches tall. He was learned, artistic, incredibly patient and meticulous. He could on occasion be too meticulous. Some of his forgeries are betrayed by being better than the originals.

Becker was clearly a charmer - three times married and able to make friends at all levels of the society of his day. He struck a medal for his friend, Prince Carl von Ysenburg, for whom he was Privy Councillor, and copied the Prince's Visigothic coins for him. Von Ysenburg was a Napoleonic general who had acquired the coins whilst serving in Spain. Other friends included Counts Rasumovsky and Wiczay, and the poet Goethe, with whom he had contact in 1815 and 1816. Goethe is thought to have bought some sixteenth century Paduan imitations from him, but not any coins of Becker's own creation. Hill[HI] saw a copy of Goethe's book on Benvenuto Cellini in which Goethe had written a dedication to Becker.

THE COLLECTOR PRECEDED THE COUNTERFEITER
The young Becker was a keen collector of ancient coins, and splashed out on an expensive gold Roman coin offered to him by a titled gentleman in Munich; a Baron, no less. The coin alas proved to be a counterfeit and Becker returned with it to the Baron. But he summarily dismissed Becker's request for a refund with the brusque admonition that it was his own fault for dabbling in things he didn't understand. The Baron's rebuff may have been the trigger for Becker's subsequent career following his failure as a wine merchant. It is said that years later he fooled the Baron into buying Becker counterfeits! Poetic revenge indeed, if true.

He had enemies, including the Italian numismatist, Sestini[SE], who called him a criminal, despite Becker's protestations that he only produced copies and any deception was by the purchasers passing them off as real. In 1826, Sestini, who had met Becker, started a catalogue of his forgeries, completed in the following year by M. Clouet of Verdun, France. This publication claimed that nearly all the Museums in Europe had been fooled into including Becker fakes in

'Beckers'

This original silver strike of a third century B.C. silver tetradrachm of Eumenes the First, king of Pergamon (top), engraved by Becker in 1824, compares well on the obverse with its genuine counterpart below it; perhaps not so well on the reverse, where Becker's Athena looks less like the genuine lady.

This Republican style piece is a Becker version of a restitutio silver denarius of Trajan.

Copying an Asia Minor original is this 'Becker' of Rhescuporis the First. (Hill 78).

A Becker copy in silver of a gold coin of Pharnaces II (Asia Minor). It has the prominent nose that is a feature of much of Becker's portraiture. This piece (Hill 75) could be from one of Becker's reference sets.

Aureus of Postumus (259-268), as reproduced in lead from Becker's dies.

Becker's version of a gold Visigothic tremissis - Suinthila (621-631).

This Tetricus I denarius copy is notable in that someone has tried to fake a Becker fake by clipping off the coin's inscription!

their collections. Becker countered the effects of Sestini's exposure by exporting his products to Turkey, where their 'discovery' would give them more credibility. A trick also employed by Caprara. One of the latter's forgeries was 'authenticated' by Becker!

Becker's skill at die cutting came from the training he received in engraving at the Munich Mint. To it however he added his own artistic expression of a high order, enabling him not only to recreate past works of art on coins, but also to produce convincing 'fantasies' generated by his imagination combined with his considerable numismatic knowledge. He claimed to produce better copies than the Paduans.

His nefarious activities seem to have started by 1806 and to be known to the extent of threatened exposure by 1808. He was forging coins and medals in the Frankfurt area of Germany from 1815 to 1825, probably his most productive period. By the early 1820's he was already known as "Antiker Becker."

Becker employed his assistant W. Zindel of Offenbach from 1826, paying him 15 florins per die. Zindel's expertise at die-cutting was almost as great as his master, whose diaries show that from the autumn of 1826 Zindel worked on most of the dies, perhaps leaving the finishing touches to Becker. They worked together for some years, as a communication between them dated 16th June 1828 shows. An Antigonus Gonatas, made under Becker's directions, was delivered by Zindel on the 22nd of May that year.

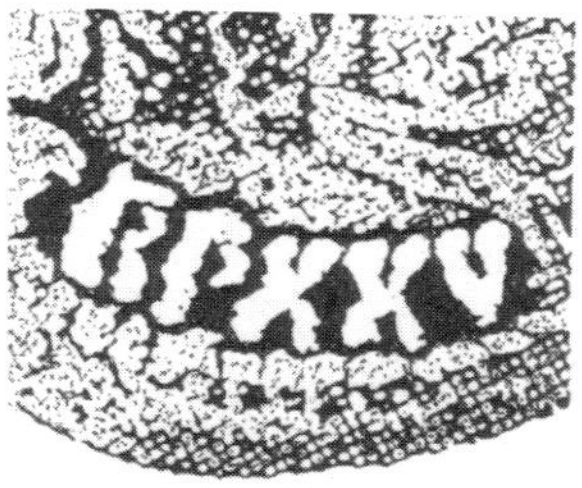

Here is a Becker mistake. This is part of the legend on a supposed denarius of Drusus, showing the erroneous inscription TR.P.XXV. This should be TR.P.XXXV. Becker later realised his error, as evidenced by pieces struck on a corrected die.

Becker was still active in the year that he died. Did he intend to defraud? The evidence accumulated by Hill and others makes it quite clear that he did. Unlike other forgers however, he also produced copies to order for museums and collectors.

AN EXTENSIVE OUTPUT

He was a prolific forger, with an output estimated at some 350 pairs of dies for ancient Greek, Roman, medieval and later coins and medals, including some common coins amongst the rarities. All known examples are of gold, electrum or silver. There is no evidence that he ever counterfeited bronze coins.

His efforts varied from brilliantly close to the original coins, to not particularly good. Some of his coins are impossible combinations of obverse and reverse. Some are complete fantasies. The gold Antipater for example has no known genuine equivalent. The Wallenstein is another illustration of the fertile imagination that accompanied his supreme skill.

Some Becker forgeries are not listed by Hill, because he only covered pieces where the dies were still extant in 1924.

THE GREEK CABINET

Considering together their individual outputs, Becker and Caprara produced nearly 200 pairs of dies imitating Greek coins. This puts them on a par with all other forgers of Greek coins, from the Renaissance to the end of the nineteenth century.

The Zancie coin, made in February 1830, may have been his last, as he died on the 11th of April of that year.

MAKING 'BECKERS'

His wife had proved unsuccessful at melting down the metal for the coins, so he paid others to do this. They provided him with different flans according to the types of coin he was currently faking. Greek coins with their high relief required fatter flans than most other coins. The metal source was sometimes ancient coins which gave added conviction to the end result. Even more convincing were the pieces he produced by over-striking low value ancient coins. This method countered what was then one of the easiest ways of spotting a 'modern' counterfeit, the edge, always the most difficult part to make look convincing. Correct colour was another difficult area that this solved. Also this method meant that the new coin would often be in the right weight area, although he does not seem to have been too bothered about getting weights to match originals.

This is a lead restrike of Becker's Albert von Wallenstein, duke of Friedland coin. It illustrates the fertile imagination that accompanied his supreme skill, as it is a complete fantasy. He dated it 1626.

Becker never cast dies, nor resorted to mechanical copying. All his dies were free-hand copies of originals or, if these were not available, of plaster or sulphur casts. Hill considered that Becker's poorer efforts could be where he was copying drawings or engravings of coins. It took him just eighteen hours to cut one die for his masterful Agrigentum decadrachm. The dies were of steel set in iron.

Hill could find no evidence of Becker ever having struck plated coins. Some of his efforts are double-struck, i.e. with the flan having shifted slightly between a first and second sledgehammer blow. Some dies had coins struck from them and then they were worked on; in one case, on a denarius of Tiberius & Drusus Caesar to correct an error. The lead metal reference sets held by top Museums are therefore only guides to the final states of the dies.

With his medieval coins, Becker did resort to the use of alphabet punches. Zeichner of Vienna was one supplier used by him. Where a very small type or detail was required, Becker would make his own punches.

To remove the newly-made look from his products, Becker would put them in his 'distressing' chest, which had acidiferous hides and metal filings. The chest was then fixed to the axle of his carriage and 'taken for a ride.' The story that he buried his coins in excrement to age them is now said to be untrue.

SALES AND MARKETING

He always claimed to be making just replicas with no intent to deceive, and he undoubtedly did sell quantities at 'replica prices'. A full set of 296 silver 'Beckers' cost a fraction of the Mionnet catalogue value of their genuine counterparts. But many were later re-sold as genuine. He dealt in artifacts as well as coins, and is known to have had three copies made of an ancient sword, which suggests that his approach to artifacts was as unconcerned about passing them off as genuine as with coins.

A London-based marketer of Becker's products was a Mr. Peacock of 22 Marylebone Street (now known as Glasshouse Street), Piccadilly. In 1829, Becker had an agent named Peters. *(Not an ancestor of mine as far as I'm aware. But I am fascinated by counterfeits ...KP).*

This mystery coin is possibly a nineteenth century copy of a Carthaginian original, or it could be a fantasy. Hard, lead-like metal with striking splits around the rim. Similar in style to some Becker pieces, but Becker is not known to have used non-precious metal on any of his creations.

At one point he seems to have been parted from much of his stock without any payment by an unscrupulous Englishman. The cheat outcheated? He was often willing to sell his dies, being regularly in financial difficulties, and in May 1824, tried, unsuccessfully, to sell the lot to Steinbüchel, director of the Imperial Coin Cabinet, Vienna. At that time they comprised 506 matrices, to produce 84 Greek and 172 other coins, making a total of 256 pieces. This had risen to 296 by c.1826 - 110 Greek, 126 Roman Emperors, 24 'Gothic Kings', 24 German medieval and 12 that spanned the sixteenth to eighteenth centuries. Up to 40 more die-sets were still to come.

After his death, the bulk of the dies, plus equipment and examples, went to the Saalburg Museum and on from there in 1911 to the Kaiser-Friedrich Museum, Berlin. Sets of lead (or lead/tin) impressions from his dies were struck there throughout the nineteenth century for the world's main numismatic centres. Impressions are also known to have been struck in bronze. By 1924, nearly all of his dies had been acquired. The Museum's 'Munzkabinett' has a display of Becker's products, including some of these dies and genuine coins paired with his fakes for comparison.

The British Museum has a comprehensive collection of his forgeries. Hill understood that, years before 1922, it too had distributed lead sets of Becker's fakes. The well-known London coin dealers, Baldwin's, have a complete set of lead 'squeezes'.

Caprara

Fake by Caprara (early nineteenth century) of a Panticapeum gold stater, c.340 B.C. Well-made, right weight and quite convincing, but Pan's head lacks the correct style.

Caprara was turning out fake Greek coins in the 1820's, probably from 1822 to c.1830, making him a contemporary of Becker. He has been described as a Becker imitator.

Although he started his counterfeiting in Smyrna, and then moved to the Aegean island of Syros, Caprara may have been Italian. It was an Italian scholar, Domenico Sestini[SE] who, in 1826, pointed the first accusing finger at him, regarding a group of Boeotian staters supposedly from Haliartos, Orchomenes and Tanagra. The cross die-linking, showing the different city types impossibly sharing dies, revealed a common source for these overweight, stylishly odd silver staters[DE]. For some, no genuine prototypes exist. Sestini's exposure of Caprara was on too limited a front to put a stop to his output, some of which was still thought genuine 150 years later. His silver coins now have a century and a half of real patination to increase their deceptiveness.

Caprara pieces are hand-engraved and struck, probably cold struck judging by the cracked edges on many of them and by the occasional double-struck examples. Artificial wear, corrosion and patina appear to have been applied, some possibly by later owners.

This Thracian tetradrachm shows that not all Caprara's dies were necessarily straight copies of originals. Here the young Hermes is looking straight ahead, with a stern expression not present in the original on the left. His cap button is missing and on the reverse the trophy facing the goat has disappeared.

This reverse side of his Thracian tetradrachm shown on the left, depicts a Capraran goat – a pun on his name.

The first known of Caprara's ninety plus forgeries, a silver Mithradates VI of Pontus, is illustrated in Mark Jones' book[JO]. Also covered therein is a silver Argos coin overstruck on a genuine tetradrachm of Athens. A Mithradates tetradrachm had been copied by Caprara and Cesati, the latter 250 years earlier but not so convincingly. Caprara created his own varieties by replacing common rulers with uncommon ones. His sources of inspiration included books such as Mionnet, evidenced by one example on which he faithfully copied a misprint. Types were paired, new values 'introduced', hoard discoveries exploited - here was a cunning man at work. Becker was asked by a collector to check a Capraran fake and pronounced it genuine – co-operation amongst crooks.

The reason for some of Caprara's unimportant bronze efforts was that when he produced them, they were regarded as rare. His last efforts, perhaps when his eyesight was failing, seem to have been a group of small, fantasy coins of Epirus, Chalcidian League, Melos, Skyros and Syros.

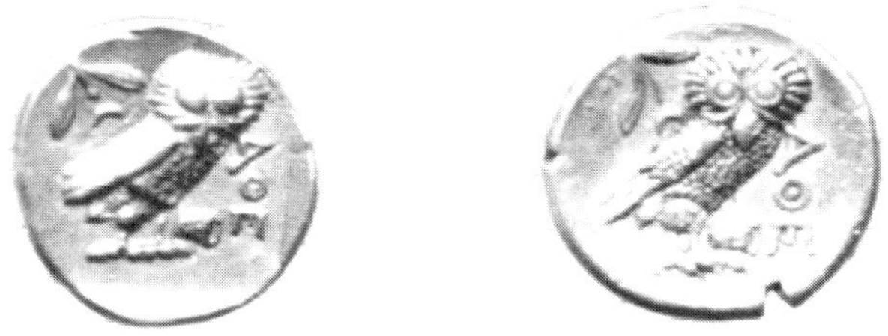

Unlike the calm (genuine) Athenian owl shown on the left, Caprara's owl has a distinctly startled look!

Luigi CIGOI (1811-1875) **BRU**
Trained as a tanner, he grew up and lived in Udine, north-east of Venice, where he became a numismatist and coin dealer, and also the chief forger of north Italian coins, such as the Ostrogothic. In addition to his main activity of medieval north Italian 'varieties', he also covered Roman Republican and Imperial, ancient Byzantine, Lombardic and Vandal pieces, plus some Papal and Papal-Imperial, Renaissance and Venetian coins of the seventeenth century. He also faked lesser-known fifth to eighth century coins. A contemporary of Emery, he is said to have produced forgeries equal in skill to Becker and Christodoulos, although he may not have cut any dies himself. Unlike most famous forgers, Cigoi appears to have been the mastermind controlling others, round and about Udine, where he based his operations. Surprisingly, he left to that city's Museo Civico his collection of genuine *and* counterfeit pieces. He was exposed as a forger by Carlo Kunz, a director of the Trieste Museum, and his forgeries became the subject of a legal action in the 1870's. The expression *A Cigoi 'atelier'* product arose because he ran a cottage industry of outworkers cutting dies to his instructions. Probably only one die survives. In addition to striking on false dies, he appears to have employed the techniques of casting and tooling genuine coins. His tannery training enabled him to age and patinate coins skilfully.

He created 'rarities' for collectors by having types and varieties of small copper and billon coins from mints such as Rome, apparently made by north Italian mints such as Ravenna. Genuine Johannes Rome bronzes were frequently poorly struck and a Cigoi copy clearly got its wrong mintmark TR (not TRM) from an imperfect original.

Edward EMERY (fl. c. 1842, d.? 1850/1)
Emery, a contemporary of Singleton and Cigoi, was a London-based plate-glass maker who is now known to have cut or had cut dies with

which he struck and sold many Anglo-Saxon**GR**, Norman and Tudor forgeries in the mid-nineteenth century. Pieces tend to be too perfect.

Silver forgery by Emery of a penny of Mary Tudor (1553-1554). Made in the early 1840's. Crowned bust l, M.D.G.ROSA. SINE:SPINA with the reverse showing a square-topped shield over cross fourchée, CIVITAS LONDON. Wgt 0.66 gm. 15 mm.

It is possible that Emery's dies were made for him by W. J. Taylor (q.v.), who also worked in London (from the 1830's) and was a medallist of doubtful repute. Baldwin's have three Emery forgery dies that were originally obtained from Taylor's estate, which ties in with this suspicion. Pagan**PA** estimated that Emery's total output of types may have been in excess of 100, but produced from fewer pairs of dies because of cross-use. Emery may have limited himself to a dozen pieces per pair of dies. Probably less than 500 now exist.

In 1842 he was exposed and a number of his dies commandeered and defaced to prevent re-use. His 'creations' began to resurface at auctions some years after his death. In his book *English Coins***BRO**, published in 1932, George Brooke unwittingly used three Emery forgeries as illustrations of genuine types, demonstrating their deceptiveness. Some of Emery's Mary copies have been described as better than the originals. He dreamt up fantasy pieces that might have been possible, and so greatly attracted collectors thinking that they were filling historic gaps. An example is a penny of Æthelbald of Wessex, son of Æthelwulf. So far no genuine coins have surfaced. He 'created' a Richard I crusade coin and 'unknown' moneyers such as Oemer and Wulgar (his idea of vulgar humour?). His main efforts appear to have been on Tudor period coins of England and Scotland, late Anglo-Saxon and early Norman coins, the latter two groups being mostly overstruck. There are also odd efforts in gold and silver copying denarii of Allectus, Carausius, Otho, Caliph Omar and a denier of Eleanor of Aquitaine.

Emery's deceptive fakes made in the mid-nineteenth century, including fantasy coins, such as this London penny of Mary (1553-1558) which was thought to be genuine until the 1960's. This type did not appear in her reign.

Representative of all the small fry of counterfeiting, who only left a record of their activities if they were unsuccessful is J. SINE, an Englishman who was prosecuted in 1846 for counterfeiting foreign coin.

William Joseph TAYLOR (1802-85) (fl.1848-82)
Birmingham born and, from 1818, trained there as a diesinker under Halliday, an ex-Soho Mint employee. By 1829 he was working in London as a medallist, die sinker and engraver. Taylor was notorious for having restruck quantities of English copper coins from genuine

> 1843 WARNING
>
> Ancient Coin Forgers: *"We have once more to caution antiquaries, silversmiths, and dealers in ancient coins, against the continued practice of the makers of counterfeit coins..A person not far from Hastings, a few months since, employed an artist to cut dies for the rare coins of Edward VI., Philip and Mary, &c... either this person, or the notorious Singleton, it is supposed, has counterfeited the Anglo-Saxon coins found at Cuerdale, and is now selling them in various parts of the kingdom by means of agents.*
>
> *"Under the names of Carpenter and Hunt, this fellow lately visited Colchester, Ipswich, &c... A late law makes this species of swindling transportation, and any person who has been duped, can take out a magi-strate's warrant to detain the criminal party for a full examination."*

Soho Mint dies he had managed to acquire. Royal Mint dies were always closely protected. Outside contractors, such as Boulton (Soho Works, Birmingham) operated much more freely. Boulton himself would often strike odd combination obverse and reverse coins as novelties for his friends. In 1850, at the auction which followed the closure of the Soho Works by Matthew Piers Watt Boulton (the founder's grandson), Taylor took advantage of the scrap lots to acquire punches and a tub of greasy, obsolete Soho Mint dies, which he then proceeded to re-use. He was located at Red Lion Street in Clerkenwell, London, and, as an established diesinker, brought his skills to work on producing false collectables.

He was the probable supplier of dies to Edward Emery (q.v.). He restruck John Milton's 1799 'Fullerton' pattern coinage for Scotland, firstly for Matthew Young (q.v.) and then for himself. In 1862, on reaching 60, he seemed to put aside his more legitimate activities in favour of profiting from the Soho dies. His straight restrikes, mules and concoctions spilled out for the ensuing twenty years. Fortunately, Peck's masterwork[PE] sheds light on the consequent mess left behind by Taylor and the other two main perpetrators, Till and Young.

Montroville DICKESON was a mid-nineteenth century U.S. copyist of Somers Island shillings and twopences. These copies are now sold in America for $200 or more each! Another mid-nineteenth century copyist, the Parisian, SAINTOT, struck copies of denarii.

In 1855, William ROBERTS took what he clearly thought to be the short route to counterfeiting and ordered a pair of dies from a Birmingham die-sinker, with which to strike Peruvian silver half-dollars. Presumably because of Birmingham's somewhat tarnished reputation, it did not occur to him that the diesinker would report him to the police.

From 1860, C. Wyllys BETTS (U.S.) produced nearly 200 fantasy Georgian copper pieces and Colonial coins, eventually donating examples of most of them to the Yale University Collection. He claimed not to be trying to fool anyone. One of his halfpennies was dated 1786.

JONS was a cheeky forger in Dunfermline, who, around 1861, took impressions of Scottish coins in the collection of the National Museum of Antiquities of Scotland, from which to make false dies. With these he overstruck Victorian silver coins, which were usually heavier than they should be for their new identities.

BILLY SMITH and CHARLIE EATON

Popularly known as Billy and Charlie[na], two notorious forgers of medieval artifacts were William Smith (also known as George Henry Smith and William Monk) and Charles Eaton. They were illiterate mid-nineteenth century mudlarks who discovered more profit in faking artifacts at their den in Rosemary Lane (now called Royal Mint Street) in Tower Hamlets, London, than laboriously trudging through the Thames mire to find real ones to sell to collectors. Their output of all types of artifact is reckoned to have been in excess of 5,000.

Of interest here are the odd coins, medallions and lead tokens they created. Their lack of knowledge makes it reasonably easy to spot their medallion products, which on some, featured early medieval figures wearing late medieval helmets and on most, garbled legends. Because genuine tokens were often crudely made, their fake tokens are much more difficult to spot. One contemporary expert examining Billy and Charlie's products said they must be genuine because *"no forger would produce anything so preposterous".* Neither he nor the other experts then vouchsafing their genuine nature had anything to say when plaster moulds stolen from the forgers' den were later shown in public, exposing the fraud finally and irrefutably.

Around 1880, A. WUESTHOFF (U.S.), a New York coin dealer, produced his own struck versions of U.S. coins in a range of metals.

OMEGA MAN (U.S.)
The conceited counterfeiter
Hancock & Spanbauer[HA] draw attention to this cheeky counterfeiter whom numismatists have dubbed the Omega man, because he could not resist adding his own mark, a symbol like the Greek Omega Ω, to the design of his forgeries of the U.S. 1882 $3 and 1907 $10 gold coins. This sign is hidden on the obverse of the $3 in the loop of the R of the word LIBERTY which appears on the headdress band, and on the reverse of the $10 piece in the eagle's trailing claw.

John COOKE & SONS are notable for two things - imitating an imitation, and concealing their own name on their imitations. The originating coin was a Venetian sequin of the Doge Alois Mocenigo III, (1722-32). Africans took to this coin to the extent of imitating it in copper, albeit with a blundered inscription. John Cooke & Sons saw a golden export opportunity and produced brass (and possibly copper-gilt) sequin and half-sequin versions, replacing the blundered inscription with their own name in pseudo-latin - *Johannes Ille Coquus Sui Filiique..*

Luigi PIZZAMIGLIO was an accidental forger, as in 1866 he found dies in a Roman antique shop for striking false copper coins of Pope Gregory III (731-41) and Zachary (741-51). Deciding they would make novel presents for his friends, he struck copies with them in a variety of metals including copper. These pieces in the right metal are now the most likely to deceive, particularly if around the correct weight of 1.5 gm.

A well-known anonymous figure in America was 'SMITH' who tooled large cents of the late eighteenth century, and possibly, early nineteenth to increase their collectability.

Written in the early nineteenth century, *'The Life of William Stuart'*, a so-called moral pamphlet, was the work of a small-time, not very successful American counterfeiter, who was imprisoned on a number of occasions.

The PARIS FORGERS' MINT

"A notice has just been received from France, to put collectors and antiquaries in England on their guard against a fresh issue from the Paris forgers' mint, of well-executed imitations of rare Saxon and English coins. One of the gang ... (bearing) the name of Noffman or Hoffman, is now on his road to this country with a large quantity of these forgeries, mixed up, to lull suspicion, with some genuine coins. It is supposed he is connected with a clever forger named Rousseau."

Extract from
The Gentleman's Magazine, 1845

"HONEST GUV'. WOULD I LIE TO YOU?"

"I found the money accidentally and was on my way to a watchmaker to find out if it was real." Victorian passer's excuse - acquitted, and on to yet more crime.

When caught counterfeiting in the 1890's, Frederick WAGNER (U.S.) told his captors that his daily output of six U.S. dimes, made in German silver (i.e. no silver), was just enough to save his family from starvation.

Coincidentally sentenced to 14 years' imprisonment after 14 years of successful counterfeiting, Thomas RAVEN was a Victorian 'entrepreneur' who thought he had a foolproof set-up hidden in the basement of a Bethnal Green tailor's shop. Two bells were rigged up so that the tailor above could press one for *coast clear* and the other for *danger*. Unfortunately for Raven, the tailor panicked when the police arrived and pressed the wrong button.

CAESARS BY THE DOZEN

"An Italian at Naples advises that he has opened a shop for antiquities. The advertisement, which is in broken English, announces that 'he make all the old ting brand new, and the new tings all old'... Collectors of coin are most of all liable to imposition of this kind. We have heard of an Italian in London, who used to complete any set of the twelve Cæsars from dies of his own."

The Gentleman's Magazine, 1833

20th Century

At the turn of the century, Reginald HUTH, a London coin collector, liked to have his own 'coins' made. One, produced for him by Pinches & Co. in 1900, to commemorate Victoria's visit to Ireland, incorrectly described as a *pattern* silver double florin, was recently offered for sale by a dealer at £550!

MEISTER was a South African immigrant who, in 1903, rewarded his host country by counterfeiting its Veld Pond coins at a shop in Johannesburg. Believed to have been deported when caught.

Constantine CHRISTODOULOS (or Christodoulou)
Born in Varosia, Cyprus, he first appears in Athens in 1900, presenting the Numismatic Museum with a handful of ancient coins. They, never having heard the expression 'Beware of Greeks bearing gifts', readily agreed to his request to have casts of a few of their rare coins. These were the masters for his early forgeries. No numismatist himself, Christodoulos was then guided and supplied with originals to copy by a local antiques dealer, for a most cunning and surprising reason. With Christodoulos unsettling the coin market with his fakes, collectors would turn to the dealer who could always 'spot' them and guarantee his offerings as genuine.

In addition to his sponsor's choices, he copied other pieces that came to hand, even including other forgers' crude efforts. He would subject the pieces to wear and false patination treatment. He had at least one assistant, and they churned out coins from his dies, some rare, some common. They also dabbled in ancient artifacts. When the dealer died, two others took over, and Christodoulos's products spread across Europe and America.

In 1914, nearly a thousand of his dies were confiscated by the Greek authorities and plaster casts taken from them. His dies were published in 1922. Years later, by a devious legal manœuvre, some, possibly all, of his dies had to be released. 'Restrikes' have since begun to appear. Christodoulos's output is estimated at over 500 different pieces. He imitated coins ranging in diameter from 8 mm to 36 mm. There are a few oval and square pieces, the rest being round.

In his book, Fake?, Mark Jones makes a key observation regarding the 'expert'. He will tend to be much less critical about pieces he finds himself, than those presented to him for an opinion. As an example, Mark quotes the 'Athenian' decadrachm Sir George Hill took to be genuine, having spotted it adorning a Greek lady's neck. It was subsequently bought by the British Museum as genuine, where it is now noted as a Christodoulos product. Apart from having a couple of extra flan rim cracks, it matches No. 294 in the book *Christodoulos the Counterfeiter* by Svoronos[SV],

TARDANI (Italian - fl. c.1890 - c.1914/5)
For many years, he was known only as 'The Carolingian forger', a specialist in faking Carolingian and medieval Italian coins. The honour of his family was said to be the reason for secrecy - perhaps a discouraging branch of the mafia! He worked in Rome, producing forgeries to rival those of Becker and Christodoulos.

The first alarm bell was rung in 1896, when Francesco Gnecchi revealed Tardani's production of Roman aurei, In 1902, Ercole Gnecchi illustrated on two plates a number of forged Italian coins, warning of the existence of others. The forgeries were being produced "almost wholesale". The then mystery forger was remarkably skilled in copying coin engravings from sales catalogues and reference books, and, by his output, was obviously a quick die-cutter.

More forgeries were notified to numismatists in 1905, 1909, 1913 and 1916. In 1919 The National Museum at Rome bought over 1,000 of this forger's dies, he by then having died. They cover Greek, Roman, Italian and Carolingian coins. Ninety per cent of the dies were electrotypes, and ten per cent were hand engraved. The latter were for the medieval coins where electrotyping would not have coped well with the often badly struck, off-flan, imperfectly preserved, thin, genuine originals. The dies were approximately 52% Roman, 23% Greek, 20% modern and 10% medieval. On at least two occasions since the dies were acquired by the Museum, they were going to be published. This is still awaited.

LUCKY HAMID

Ninety years' ago, in the sultanate of Darfur in the Western Sudan, Hamid Muhammad, the chief silver smith, was in deep trouble. Dies for forging piastres had been found in his house. Genuine coins of the time were made to order in Egypt and arrived at annoyingly irregular intervals - a thought that occurred to the Sultan, whilst contemplating Hamid's beheading. Why not get his own silver smiths to manufacture his coinage. "*We would if we could*", came the reply, "*but only Hamid has the skill.*" And so Hamid the forger, became Hamid the Mintmaster, eventually turning out coins of such poor quality that the Sultan's subjects had to be threatened with beheading if they did not accept them!

Tardani believed that collectors would be more convinced by hoards than individual pieces. He created and sold his spurious Bolsena 'hoard' of early 9th to mid eleventh century coins in 1909, mostly, it seems, to an Italian dealer called Alessio Gilli, who in the same year sold one piece to the King of Italy! The 'hoard' included a fused-together group of coins to add authenticity, nullified by the unbelievable consistency of fabric, style and condition over the two and a half centuries spanned by the coins. There were also fantasy denarii of Pope Leo IX (1049-54) and Henry III for whom no genuine coins are known. It is said that all collections of Italian coins made in Italy in the early years of this century are tainted with 'Tardanis'.

He modelled his coin fabric on pieces from around 900, not appreciating that from fifty years later, the coins were smaller and thicker. So his imitations of earlier coins are close in fabric, later ones are not. He artificially aged his products in acid baths. He also went in for tooling, changing the mint names on genuine fifteenth and sixteenth century papal ducats and double ducats.

A Frenchman, Louis FARRIGAULT of Châtellerault is thought to have produced forgeries of rare early Capetian deniers and obols, Carolingian and Merovingian coins in the 1920's and 1930's. Farrigault came along slightly after Tardani. The metal he used is not a close match to genuine coins.

A numismatist, W.C. WELLS (fl. c.1915-1920), is suspected of being the faker of Castlecomer Colliery 5s. 5d. countermarks on Spanish dollars. The die still exists.

'THE GENEVA FORGER' (fl. early 1900's-1930's) appears to have been a Geneva craftsman who worked in bronze and ran a small antiques business in the 1920's. His efforts initially fooled Museums, dealers, collectors and 'authorities'. When the truth was revealed, one dealer bought back all he had sold, and made a presentation of 76 pieces to the British Museum. The forger appears to have confined himself to a restricted range of counterfeits, copying bronze coins of the late third and early fourth centuries only, and of just five historic figures: Nigrinianus, Julian the Corrector, Domitius Alexander, Valerius Valens and Martinian. Genuine coins are so rare that comparisons *are* difficult. These forgeries have been die-cut closely to the styl e of the originals, with the fabric also close, so Carson's illustrations of 25 of them provide an invaluable guide[CA]. He examined 103 examples, finding them all bearing a similar patina and lack of wear. Too many have edge splits, die-flaws and 'corrosion' to be real. Each repeated type example has come from one pair of dies, which does not conform to any normal coin finds. Mr Geneva had a friend who also produced forgeries, such as a Magna Urbica aureus and an Orbiana denarius. Mr Geneva's products continued to appear in the 1930's, whereas this friend died in the 1920's. This, plus differences in style, as exemplified by some of the Geneva Museum examples, set the two apart.

Bekhraj NEWAR (fl. c.1925-7) used good quality iron-dies to churn out tens of thousands of false Tibetan copper Sho-kangs. He was caught in his Calcutta workshop, together with all his manufacturing apparatus and sentenced to six years' imprisonment.

The 'BEIRUT' School

Since around 1950 and continuing through 1974, the so-called Beirut School in Lebanon has been turning out pressure-cast and die-struck forgeries, some possibly from cast dies. They are mostly common Byzantine solidi or histamena gold coins[OH], which can be sold more readily to naive tourists and non-specialist dealers. One tremissis is known. The forgeries have mainly been detected by their shoddy workmanship and by die linking. From the late 1960's to the early 1970's, quantities of 1887 UK £5 coins and U.S. $20 pieces were coming from Beirut.

In 1976/7, a fake gold and silver smuggling gang was caught and convicted in Lancashire. The seven men received sentences ranging from 4 years down to a £1000 fine. The source of their coins was a master coiner in Beirut, via an American whose previous experience as an airline pilot and gunrunner seems somehow appropriate. When they were caught, the American had already been deported. The activities of the 'School' (sometimes referred to as the Beirut Mint!) were curtailed in the early 1980's by the dire political situation in the Lebanon. Some Athens' products, e.g. an Athens' copy of a Heraclius gold coin, may have found their way on to the market via Beirut.

GIVE A DOG A BAD NAME...

An aptly named Edinburgh man, James STEELE, one of the most skilful forgers of the twentieth century, was nicknamed 'Gentleman Jim' because of his helpful attitude towards the police once he had been caught. In fact he was caught twice; once in 1930 and again in 1964. In 1930, it was halfcrowns, some 1,350, for which he got 3 years' penal servitude. In 1964, florins, 14,000 of which got him two years' imprisonment, he then being 80 years' old.

He did not see through his first attempt at forgery, soon after the end of the First World War, because he discovered halfway through making his fake sovereign dies that sovereigns had ceased to be legal tender! He engaged in the manufacture of the halfcrowns in 1930 with an accomplice, Robert Ramsay, producing copies so good that only experienced cashiers could detect them. Ramsay suffered the same sentence as Steele and is not heard of again. Steele returned to counterfeiting "*to supplement my pension, as I did not want to apply for National Assistance*". He obtained the metal for all his florin production from ICI, paying 10 shillings per strip from each of which he produced 40 florins. His florins were so good that they were not detected, and he may have got away with it completely, but for his neighbours complaining about the noise he was creating in his small back room. The Royal Mint said that his diecutting and toning of the end products with powders he had developed, were of an extremely high level of skill. When asked why, with that skill he had not applied to work at the Mint, he replied *"because counterfeiting's more satisfying. You see the whole job through from beginning to end."*

José BERAHA or Beraha ZDRAVKO (1907-) (fl. 1951-1955?) minted British gold sovereigns dated 1926, a year in which there were no official sovereignsd. From 1951 he churned out these imitations, having first established that the prototypes were no longer legal tender. He set up a minting operation in Milan that turned every two kilos of gold into 270 sovereigns, compared to the Royal Mint's 273. In other words, his sovereigns had slightly more gold than the officially struck ones. Because of the premium put on coins, this still left an acceptable margin of profit. His mint comprised a furnace, stamping machine, master dies and working moulds, roll bars and polishing machines. He spent seven months in jail in the early 1950's awaiting possible extradition from Switzerland to Italy. The extradition request was then turned down, because the sovereigns he had been replicating were not current coins of the British Realm.

In 1959, Dr SCHMIDT, a German, acquired a spark erosion machine with which he said he produced 150 facsimile German Reichsgoldmünzen, as close as he could to their alloy and legal weight. Experts could only tell them from genuine coins by chemical tests. His sister passed the fakes to banks who accepted them as genuine. Brother and sister were each sentenced to six months' imprisonment. Schmidt was at one time planning to 'restrike' various ancient Greek coins.

THE HASLEMERE HOARD FORGER

In the mid 1980's, the Haslemere Hoard was revealed as completely counterfeit - a modern fabrication, probably made some time in the 1960's. A full investigation was published by Robert Van Arsdell[VA] in 1986. He considers the forger a fairly incompetent die-cutter and is not surprised that the less demanding and more abstract designs were attempted. A design problem experienced by the forger was his inability to cut the smooth curves of the originals in his dies. Instead, he resorted to 'step' cutting them. Van Arsdell points to the creation of 'new' types in the hoard as clear evidence that modern collectors were being targeted.

In the 1960's, forgeries were flowing from Northern Italy. A 1962 police raid on a Milan works found the staff churning out quantities of Latin American counterfeits. Two years later, not far from Bologna, a factory spreading counterfeits all round the World, was pounced upon. American, Austrian, Belgian, British, Indian, Iranian and Turkish counterfeits were amongst over 20 countries represented in the large stock found in 1969 in the secret premises of an Iranian goldsmith. Two of the six in the gang escaped the police raid, leaving behind two counterfeiting machines - one manually operated and one electric..

Suspect coins being offered for sale in 1968, led to the flat of one Anthony DENNINGTON being raided, where the police found counterfeiting apparatus, moulds, etc., for imitating gold and silver coins across the British series from William I to George III, plus one Athenian tetradrachm. He was in his mid 30's when in 1969 he was tried, convicted and sentenced to two years' imprisonment for coin counterfeiting. His conviction was recorded in The Times of 10th July 1969. Cadmium present in supposedly ancient coins is a giveaway, being a metal whose use began in the nineteenth century. This was a factor in Dennington's trial at the Old Bailey. Marion Archibald of the British Museum was called as an expert witness. A supposed William I penny was shown to contain cadmium, demonstrating irrefutably that it was a fake. Apparently, Dennington would obtain coins on loan from Spink, make moulds from them and then return them to Spink as "not quite what I require!" He is known to have used a British Museum electrotype as a master for one of his efforts.

The 1970's self-confessed Banknotes forger, Charles BLACK, was also connected to gold-plated half sovereigns. In his autobiography, *Counterfeiter. The Story of a British Master Forger*, published in 1989, he mentions advising on the use of a heavy hydraulic press to stamp out half-sovereigns. Dies from Beirut simulated the coins on copper flans that were then gold-dipped and set into rings to conceal their incorrect weight. During a Moroccan holiday in the 1970's, the author was approached in Tangiers by a man purporting to be a sailor just off a ship out of funds and so 'willing' to sell his valuable half-sovereign ring for a mere pittance! Most likely a Beirut 'special'.

In his sixties, Francis HENNING (U.S.),, a mechanical engineer, built a remarkable one-to-one pantograph machine with which he made 1944 nickels. They were of high quality apart from his oversight of using two differently dated coins for the two halves. This resulted in the wartime mintmark 'P' being omitted. The dies supposedly ended up in the Copper River.

THE GALVANO BOYS

The International Bureau for the Suppression of Counterfeit Coins dubbed one counterfeit group, The British Museum gang, and had to hastily retract this description which, although meant to refer to the gang's use of British Museum electrotypes for their master dies, was widely misinterpreted. They then called the gang The Galvano Boys.

MINT MAN WHO MADE A MINT

In 1975, the deputy director of the Karlsruhe mint and a craftsman were arrested for making hundreds of thousands of rare coins without permission. It is difficult to see how such quantities could leave any of the coins still classified as rare! In fact it was a collector, surprised by the sudden excess of supposedly rare coins, who suggested that officials should check into the matter. Original dies appear to have been used to churn out the pieces. 1950 fifty pfennig coins, pre-1960 five mark coins, and pre-1967 two pfennig coins were some of the 'rare' coins in question.

SLAVEJ (or Slavei) (Bulgarian) produces unmarked imitation coins, specialising in Roman denarii probably hand-engraving dies and machine pressing from them. Details are clear, suggesting that they are machine-struck on hand-engraved dies. Edges are artificially rough and 'silver' high points show through a strangely even patina. At least one of his struck pieces has been cast later by someone else.

THE BRISTOL FORGER

This unnamed forger of Celtic coins died in 1992. His pieces are discussed and illustrated in Chris Rudd's article[RU].

14

A Risky Business

A Justice of the U.S. Supreme Court observed that "Counterfeiting is an offense never committed by accident, nor by ignorance, nor in the heat of passion, nor in extremity of poverty. It is a... sneaking offense."

The sneaks' products appeared hard on the heels of the very first coins, to be followed almost immediately by preventative devices and measures and laws for discouragement and retribution, usually of a draconian level, making counterfeiting a very risky business indeed!

ANCIENT GREECE
If, as is now generally thought, coinage commenced c.625 B.C., then Solon's edicts of c.583 B.C., against forgers of public money, appeared less than fifty years later. In most Greek states, the introduction of coinage was quickly followed by the establishment of counterfeiting as a capital offence. The Monetary Pact between Mytilene and Phocaea prescribed the death penalty for counterfeiting and for mint officials issuing sub-standard coinage.

In 375/4 B.C., the Athenian Law was introduced to protect Attic silver coinage from forgeries. It provided for the confiscation and mutilation of all plated or base imitations of the official coinage. Also to reject all foreign imitations, as there was at that time no way of telling if the silver content was up to the high Athenian standard, i.e. between 99.3% and 99.9% pure silver. *"Let the Certifier sit among the (money changers) tables certify according to these conditions every day .... If anyone brings to him coinage with the same stamp as the Attic (foreign imitation), let him return it to the one who brought it. But if it is bronze beneath or lead beneath or counterfeit, let him cut across it at once, and let it be sacred to the Mother of the Gods and let it be deposited with the Council. If the Certifier ... does not certify according to the law, let the public collectors beat him with fifty blows of the whip."*

Moses' Law forbade counterfeiting.

ROMAN REPUBLIC
Sulla's Law, c.81 B.C., the *Lex Cornelia de falsis*, refers to the offence of buying or selling tin or lead counterfeits for illegal purposes. Many Roman Republican coins bear Bankers' marks, not so much to test for plating as to indicate approval of genuine pieces.

IMPERIAL ROME

The *Lex Julia peculatus* of Augustus equated coining with treason. Severe laws against coining were embodied in the Theodosian code. The Romans made it an offence for the mint to issue cast instead of struck coins.

Until the fourth century A.D., there was no Roman Law expressly forbidding the counterfeiting of copper, brass or bronze coinage. By then, it was a capital offence to melt down coinage to separate silver from bronze, as well as for counterfeiting. It embodied clear class distinction; banishment for the elite - as happened to Hikesias the banker - but crucifixion, the mines or the Arena for the proletariat and slaves.

In 317, under Constantine I, death by burning was introduced, when forgery once more became regarded as treason. This applied only to the precious metal coinage until 371. In 349, Constans introduced a law that forbade the extraction of silver from the bronze coinage on pain of death. Constantius II then made extraction uneconomic by reducing the silver content to less than 1%. A writer of this time suggested putting all mintworkers on an island to counteract their propensity to fraud.

The Roman Law of Counterfeiting from the post-Diocletian empire has been investigated by Grierson[GR].

ANGLO-SAXON

Alfred's laws contained no forgery penalties; Æthelstan, King of Wessex (924-939), introduced these in The Grateley Decree, to cover coin forgery at the Royal Mints. Following conviction, the moneyer's guilty hand would be cut off and displayed at the Mint. The accused could choose trial by ordeal. The Decree seems to have worked well for a while, with the exception of Hiberno-Norse imitations.

Once you were a moneyer, the authorities liked you to remain one - under their control. The English moneyer, Robert, for instance, was fined a 'sconce' (a fairly mild fine - a tun of wine) for relinquishing his office without permission. Many moneyers were said to be of dubious character, and to disappear into the woods at night with the official dies to knock out some base metal pocket money. Æthelred invoked the death penalty for such moneyers "*who work in a wood or elsewhere*", unless given the King's Pardon. Oddly, for striking false coin, his code imposed just a twelve ores fine.

11th Century

Contemporary forgeries are not so common at the start of the Norman period.

12th Century

Article 13 of the First Lateran Council (1123), states that he who manufactures or knowingly trades in false coins is an oppressor of the people and a troubler of civic order.

Despite the dire consequences, counterfeiting increased, so that by 1125 the Anglo-Saxon Chronicle records "*In this year King Henry (I) commanded all the moneyers in England to lose each of them the right hand, et testiculis infra.... (testicle). And the Bishop Roger of Sarum (Salisbury) sent over all England, and bade them that they should all come to Winchester at Christmas.*" Almost all who attended were duly mutilated. This harsh punishment suggests that the king had concluded, like others before him, that those most responsible for the forgeries were the makers of the legitimate coinage! Hand amputation continued up to c.1200. Later, forgers lost an ear for a first offence; death for a second offence.

13th Century

Edward I's regulations of 1291, replacing those of 1284, set out staged penalties:
First offence - all bad money confiscated.
Second offence - all bad money and all other goods on the person confiscated.
Third offence - all goods confiscated and death (hanged, and then occasionally drawn and quartered for good measure).

By this time, although the death penalty was rarely being carried out, there are some recorded hangings - John le Havekere in 1279; two Irish forgers in 1295; two Flemish merchants in 1300, despite bringing in less than £12 of counterfeit money,

If you crossed London Bridge, your money would be checked, which may account for some of the medieval counterfeit coins that turn up on the Thames foreshore.

Edward failed to stop the importation into England of the debased silver imitations of English silver pennies, known as Crockards and Pollards, and so, in 1299, allowed them to pass as halfpennies. As the silver content of each was worth more than a halfpenny, they had disappeared within a year, mostly into the melting pot.

In medieval Europe, mintworkers were encouraged not to indulge in lightweight production, debasement, clipping or moonlighting by the draconian punishment of losing a hand! This Continental woodcut comes from the early 1500's.

14th Century

Legislation against imported imitations appeared in 1346, 1347, 1348 and 1351. Black money (turneys) was a problem in England at that time.

From the Middle Ages, the Trial of the Pyx was used to ensure that the required standard was maintained for the official coinage. If mistakes occurred, the mintworkers could suffer condemnation as traitors and suffer mutilation, fines and exile. One wonders why any took up such an occupation in the first place.

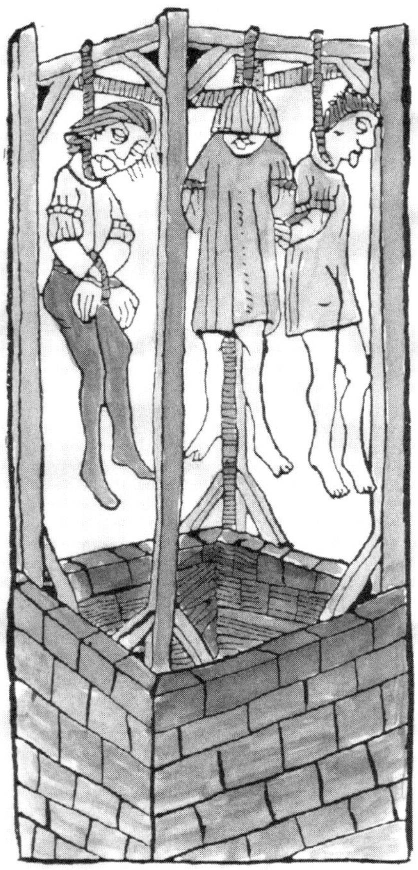

Counterfeiting the King's money was, according to Edward III's Statutes, treason, and for that you could suffer a variety of unpleasant deaths, including impaling on a stake.

A 1554 diary records a hanging of eleven men at Tyburn for *the coining of naughty money.*

15th Century

The death penalty for forgery continued to apply throughout this century.

There are not many counterfeits from the late medieval to early modern period. Firstly, treason (without the benefit of clergy) was a frightening charge and secondly, each coin represented too much value not to have been closely examined. So forgeries would have been weeded out, leaving the few really good, die-struck, well-plated examples in circulation, to arrive at the present day mostly via hoards. The thinness of the coins of those times made cast forging difficult without resulting in an easily spotted thick imitation.

Starting c.1464, possibly even earlier, and recurring up to the mid nineteenth century, laws were passed to force employers in certain trades to pay their workers *only* in legal coinage. These laws were seldom effective.

Henry VII introduced a law making it high treason to counterfeit English coin or import continental imitations. In 1489 it also became high treason to counterfeit *permitted* foreign coin.

By c.1500, most of Europe had reverted to burning as a jolly way of punishing counterfeiters. In England, it was hanging for men and strangling for women, followed by burning in many instances. This continued to the end of the eighteenth century.

16th Century

Two counterfeit hoards of this period have been found in the Thames, and another in a cesspit, suggesting that the severe penalties for getting caught prompted occasional 'sacrifices' of the evidence. Anyone receiving counterfeit gold or silver coins, was ordered to cut them through the middle, deface or break them so they "could not pass."

In 1553, in the reign of Mary Tudor, counterfeiting the foreign coins then approved as normal currency, was once more said to be treasonable. By 1572, under Queen Elizabeth, an Act of Parliament again made counterfeiting of these foreign coins "musprision of treason" with penalties of life imprisonment, forfeiture of goods, and lifelong loss of land profits.

Removal of the rose and date of an Elizabethan three farthings coin (1561-77) allowed it to pass as the fractionally larger penny.

In *The Scornful Lady*, the Jacobean playwrights Beaumont and Fletcher, had a character, Lovelace, say "He had a bastard, his own toward issue, Whip'd and then crop'd, for washing out the roses in three Farthings to make them pence."

17th Century

In Charles I's reign, renewal of the farthing patent (11th July 1625), specified that "*The making or uttering of any other tokens, whether made or counterfeited within the realm or 'beyond the seas' is forbidden.*" Most of the contemporary references to tokens seem far more concerned with the prevention of the making and circulating of counterfeits than with the genuine tokens.

The small size of the farthing tempted many into counterfeiting. Not surprising when eighty false farthings could be produced from a pennyworth of metal. "*In the early part of the reign of Charles the First, one William Hawks and several others were fined, placed and exposed in the pillory in London, for counterfeiting (the) Royal token farthing...*"

"*...reason for the changed position of the sceptre is uncertain: it may have been merely to confuse the counterfeiters.*"

CROMWELL WARNS
Graining and edge inscriptions were devices intended to prevent clipping. Cromwell's pattern crown, which probably circulated, bears the edge inscription HAS NISI PERITURUS MIHI ADIMAT NEMO - *the penalty for clipping this coin is death.* DECUS ET TUTAMEN, first used in Charles II's reign, means *an ornament and a safeguard.* It is a quote from Virgil suggested for use in this way by the diarist, John Evelyn. Many modern pound coins have DECUS ET TUTAMEN as their edge inscription. In one of his diary entries, Evelyn noted that there were frequent executions in London of coin clippers.

Small centre plugs of brass were introduced as a preventative measure into the tin coinage of Charles II and continued with James II and William and Mary coinage. A House of Commons resolution of 1692 shows that tin coins were still considered too easy to counterfeit. Many fakes simply ignored the centre plug, relying on public carelessness or indifference to overlook this clue.

In 1696, Sir Isaac Newton became William III's Warden of the London Mint. His endeavours to quell the malpractices that then abounded, resulted in many arrests and nineteen executions in the following year alone.

Where any money, whether silver or copper, was produced in Court by way of evidence during the course of a prosecution, it was provided by *statute 8 and 9 William III c. 26*, that the judge should cause it to be cut in pieces in open Court, or in the presence of some justice of the peace, and "*delivered to or for such Person or Persons to whom the same of Right shall appertain.*" No doubt this intriguing provision gave rise to many a knotty legal problem. The *statute 9 & 10 William III c. 21*, empowered, but did not compel, any person (including justices) to break or deface pieces of silver money suspected of being counterfeit, it being provided that if the broken pieces turned out to

(549)

Anno Octavo & Nono

Gulielmi III. Regis.

An Act for the better Preventing the Counterfeiting the Current Coin of this Kingdom.

Whereas notwithstanding the good Laws still in Force against the Counterfeiting of the Moneys and Coins of this Realm, yet the said Offence doth and is like daily to Increase, to the manifest Wrong and Injury both of His Majesty and all His Loving Subjects, being very much occasioned for Want of a Due and Condign Punishment, to be Inflicted upon such Artificers and others, who without any Lawful Authority do Make or Use Puncheons, Stamps, Dyes, and other Engines and Instruments, which are commonly used or may be made use of, in

Pppppp 2 in

be good coin: "*it will be at the breaker's peril, who shall stand the loss of it.*" Any dispute as to whether a broken coin was good or bad could be determined by the "*Mayor, Bailiff or Bailiffs, or other Chief Officer of any City or Town Corporate*," or by a justice of the peace in a County.

The Plate Act of 1696 commanded that all possessing presses that could be used for coinage, must hand them in to the Mint. They would then be recompensed. From May 1697, the death penalty came into force for making coining tools, taking coining gear from the Mint, colouring or gilding metals to look like current coin, and for handling counterfeits. In the same year, James Roettier(s) was found guilty of smuggling coin dies of Charles II and James II to France and was dismissed from the Mint.

From the 1st December, the 1697 Act *to prevent the further currency of any Hammered Coin of this Kingdom, and for recoining such as is now in being* required all hammered coinage to be handed in for melting down and recoining. It finally put hammered coinage to rest, thereby ending the easy times for counterfeiters who now had to try and imitate precise, machine-made pieces.

William's 1698 Act was entitled optimistically "*An Act for the better Preventing the Counterfeiting, Clipping, and other Diminishing the Coin of this Kingdom.*" It was designed to counter clippers by making clipped money unacceptable. Also in 1698, a bounty of ten pounds each was put on the many English coiners who had moved to Ireland as a safer place to pursue their 'trade'.

18th Century

Counterfeiting legislation was now beginning to appear at regular intervals. Queen Anne's Act of 1714. (made perpetual 4 Geo.I.cap.9.): "*By an English stat. 8 Annit is enacted, cap.45, that if any person shall mark on the edges any counterfeit coin resembling her majesty's coin, or other coin made, or which shall be made current in this kingdom, with letters, grainings, or other mark like those on the edges of money coined in the queen's mint, or other current coin in this kingdom, every such offender, his aiders and abettors, shall be guilty of high treason. Cap.46. If any person shall colour, gild, or case over with gold or silver, or any wash or materials producing the color of gold and silver, any coin resembling her majesty's coin, or other coin made, or which shall be made current in this kingdom, or any figured blanks of base metal, or coarse gold or silver, of the size of milled money, or gild over silver blanks of fit size, and figure, to be coined into pieces resembling the current gold coin of this kingdom, every such person, his aiders and abettors, shall be guilty of high treason. Cap.47. If any instrument or engine, used or designed for coining or counterfeiting gold or silver money, shall be found concealed in the house or possession of any person not employed in some of the queen's mints, any person may seize the same, and carry them to some justice of the peace, to be produced in evidence against that person who shall be prosecuted for such offences. Cap.51. Any person to whom any gold or silver money shall be tendered, any pieces whereof may be suspected to be counterfeit, may cut, break, or deface the same, and thereupon appearing to be counterfeit, the tenderer shall bear the loss, but appearing to be lawful, the person who cut it shall take it at its currency. Cap.52. If any dispute arise, whether the piece so cut be counterfeit, it shall be determined by the chief officer of the place where tendered, if a city, or town corporate; or if not, by the next justice of peace of the county, who may administer an oath as they shall see convenient for determining any question relating to the said piece. Cap.53. All officers concerned in the receipt of her majesty's revenue, may cut or deface every piece of counterfeit or unlawfully diminished silver money tendered them for her majesty's use."*

George II passed several anti-counterfeiting Acts:
16th January 1732
"*An Act to prevent the copying or counterfeiting any of the Gold coins, commonly called Broad Pieces.*"

The Act of 1742 (29th September) made forgers of brass or copper money liable to two years' imprisonment. Offenders also had to produce sureties to guarantee two further years' good behaviour. Lawbreakers at the time considered this a mild risk.

(It is) "*High Treason to wash over or alter the impression of either Side of any real or counterfeit Shillings or Sixpences, to make them resemble Guineas and Half-Guineas, or in like Manner to make any real or counterfeit Halfpenny or Farthing to resemble Shillings or Sixpences.*
" - *And whoever shall tender in Payment, any counterfeit Money, knowing it to be so, upon Conviction shall suffer for the first Offence 6 Months Imprisonment, and find Security for their good Behaviour for 6 Months more; for the second Offence, 2 Years Imprisonment, and find Security for 2 Years more; and for the third Offence, shall be adjudg'd guilty of Felony.*
"*Whoever shall utter any counterfeit Money, and shall either the same Day, or within 10 Days after, utter more and shall have in their Custody one or more Pieces of counterfeit Money, upon Conviction shall suffer a Years Imprisonment, and find Security for 2 Years more; and for the second Offence be adjudged guilty of Felony. And whoever counterfeits Halfpence or Farthings, and is convicted thereof, shall suffer 2 Years imprisonment, and find Security for 2 Years more.*
" - *This Act appoints a Reward of £40 for the Discovery of every Person that shall be convicted of any of the Treasons or Felonies above mention'd, and £10 for every Person that shall be convicted of counterfeiting any Halfpence or Farthings; and if any Person after this Day being out of Prison, shall discover 2 or more Accomplices that have since this Day committed any of the offences beforementioned, upon their Conviction is entitled to his Majesty's Pardon*".

July 1751 saw an Act to "*Implement the Act of 1742*"!

At this time, a woman could escape the death penalty by revealing that she was pregnant, and that the law, if carried out, would be

killing an unborn innocent child:
October 1733
"*The Sessions ended at the Old Bailey, when the following Criminals receiv'd Sentence of Death... Margaret Berry, for Coining... pleaded her Belly, and was found quick with Child*".
December 1733
"*Elizabeth Wright pleaded her Belly, but was found not quick with Child.*"

The intrinsic value of the counterfeit guineas circulating in York in the mid-eighteenth century was roughly a quarter that of the real guineas - a handsome margin of profit. In England, as the production of base metal coinage was not a Royal prerogative, counterfeiting it was only regarded as a misdemeanour. Consequently, forging copper and bronze coins became a popular, less risky activity. Profits, although considerably less per item than with silver or gold coins, were achieved by the sheer volume produced. By the middle of the eighteenth century, there were more counterfeit than genuine base metal coins in circulation.

Despite George II's legislation, copper coin counterfeiting from 1770 to the end of the century was worse than ever. Generally, the Act was not enforced. A 1770 Proclamation threatened branding on the cheek with the letter R (for reprobate?) for clipping or filing, and in 1771 a new Act (24th June) made counterfeiting copper coins, or trying to sell them at under their nominal value, a felony. Warrants could then be issued for premises to be searched for coining equipment. This seems to have been as ineffectual as the previous Act. Evasions slipped through the definition to make handsome profits for the manufacturers, even at considerably discounted prices, due to the low intrinsic value of the genuine coinage, and the light weight of the evasions.

In Somerset in the eighteenth century, of people arrested for counterfeiting halfpennies, only a third ever went to trial. There was at the time a general tendency of juries to acquit coiners because of the extreme severity of the law. Not all escaped the ultimate penalty. James Oldfield was executed for coining, at Tyburn on the 28th of April 1770.

6th November 1772
An Act for the better preventing the counterfeiting, clipping, and other diminishing the gold coin of this kingdom.

The Mint Records note many prosecuted for clipping and coining. Often these were due to paid informers, some of whom were adept at making innocent people appear to be coiners.

Coiners of the late eighteenth century knew they were engaged in a hazardous business, and they had an expression for a cowardly compatriot - "*his arse makes buttons (counterfeit shillings); he is ready to bewray himself through fear.*" The main weapons to combat them were draconian penalties, confiscations and coins so hard to copy as to discourage attempts. Private possession of screw presses was made illegal and any found were destroyed.

From Baker's History of Scarborough:
"*1781. Base Coin: The Deputy Recorder informed the Court that he had in his hands the nett sum of £1 16s 0d arising from the sale of eight stone and five pounds of base and counterfeit half-pence seized from David Estell, tailor, in the time of Plaxton Dickenson and Jonas Sutton (1778), bailiffs and justices of the borough, after allowing 3s. for cutting and defacing.*"

At the Old Bailey in December 1795, John Gilbert was sentenced to one year's imprisonment and fined one shilling for selling 357 half-penny forgeries for eight shillings. If genuine, their value would have been fourteen shillings and tenpence halfpenny.

In 1798 it was laid down that counterfeit *copper* coin, "*by Order of the Court where [the] Offender or Offenders shall be tried, or by Order of some Justice of the Peace in case there be no trial, be defaced or destroyed*, or otherwise disposed of, *as such Court or Justice shall direct" (37 George III c. 126, s. 7).*

21st June 1798
"*An Act to prevent the exportation of base coin to His Majesty's colonies in the West Indies and America.*"

12th July 1799
"*An Act to prohibit the Importation of light Silver coin from Foreign Countries.*"

GEORGIAN TERMS OF ARRAIGNMENT
"*That A.B. of etc. not having God before his Eyes but being seduced by the instigation of the Devil, on the Day, etc., in the Year of the Reign, etc., at the Parish of, etc., in the said County, did falsly and traiterously forge, counterfeit and Coin twenty pieces of Brass and Copper, and other mixed metals, to the Resemblance and Likeness of good, lawful and currant Money of the King and Kingdom of England, to the great Prejudice and Deceit of the subjects of our said Lord the King, and against the Peace, etc., and also against the form of the Statute, etc.*"

In the eighteenth and early nineteenth centuries, counterfeiting was rife and punishments permanent, as these contemporary magazine extracts graphically illustrate.

THE GENTLEMAN'S MAGAZINE
1732
"... *sentence of death.. for coining counterfeit Half-Crowns and Shillings.*"
1733
"... pleaded her belly, but was found not quick with Child . She confessed that she had practiced Coining for 8 Years past". She was

drawn in a sledge to Tyburn, chained to a stake, first strangled and then burnt. A male coiner was hanged and slashed across the body.
1738. "*One Mrs. Carter, and her Servant Maid, have been committed to New-Prison for diminishing Guineas by filing them, some to the Value of 1s. 6d., and others to 1s. the Husband escaping who is equally guilty, and for apprehending of whom, or Francis Kelham his Accomplice, or any other Person concerned in filing Guineas, His Majesty has promised on Conviction a Reward of £100. besides what is allowed by Act of Parliament.*"
"*Executed at Tyburn, Jonathan Thomas for filing Guineas, who was drawn on the Sled.*"
"*A Man and his Wife were try'd at Hick's-Hall, for counterfeiting Sixpences, by filing the Britannia Side of Copper Farthings, and silvering them over; and were adjudg'd to imprisonment and hard Labour for one Year.*"
1739
"*Condemn'd for High Treason in diminishing the Coin.*"
1741
"*Several evil dispos'd Persons have practis'd the making of Shillings and Sixpences to resemble Guineas and Half Guineas by putting Scepters upon the Reverse, and guilding them over.*" Readers were advised to make sure that there was no Robe or Drapery on the Shoulders of guineas presented. These only appeared on the silver coins.

SCOTS MAGAZINE
1748
"*.. committed to prison for coining and uttering bad halfpence, the tools being found at their lodgings, which they had exercis'd above 20 years.*"
1750
"*.. for coining, to be transported for life.*"
"*.. convicted for coining halfpence, and sentenced two years imprisonment in Newgate.*"
1751
"*One Wood, a [h]awker, having published advertisements at Birmingham for the sale of goods to be paid for in counterfeit halfpence, was taken into custody, but released on consenting to the cutting of what halfpence he had taken, which amounted to £7. The halfpence were cut by a brazier, and sold as metal, and his advertisements burnt.*"
"*Was seiz'd at an inn, and carried to the Tower, about 400 weight of bad half-pence; 60 of these weigh about a pound, and consequently the makers get 2s. 6d. for what is not worth above 9d.*"
1752
"*I have also wronged my country by coining money.*" Highway robber's confession.
"*A notorious gang of coiners were examined before Justice Fielding, when it appeared that they had in a cellar in one of their houses, a press fixed for striking off moidores. The date of these moidores is 1721. The solicitor of the mint directed their press to be sent to the tower, which weigh'd 900 weight, and was in as good order as any at the mint.*"

"A woman was apprehended for putting off counterfeit guineas, 50 of which it is said were circulated at Horn-Fair by her and her gang."
1754
Ayr. *"Timothy and Patrick Harley, were accused of uttering counterfeited coin, knowing it to be so. The Advocate-Depute consented to restrict the libel to an arbitrary punishment: The libel being found proven, the pannels are sentenced to be whipped through the streets of the town on Friday the 26th curt. and to be transported for seven years."*
Warning of counterfeit halfpence and farthings - *"the letters flatter than is true."*
1758
"Information was brought ... that a considerable quantity of French money called deux sous, were made and concealed in the house of one Cartwright in the Strand, upon which Mr. Welsh, by an order from the secretary of state, went to the said house, assisted by a messenger, and two constables, and seized near 14 Cwt of them; two persons were taken into custody for this offence, and bound over to answer at the next sessions the complaint of the solicitor of the mint."

"Richard William Vaughan, late a linnen-draper at Stafford, was committed to Newgate for counterfeiting the notes of the bank of England. He had employed several artists to engrave the different parts of the note, by one of whom the discovery was made. He had filled up to the number of 20, and deposited them in the hands of a young lady, whom he courted, as a proof of his being a person of substance. This is the first attempt of the kind that ever was made."
He died for love - at Tyburn.

1764
"Timothy Rhodes and his wife were lately committed to Ilchester goal, for making base shillings: The discovery was made by their apprentice, who being questioned in passing one of them, ignorantly said, 'he'd go whome and chaunge it, for that his maister made 'em'."
1770
"At Kylsyth, in Scotland, a cart, with a chest upon it, was seized in the street. In the chest, were three bags of counterfeit half-pence, and a bundle, containing two bags of the same, all of base metal and by appearance lately cast, as they were partly joined two and two together."
1772
"At this Sessions, John Davis, for selling to Hugh Evans 84 pieces of counterfeit money resembling shillings, for three guineas, was branded in the hand, and ordered to be imprisoned."

1773
THE SETTING OF GOLD COIN STANDARDS
"This day the Royal Assent was given to a bill .. for preventing the counterfeiting or diminishing the gold coin. By this bill, the several receivers of the public revenue are empowered to cut and deface all unlawfully diminished coin that shall be tendered to them in payment; and all gold coin under the weight here specified, is to be considered by them as unlawfully diminished:

	dwts.	gr.
Guineas coined prior to 1st Geo. III	5	3
Half guineas during the above period	2	13
Guineas coined during the reign of his present Majesty, prior to 1st Jan. 1772	5	6
Half guineas during the same period	2	14
Quarter guineas	1	7
Half guineas coined subsequent to do.	2	14
Gs coined subsequent to 1st Jan. 1772	5	8

"*But for accommodating the holders of light money, the receivers are empowered to accept all such cut money in payment, at the rate of £3. 18s. per ounce; and the Bank of England will purchase cut money at the same rate.*"

"*The new guineas now in circulation are already counterfeited or diminished. Out of 120 of them, brought this day to the Bank, 80 were cut that were deficient in weight.*"

1774

"*Information having been given to Sir John Fielding, that a company of coiners made a business of coining halfpence in a house on Fish-street-hill, that magistrate applied to the Lord Mayor for his warrant to apprehend them, which he obtained, and sent five of his people, well-armed, to take them by surprize. There were no less than eight of them at work, who, when they found themselves discovered, endeavoured to make resistance, and one of them received a ball in his head before he surrendered.*

"*The night before, they had sent a child for some beer, with new halfpence to pay for it; and the landlord observing to the child that they were warm, she innocently replied, that her daddy had just made them. A cart-load of implements were found in the house, and carried to Bowstreet.*"

1775

"*Consideration of the Means of preventing fraudulent Practices on the Gold Coin.*" Written at Geneva in 1773 by Lord Viscount Mahon, F.R.S, 4to. pp.17. 1s. Shropshire.

1783

"*Mary Holt, whose husband was executed at Tyburn a few years ago for burglary, has since been taken up for circulating counterfeit shillings and six-pences, which clearly appear to have been cast in the moulds seized upon Dowgate Hill.*"

1786

At this time, coining silver was regarded as high treason, and a capital offence for both men and women. For some strange reason, women were executed differently from men.

"*Phoebe Harris, the female convict, was led by two officers to a stake, about eleven feet high, fixed in the ground, near the top of which was an inverted curve made of iron, to which one end of a halter was tied. The prisoner stood on a low stool, which, after the Ordinary had prayed with her a short time, was taken away, and she hung suspended by her neck, her feet being scarcely more than twelve or fourteen inches from the pavement. Soon after the signs of life had ceased, two cartloats of fagots were placed round her, and set on fire; the flames soon burning the halter. She then sunk a few inches, but was supported by an iron chain passed over her chest, and affixed to the stake. It was more than three hours before the fire was extinguished.*"

1787

"*It was then determined immediately to commence a new coinage; and in order to put a total stop to counterfeit half-pence and farthings, which is now so great a burthen to the public, it was resolved that, in the new arrangement, one pound of copper should be made into twenty-four half-pence, instead of eight and forty, which has been the practice hitherto, and the farthings in the same proportion of size and weight.*"

1788

In this year, the sentences announced became more vicious, "*the man to be hanged and quartered, the woman to be burnt alive*", but the actual executions were as before.

1789

Denton was an accomplished craftsman from northern Yorkshire, who imitated "*the current coin in a manner that deceived the best judges, and held the court seven hours upon his trial, and at last he was acquitted of coining; but convicted on having the implements for coining in his possession,*" and executed the same day.

19th Century

18th April,1804 - "*Two individuals had passed 20 dollars with false stamps and had in their possession 30 more; the Bank wanted to know how to prosecute them. The case put to Piggott (Sir Arthur Piggott, the Bank's counsel) was that dollars worth from 4s 3d to 4s 9d each were circulated 'for the accommodation of the public' at 5s each with the promise of redemption at the latter price. The difference was sufficient to tempt people to forge the stamp on the coins and pass them off as being issued from the Bank. Now the bank admitted that the issue was one of 'Public convenience, not supported by any Act of Parliament or Proclamation', but they claimed that, whether or no they were issued with authority, the imitation of them was a cheat and punishable at Common Law, as individuals would accept them thinking that the security of a 'public body' guaranteed their genuineness.*" Piggott said the Bank had no more rights than any other individuals, so a bill was hurriedly put forward and became law on the 10th July and an announcement was issued to the public two weeks later saying "*In future any one who shall make, coin or counterfeit, or cause or procure to be made with intent to resemble or look like dollars would be judged guilty of a Felony and be transported for up to seven years.*" Importing counterfeits was considered to be an equivalent offence.

At the start of the nineteenth century, prosecutions for coining diminished. In Somerset, between 1810 and 1855, there were 238 prosecutions, mostly for uttering. Sentences ranged from four days to two years. Anyone found in possession of about 30 base sixpences, shillings and halfcrowns would get 12 months' imprisonment. The

English Coinage Act of 1810 covered base metal and colonial coin counterfeiting.

The Bank was on weaker legal ground with token forgers compared to dollar forgers, so it indemnified its Birmingham Agent, Payne, against breaking in on suspected forgers and finding no evidence of their efforts. When doing so, he was to ensure that he had a fully motivated team to catch the perpetrators off-guard and, hopefully, in the act of coining or forgery. Birmingham was notoriously the centre of such illegal operations at that time.

26th June 1811
"*An Act to prevent the counterfeiting of Silver Pieces denominated Tokens, intended to be issued and circulated by the Governor and the Company of the Bank of England, for the respective sums of Five Shillings and Sixpence, Three Shillings and One Shilling and Sixpence; and to prevent the bringing in to the Kingdom or uttering any such counterfeit Pieces or Tokens.*"

Bath Chronicle, 15th August 1811.
"*Bank Tokens. Counterfeiters are liable to seven years transportation; Utterers, first time, six months imprisonment; second time, two years imprisonment; third time, fourteen years imprisonment.*"

An alternative third time punishment was fourteen years' transportation.

In July 1812, a bill was drafted to double the penalty for uttering forged 3s Bank Tokens from six months to twelve, making it the same as for forged sixpences. One Bank token forger escaped prosecution because if found guilty he would only face imprisonment and he was already a French prisoner of war in Portchester Castle!

The forgery of Banknotes, presumably because of their higher 'value', appears to have been regarded as more heinous than coin counterfeiting. In the early nineteenth century it was still a capital offence. It got William Booth publicly hanged at Stafford in 1812. The year before he had been producing penny tokens at Perry Barr which obviously led him astray into more precise but less legal engraving.

1815
"*List of Crimes punished with Death by the Law of England, includes:*

Edward III	*High treason, which comprehends the offence of counterfeiting the coin.*
William & Mary	*Buying, selling, or having any mould for coining.*
George II	*Gilding a shilling to make it look like a guinea.*
George III	*Coining of a half-penny or a farthing. Uttering counterfeits, third offence.*

1820
"*Statement of the number of Criminal Offenders in his Majesty's Gaol -*

of Newgate, who were convicted at the Old Bailey Sessions in the year 1819.
- Uttering forged notes - 14 (4 executed in 1819)
- Having possession of forged Bank-notes without lawful excuse - 80 (none executed)
-Uttering counterfeit coin - 10 (none executed)."

In Britain in 1820, 46 people were executed for forging or uttering counterfeit coins.

When William IV came to the throne in 1830 "*there were .. at present sixty-one Acts relating to the crime of forgery, where death was inflicted.*"

In the Royal Mint collection is a punch for the production of a counterfeit coin of George IV, c.1830. Two men, Buckle and Andrews, were arrested while working on it, tried and executed - Britain's last execution for forgery.

In 1831, coining ceased to carry the death penalty in Britain, formalised in the 1832 Act, "*for consolidating and amending the Laws against Offences relating to the Coin" (23rd May).* This set out all the anti-counterfeiting Acts from Edward I's time and repealed and consolidated them into this one Act.

The top punishment was thenceforth "*to be transported beyond the Seas for Life or for any Term not less than Seven Years, or to be imprisoned, with or without hard Labour, for any Term not exceeding Four Years.*" This applied not only to forgers but to anyone gilding, silvering, filing or altering any coin to make it pass for a higher value.

The punishment for clippers and diminishers was "*to be transported beyond the Seas for any Term not exceeding Fourteen Years nor less than Seven Years, or to be imprisoned for any Term not exceeding Three Years.*" Distributors or importers could face transportation for not less than seven years or imprisonment not exceeding four years. Utterers could be imprisoned for up to a year, rising to two years if carrying more than one counterfeit. A second offence could bring the top punishment down on them. Offences involving copper coins were less severe. The Act also covered the possession of counterfeiting tools and the illegal possession of Mint tools. People were permitted from then on to cut, break or deface any counterfeit presented to them.

PUNISHING THE COINS

A nineteenth century Polish count stamped all the coins in his collection that he judged to be not genuine with a minutely lettered word – FALSVS.

A 'credible witness' was all that was needed in Court to prove that a piece was counterfeit.

1833
"The new sixpences lately coined have the word sixpence impressed on them, to prevent their being passed, when gilt, as half sovereigns, a fraud which had been committed to a great extent by passing gilt sixpences of a former coinage."

VICTORIAN PREVENTATIVE MEASURES
4th August 1853
An Act for the punishment of offences in the Colonies in relation to the Coin.
- an Act for preventing the sale of medals resembling coins.

By the passing of the Coinage Offences Act, 1861, it became obligatory upon justices to deliver up false and counterfeit coin either to the Mint, to the Treasury Solicitor, or to any person authorised by them to receive it. This is still the law by virtue of the Coinage Offences Act, 1936, but in the eighteenth and early nineteenth centuries the position was dependent on whether the forged coin was of silver or copper, and upon whether it had been "brought into court" or not.

> ME HAWKEYE - YOU NO TRY!
>
> Once upon a time, shop-keepers would nail counterfeits to their counters - in the hope, no doubt, of discouraging customers from presenting others to them.

10th July 1864
An Act to prevent the counterfeiting of Silver Coin.

25th August 1883
The 1883 statute, known as The Counterfeit Medals Act, prohibited the manufacture, possession and/or sale of any medal or similar object resembling a coin of the realm.

A draft clause for prohibiting the importation of imitation coins appeared in 1889.

A Proclamation of 1890 classified British gold coins as 'current' if minted after Victoria's accession in 1838. It spelt out in detail how the laws covered the importation of imitation coins intended to pass as if of currency value, either as they were or after treatment of any sort, e.g. gilding.

One counterfeiter got seven years' transportation; served it, returned to England, and resumed his old ways! He 'uttered' in the Bolton and Blackburn areas, preferring to buy counterfeits rather than make them any more, being chronically but unsurprisingly afraid of being caught when engaged in manufacture.

20th Century

In 1935, International Police forces published a joint effort to fight counterfeiters. A world war then interrupted and it was not until Interpol's publication of 1963 that a further effort was made. This covered paper and metal money, providing a reference to what it should be like for the then current money of many countries.

The Counterfeit Currency (Convention) Act of 1935 embraced current foreign coinage as well as British. The Coinage Offences Act of 1936 declared it an offence to counterfeit, file or alter *current coin*, or to utter, trade in or own counterfeit current coin. The maximum penalty for some of these offences was life imprisonment. Although the Act had one definition of 'current' as "any coin made in Her Majesty's mints", i.e. *including* coins not currently legal tender, this definition has not been accepted by at least one foreign court. The Act also stated that it was an offence to buy, sell, receive, pay, put off, offer to buy... any false or counterfeit coin at a lower cost than its denomination without lawful authority or excuse.

SECTION 8 of the Coinage Offences Act contains the following provision:
Every person who, without lawful authority or excuse (the proof whereof shall lie on him) makes, sells, offers for sale or has in his possession for sale, any medal, cast, coin or other like thing made wholly or partially of metal or any mixture of metals and either (a) resembling in size, figure and colour any current gold or silver coin; or (b) having thereon a device resembling a device on any such current coin; or (c) being so formed that it can by gilding, silvering, colouring, washing or other like process be so dealt with as to resemble any such current coin, commits an offence. The reference to gold and silver seems to exclude pound coins, and also to exclude simple possession of the objects. In the UK, a counterfeit gold coin is not a coin and therefore should by law be hallmarked. To be hallmarked, it must conform to one of the four permitted standards of fineness for gold - 22, 18, 14 and 9 carat. No genuine gold coins match these standards.

A target of the Paris Conference of 1965 was to encourage Governments to create a specific offence covering the counterfeiting of coins no longer legally current, i.e. those aimed at collectors, dealers and museums. The U.S. Hobby Protection Act of 1973 requires manufacturers and importers to mark reproduction coins with the word 'copy'.

THE 'FUNNY MONEY" SQUAD

Currently, as laid down by the 1986 Act, the penalty for counterfeiting coin of the realm is a maximum of ten years' imprisonment or an unlimited fine or both. In Britain in 1989, about 2,500 counterfeit coins were being recovered annually by the police. There is a Counterfeit Currency Squad, known as the 'funny money' squad and a Forgeries and Counterfeits Display in Scotland Yard's Black Museum. The Royal Mint, although no longer actively pursuing counterfeiters, still provides an expert advisory service to the police and courts.

Most current laws are designed to protect against the counterfeiting of current coinage. Security devices are designed to prevent currency fraud. The author knows of none intended to counter the forgers targetting collectors.

EUROPEAN PUNISHMENTS

With the demise of the Roman Empire in Western Europe, coinage became less significant, and the crime of forging was downgraded to theft with the lesser punishment of a hand being amputated. This lasted until the importance of coinage returned at the start of the thirteenth century. From then until the sixteenth century in France, the Low Countries, North Germany and Switzerland, counterfeiters were boiled in cauldrons. Roman law then returned, bringing back with it burning as punishment.

ORDEAL BY FIRE

In other parts of Europe, a person suspected of counterfeiting had to undergo trial by fire. His hand would be placed in fire. If he withstood the pain, he was innocent. If he felt pain, he was guilty!

The customary punishment for a woman was burning. Men could suffer drowning, hanging, drawing and quartering, blinding - and still counterfeiting continued.

There were some discouraging ways in which a forger could lose his life, depending in which part of Europe he was caught.

Country	Death by
England	Hanging
France	Breaking on the wheel
Germany	Boiling in Oil
Russia	Molten lead down the throat
Elsewhere	Beheading

(left) this shows what used to happen to some continental coiners in medieval times. They were boiled alive after having been given a break!

This plated counterfeit of a gold ecu au soleil of Louis XI of France (1461-1483), was found at Logne Castle in France where it had been struck with forged dies. The castle was destroyed in 1521 as punishment for coin forgery.

FRANCE

In 1356, the Chevalier Bouchard de Poissy, found guilty of forging a seal, was fined 4,000 livres and banished from Paris. In 1521 Logne Castle in France was destroyed to discourage the counterfeiting that had been going on therein.

Louis IX: Convicted forgers should be hanged "*and presented to the wind.*"

In the early nineteenth century, forging legal tender in France was punishable by death. By mid-century this had become life imprisonment. By the middle of the twentieth century, the cessation of gold coinage as legal tender led to a rash of false napoleons made exactly to the genuine specification to profit from the greater value put on the gold in coin form compared to bar. This loophole was closed in the mid 1960's by invoking a penal clause for punishing "*those who have counterfeited the seal, punch or mark of whatsoever authority...*"

The skilful counterfeiters of the five franc nickel coin of 1932 were less skilful at evading capture, and then again more skilful at evading punishment, by pointing out that the law against counterfeiting did not cover nickel. It did soon after.

GERMANY

The early Germanic law, EDICTUM ROTHARI, stipulated that anyone minting coins without Royal permission risked having a hand cut off.

IRELAND

"*There being divers coiners in the city of Cork, the towns of Yoghil, Kinsale and Killmallock, viz. John Fannin, John Crone, Patrick Martel, William Synnot, Mortagh O Haurighan, Nicholas Rewy, and others, who make false coines without authority, only the said John Fannin shews letters patent which are not of record, to the great damage of the said city, towns and counties; it is enacted, that if the said coiners do not appear before the deputy in parliament the first day of the next prorogation or adjournment, that they shall be attained as traitors, and their lands, tenements, goods and chattels, forfeited; and, that it shall be lawful for James earl of Desmond, the mayors of Cork and Yoghill, and the soverains of Kinsale and Killmallock, to apprehend them and execute the law on their persons as traitors attained; and that no body shall maintain, support, harbour or succour them, under the penalty of forfeiting their goods and chattels, lands and tenements to the king, and their bodies to be at his will; and all letters patent shown by the said coiners to be void.*" 1472 Report.

THE ISLE OF MAN

Most penal codes made forging copper coins a lesser offence. The exception was the Isle of Man, where the 1646 Act of Tynwald decreed death by hanging and forfeiture of all property for counterfeiting base-metal farthings and halfpennies (duckatoons).

ITALY

In the sixteenth century, Tobbia, a noted Milanese goldsmith, was condemned to be burnt for counterfeiting the current coin. Because of his artistic skills with gold, he was reprieved by the Pope who then employed him.

SWITZERLAND
The Swiss Penal Code covers the forging of non-current coinage as "*falsification of merchandise.*"

The earliest known publication warning against counterfeit coins, was a leaflet issued at Augsburg in 1480.

As coinage spread around the world, so did the need to protect it.

ISLAM
Early eighth century mintworkers had their hands branded or tattooed - and cut off if they forged!

CHINA
At one time, Chinese counterfeiters were so successful that the Government, in despair, offered the best of them lucrative jobs at the Royal Mint! The oldest known example of paper money comes from fourteenth century China, where counterfeiting was always rife. It carried a warning to counterfeiters that they will be beheaded.

USA
Virginia 1645 Act - death penalty for counterfeiters and passers.

In 1682, William Penn and friends, not long arrived in Philadelphia, were annoyed to find false money circulating in the Quaker community. Three were caught, charged with and convicted of "*Quining of Spanish Bitts and Boston money*", even though the silver was as good as in the coins copied.

1692 Act
"An Act Against the Counterfeiting, Clipping, Rounding, Filing or Impairing of Coynes."

(left) the mildest physical punishment meted out by soft-hearted judges in America in the eighteenth century America, was a period in the pillory. However, this was usually accompanied by flogging.

Colonial Penalties included gallows hanging, ear-cropping, hand-lopping, hot-iron branding and life sentences. Virginia 1714 Act – counterfeiting of all current coins (including foreign) to be high treason. Amended in 1729 to include copper coinage.

U.S REGULATIONS
Section 8.16.020 Unlawful to produce false coins.

It shall be unlawful for any person, with intent to cheat or defraud the owner, lessee, licensee or other person entitled to the contents of any vending machine, slot machine, coin-box telephone or other receptacle designed to receive or be operated by lawful coin of the United States of America in furtherance of or in connection with the sale, use or enjoyment of property or service or the use or enjoyment of any slot machine, telephone or other facilities or service, or knowingly or having cause to believe that the same is intended for fraudulent or unlawful use on the part of the purchaser, donnee or user thereof, to manufacture for sale, sell or give away any token, slug, false or counterfeited coin or any device or substance whatsoever, intended or calculated to be placed, deposited or used in any such vending machine, slot machine, coin-box telephone or other receptacle. (Ord.21 § 1 (part), 1953)
Any person who shall violate any of the provisions of this chapter shall be guilty of a misdemeanor. (Ord. 1492 § 4, 1994: Ord. 117, 1955; Ord. 21 § 2)

The U.S. Secret Service was founded in 1865 to fight counterfeiting. It has since diversified! It publishes a booklet entitled *Know Your Money.*

SOUTH AFRICA
In 1891 in the South African Republic, the penalty for contravening the Mint's exclusive right to coin money, was a fine of one thousand pounds sterling or imprisonment with or without hard labour, for a period not exceeding five years or with both - for every contravention.

VENEZUELA
In Venezuela, you cannot be guilty of forgery if you create a new type of coin "*with original characteristics, completely different from existing coins, even when an endeavour is made to pass them off as coins.*" Coins of any country that have ceased to be current are not covered by Venezuela's forgery laws. If you make or own counterfeiting equipment, you risk 6 to 30 months' imprisonment. If you successfully inform on a coiner, you get his metal.

Some countries ordered counterfeit coins to be spiked.
Other countries extended this idea to the actual coiners.

References

CHAPTER THREE
Celtic Tribal Platers

14

[HE]HEDGES, E.S. & ROBINS, D.A., 1963. Examination of an Ancient British Bronze Coin. NC 7th Series, Vol. III. London: RNS, pp. 233-6. *Metallographic examination of a Potin.*

15

[CA]CASEY, J. & REECE, R. (eds), 1988- 2nd Edition. Coins and the Archaeologist. *A functionalist approach to pre-Roman coinage* by John Collis, pp. 4-7.

[HA]HASELGROVE, C., 1984. Celtic Coins Found in Britain, 1977-82. London: Institute of Archaeology reprint from Bulletin No. 20.

HOBBS, R., 1996. British Iron Age Coins in the British Museum, London: British Museum Publications. *Numerous references to contemporary counterfeits.*

VAN ARSDELL, R.D., 1989. Celtic Coinage of Britain. London: Spink. *Van Arsdell lists ancient plated coins for 82 different types, and 39 types for which modern forgeries were known. He logs 26 types awaiting scientific verification.*

CHAPTER FOUR
Rampant Roman Counterfeiting

17

[CR]CRAWFORD, M.H., 1968. (Roman) Plated Coins - False Coins. NC 7th Series, Vol. VIII, pp. 55-9, pl.XIV.

[KE]KENT, J.P.C., A Brief Technical History of Coining in Britain. BANS 14, p. 44.

18

[KE]KENT, J.P.C., A Brief Technical History of Coining in Britain. BANS 14.

21

[SE]SELLWOOD, D., 1981. NC 1981, p. vii, pl. 38-9. *Illustrates test cuts.*

24

[SU]SUTHERLAND, C.H.V., 1963. A Late Julio-Claudian Aes Hoard from Worcester. NC 7th Series, Vol. III. London: RNS. pp. 57-9.

25

[SY]SYMONS, D., 1984. A Roman Plated Denarius. SCMB 10/1984, pp. 250-1.

26

[OR]ORNA-ORNSTEIN, J. & KENYON, R. North Suffolk. Coin Hoards from Roman Britain, Vol. X. London: British Museum Publications, pp. 37-46, pl. 2-5. *Detailed examination of the Waveney hoard of plated Claudian denarii, with illustrations of 110 pieces.*

27

[BR]BROWN, R.A., 1981. An Unusual counterfeit Denarius of the Reign of Nero. NC 141, pp. 145-6, pl. 27b.

[TA]TAMEANKO, M., 1999. The "Hudaea Navalis" Coin: A spurious record of historical fact. Coin News, August 1999, pp. 25-7.

Abbreviations

BANS	British Association of Numismatic Societies	OUP	Oxford University Press
BNJ	British Numismatic Journal	RNS	Royal Numismatic Society
CUP	Cambridge University Press	SCBI	Sylloge of Coins of the British Isles
NC	Numismatic Chronicle	SCMB	Seaby's Coin & Medal Bulletin
		SNC	Spink's Numismatic Circular

33

[BO]BOON, G.C., 1965. Light-weights and 'Limesfalsa'. NC 7th Series, Vol. 5, pp. 161-74, pl. XVI-XVII. *Detailed investigation of these lightweight cast aes copies of the late 2nd, early 3rd centuries, plus illustrations of 25 Limesfalsa.*

38

[DA]DAVIES, J.A., 1988. Barbarous radiates: a study of the irregular Roman coinage of the 270s and 280s AD from southern England. (PhD Thesis) Reading University 1988. *(Copies can be obtained from The British Library Documents Supply Centre. The only problem is the poor reproduction of the photos). Die and style links are examined in detail, pp. 103-44 (+).*

39

[WE]WEDER, M.R., 1994. The Coinage of Aurelian and Roman Imperial Mint Forgeries. NC 154, pp. 243-66. *In-depth look at Claudius II and Divo Claudius imitations.* A Review of Robert Göbl, Die Münzprägung des Kaiseres AURELIANUS (270/275). Vienna, 1993.

45

[HI]HICKS, A.J., 1998. Excavations at East End, Ash, 1992. AC CXVIII, pp. 91-172. *Many late Constantinian copies of 330-48 prototypes. Thought to have been produced c. 341-347.*

[KE]KENT, J.P.C., A Brief Technical History of Coining in Britain. BANS 14.

INSCRIPTION ANOMALIES

The ten volumes of Roman Imperial Coinage contain much information about Roman counterfeits, such as this example: *Aureus of Claudius (AD 41-54) inscribed DE BRITANN on the reverse. Forgeries exist with an extra letter added to the inscription - DE BRITANNI - plus an unusual obverse.*

CHAPTER FIVE
The Anglo-Saxon Lull

49

[ME]METCALF, D.M., 1966. A Coinage for Mercia under Æthelbald. BANS No. 12, pp. 30-9. *An analysis of B111 sceattas, including details and illustrations of contemporary copies, from p. 32.*

50

[BLU]BLUNT, C.A. & THOMPSON, J.D.A., 1958. Forgery in the Anglo-Saxon Series. BNJ 28, pp. 18-25, pl. 1. *Æthelbald, Æthelwulf, Alfred, Æthered, Iaenberht, Edwig, Offa. The forger altered his dies so skilfully and to so little purpose that he seems to have been showing off.*

53

[JE]JENSEN, S.S. 1985. Hikuin 11. Essays in Honour of Brita Malmer. Stockholm. *Non-English articles given English summaries. Includes a look at 'peck-marks' on Anglo-Saxon coins in Scandinavia, by Dr. Metcalf; English dies in Scandinavia, by Dr. Blackburn; Æthelred II imitations in Europe, by Dr. Suchodolski, etc.*

54

[BLA]BLACKBURN, M., & CHOWN, J., 1984. A die-link between the Sigtuna coinage of Olaf Skötkonung and some Long Cross imitations reading 'OCLOD'. NC 144, pp. 166-72, pl. 30.

[SC]SCBI 2, pl. XXXI.

[ST]STEWART, I., 1978. A Lead Striking of William II's Last Coin-type. NC 138, pp. 185-7. *He describes the piece as having a pumice-like texture reminiscent of the base-metal core of medieval forgeries that had once been plated.*

CHAPTER SIX
Post-Conquest problems from the Continent

57

[ST]STEWART, I.S., 1958. A New Norman Forger. BNJ 58, pp. 190-1, pl. XIV.

63

[MU]MUNRO, J.H., 1981. Mint Policies, Ratios and Outputs in the Low Countries and England, 1335-1420: Some Reflections on New Data, NC 141, pp. 71-ff.

[WO]WOODHEAD, P., 1996. English Gold Coins and their Imitations, 1257-1603. SCBI 47. London: Spink. *Contains in-depth descriptions and extensive illustrations of these imitations.*

CHAPTER SEVEN
Golden Reflections

66

[AR1]ARCHIBALD, M.M., 1970. Wyre Piddle (Worcs.) 1967 Hoard of Fifteenth-Century Silver Coins. NC 7th Series, Vol. 10, pp. 133-62, pl. 11-12.
[AR2]ARCHIBALD, M.M., 1980. The Queenhithe Hoard, BNJ 50, pp. 61-6. *This hoard is also known as The Bull Wharf Hoard.*

CHAPTER EIGHT
Tudors, Stuarts and advancing technology

69

[BO]BOON, G.C., 1976. An Early Tudor Coiner's Mould. Reprinted from the Transactions of the Cumberland & Westmorland Antiquarian & Archaeological Society, Vol. LXXVI - New Series. *Plates I & II show the mould and impressions taken from it.*
[CH]CHALLIS, C.E., 1978. The Tudor Coinage. Manchester: Manchester University Press.

71

[PR]PRIDMORE, F., 1962. Documentary Evidence Relating to Countermarking. SNC January 1962, pp. 1-3. SNC February 1962, pp. 30-2.

72

[WE]WEIGHTMAN, A.E., 1907. The Royal Farthing Tokens, Part I, 1613-1636. BNJ, 1906, pp. 181-217, pl. I & II.

76

[NA]NATHANSON, A.J., 1975. Thomas Simon, His life and work. London, Seaby.

77

[RO]ROWE, C.M., 1966. Salisbury's Local Coinage. Salisbury: Tisbury Printing Works. *Tradesmen's tokens issued in Salisbury during the middle of the seventeenth century.*

81

[MI]MITCHINER , M.B. & SKINNER, A., 1986. Contemporary Forgeries Of Late Seventeenth Century English Tin Coins: the Implications for the Study of Leaden Tokens. NC 146, pp. 178-84, pl. 23. *William III forgeries.*

83

[MI]MITCHINER, M., 1998. Jetons, Medalets and Tokens, Vol. 3. London: Hawkins, pp. 1761-4. *Illustrates over 40 Anne counters.*

CHAPTER NINE
Georgian Epidemics

102

[SHE]SHERLOCK, R.J., 1958. A Hoard of Forged Bank of England Tokens. BNJ 28, pp. 423-4.

103

[SHA]SHARP, M., 1989. A Hoard of Defaced Forged Halfpence of the Reign of George III. BNJ 59, pp. 214-6, pl. 18.

104

[DA]DALTON, R. & HAMER, S., 1910, reprinted 1977. The Provincial Token-Coinage of the 18th Century, Massachusetts: Quarterman, pp. 350, 366.
KENT, J.P.C., 1957. Forgery in the reign of George III: the problem of medley halfpence; mss in BM Dept of Coins & Medals. (read to the BNS in May 1957).

109

[BE]BELL, R.C., 1975. Unofficial Farthings.

CHAPTER ELEVEN
Scotland
121
[FE]FERGUSON, W.B. & JONES, I., 1998. Imitation Pennies of the Second Coinage of Alexander III of Scotland. SNC November 1998, pp. 391-3.
122
[HO]HOLMES, N., 1998. Scottish Coins; a history of small change in Scotland. Edinburgh: NMS Publishing. *Illustrates ten Scottish counterfeits and a stone mould for casting Charles I or II counterfeit turners.*
[HO1]HOLMES, N.M.McQ., 1998. Scottish Coin Hoards: Culross, Fife, 1996. BNJ 68, pp. 90-4. *121 billon plack counterfeits of James VI - 1583-1590 period.*
[MU]MURRAY, J.E.L., 1987. The (counterfeit) Coinage of the Marians in Edinburgh Castle in 1572. BNJ 57, 1987 (1988), pp. 47-53, internal pl.
[RA]RAMPLING, D.J. & MURRAY, J.E.L., 1989. The Coinage of the Marians in Edinburgh Castle in 1572 – An Addendum. BNJ 59, p. 213, pl. 17.

CHAPTER TWELVE
Ireland
126
[BL]BLACKBURN, M.A.S., 1975. Hiberno-Norse imitations of Watchet *Long Cross* coins. NC 135, pp. 195-7, pl. 18, 3-6.
128
[SE]SEABY, W.A. & BRADY, G., 1973. The Extant Ormonde Pistoles and Double Pistoles of 1646. BNJ 43, pp. 80-95, pl. II. London: BNS. *Covers counterfeits.*
130
[MI]MITCHINER, M., 1998. Jetons, Medalets and Tokens, Vol. 3. London: Hawkins, p. 1786. *Illustrates Roche's Voce Populi halfpenny and two halfpenny forgeries - 1769 and 1775.*

CHAPTER THIRTEEN
The Coiners
136
[LA]LAWRENCE, L.A., 1905, 1906, 1907. Forgery in Relation to Numismatics, Part I (Anglo-Saxon), BNJ 2, 1st Series, pp. 397-409, pl. I-V. ; Part I (cont.) (Anglo-Saxon to Norman), BNJ 3, 1st Series, pp. 281-290, pl. I-VI. ; Part II (Edward I. to Elizabeth). BNJ 4, 1st Series, pp. 311-6, pl. I-V.
141
[KL]KLAWANS, Z.H., 1977. Imitations and Inventions of Roman Coins. Renaissance Medals of Julius Caesar and the Roman Empire. Santa Monica, USA: The Society for International Numismatics. *Illustrates most of the imitation sestertii known as 'Paduans', produced by Cavino and others in Padua, Italy in the mid to late sixteenth century.*
142
[JO]JONES, Mark (Ed.), 1990. Fake? the Art of Deception. London: Trustees of the British Museum, pp. 137-8. *The coins referred to in the text, the Aeneas, the Lysander, etc. are illustrated in this book.*
[VA]VASARI, G. Life of Belli. Part of his Lives, published by Bohn, London (Standard Library Edition - 1850-2), pp. iii, 477-8.
[VI]VICO, E., 1691 (reprint of 1555 Venice edition). Discorso sopra le medaglie deglie antichi. In Miscellanea italica erudita, Vol. II. Parma.
144
[BE]BELLESIA, L., 1995. La zecca dei Pico, Publi-Paolini. *Mirandola.*
145
[FR] FREEDMAN, D.S., 1969. New Evidence concerning the authenticity of the 1655 Half-crown. BNJ 38, pp. 190-3.
146
[HO]HOBLYN, R.A., 1878. 18 April. Exhibited a "complete set of the coins struck in 1828 by Mr. M. Young

from original dies obtained by him from a member of the Roettier family". NC N.S. Vol. 18 (1878). Proceedings (1877/8), p. 9.

149

DO DOLLEY, R.H.M., 1963. Two 'Unique' Plantagenet Pennies from Midlands Mints (portions from paper read at Coventry Congress, 1961). BANS No. 9, 1963, pp. 29-36, 4 coin illus.
A) The 'Oxford' Short-Cross Penny of Henry III (John White forgery).
B) The 'Lichfield' Short-Cross Penny of Richard I (probable John White forgery).

156

MIa MITCHINER, M., 1998. Jetons, Medalets and Tokens, Vol. 3. London: Hawkins, p. 1907. *Tells Milton's story and lists his output.*

TH THOMPSON, R.H., 1969. The Dies of Thomas Spence (1750-1814). BNJ 38. Oxford: BNS, pp. 126-62, pl. VI-VIII + plan; 1971. BNJ 40, pp. 136-8.

157

MIb MITCHINER, M., 1998. Jetons, Medalets and Tokens, Vol. 3. London: Hawkins, pp. 1978, 1988, 1990-1, 1995. *Contains Lutwyche references.*

161

HI HILL, Sir G.F., 1995 reprint of 1924 edition. Becker the Counterfeiter. Parts 1 and 2 in one volume. New York: Durst. Also 1955 Spink reprint. *Lists, describes and illustrates over 350 of Becker's Greek, Roman and medieval pieces.*

SE SESTINI, D., 1826. Sopra i modernai falsificatori di medaglie greche antiche (On modern forgers of ancient Greek coins). Florence.

167

DE DEMETRIADI, V. & HEPWORTH, R.G., 1984. Forgeries of Boeotian Autonomous Staters. NC 144 (1984). London: RNS, pp. 186-91, pl. 33. *This illustrates actual forgeries. One shows an undertype from the following century!*

JO JONES, M., 1990. Fake? The Art of Deception. London: Trustees of the British Museum, pp. 145-6. *Illustrates what is said to be Caprara's first known forgery - a silver piece of Mithradates VI of Pontus.*

SE SESTINI, D., 1826. Sopra i modernai falsificatori di medaglie greche antiche (On modern forgers of Ancient Greek coins). Florence. *He also covers Caprara.*

168

BRU BRUNETTI, L. 1966. Opus Monetale Cigoi. Trièste. 158 pp. 14 plates. *Describes and illustrates nearly a thousand Cigoi forgeries of false Roman Republican & Imperial, Byzantine and medieval Italian coins.*

169

BRO BROOKE, G.C., 1932; 1950, 3rd Edition, revised by C.A. Whitton. English Coins. London: Methuen.

GR GRIERSON, P. & BLACKBURN, M., 1986. Medieval European Coinage. 1. The Early Middle Ages (5th-10th centuries). Cambridge: CUP, pp. 337-8. *Anglo-Saxon forgeries. Two Emery fakes illustrated, pl. 64.*

PA PAGAN, H.E., 1971. Mr Emery's Mint. BNJ XL, pp. 139-70, pl. I-II. *The most comprehensive account of Emery's activities and output, with a fine selection of illustrations of his forgeries.*

170

na n.a., 1931. Varia: Mud-rakers as Forgers (during excavations for Shadwell Dock in 1858, and later by 'Billy and Charlie', Rosemary Lane, Tower Hill, still being offered as genuine antiquities) Morning Post, 31 Aug 1931). SNC Vol. 39, 1931. November-December 1931, Parts 11-2, col. 477.

PE PECK, J. Wilson, 1970 2nd ed'n. English Copper, Tin and Bronze Coins in the British Museum, 1558-1958. London: British Museum, pp. 221-8, 361-71.

171

HA HANCOCK, V. & SPANBAUER, L., 1979. Standard Catalog of Counterfeit and Altered United States Coins. New York: Durst, pp. 21-2, 84, 96.

173

SV SVORONOS, J.N., 1974 (reprint of 1922). Christodoulos the Counterfeiter. Chicago: Ares Publishers Inc. Also a 1963 reprint in French. Synopsis de mille coins faux du faussoire C. Christodoulos. Athens

(1922); Basel and Amsterdam (1963).

174

CA CARSON, R.A.G., 1977. The Geneva Forgeries. New York: Attic Books.

175

OH O'HARA, M.D., 1974. Some Forgeries of Byzantine Gold Coins, Special Supplement to Bulletin-Circular No. 62 - May, 1974 of the International Association of Professional Numismatists. *This enlarged reprint of SCMB article, October 1973 describes and illustrates false Byzantine coins from the 'Beirut' and other 'schools'.*

176

VA VAN ARSDALL, R.D., 1984. Yet Another Surprise from the Haslemere Hoard. SNC September 1984, pp. 216-7.

VAN ARSDELL, R.D. 1985. The Hallmark of the Haslemere Forger. SNC April 1985, p. 79.

VAN ARSDELL, R.D. 1985. False Coritanian Staters from the Hand of the Haslemere Forger. SNC October 1985, pp. 259-60.

VAN ARSDELL, R.D., 1986. The Forgery of the "Haslemere Hoard". BNTA Special Publication No.1 British Numismatic Trade Association.

VAN ARSDELL, R.D., 1988. Celtic Chicanery. SNC 96, April 1988, p. 78.

178

RU RUDD, C., 1992. The Bristol Forger (of Celtic coins, d. 1992). C & M Vol. 29, No. 9 (September 1992). pp. 33-4, 6 photo pairs.

CHAPTER FOURTEEN
A Risky Business

180

GR GRIERSON, P., 1956. The Roman Law of Counterfeiting. Essays in Roman Numismatics presented to Harold Mattingly edited by R.A.G. Carson & C.H.V. Sutherland. Oxford: OUP, pp. 240-61. *Contains a full account of the legal aspects of coin forgery in the Roman world.*

Glossary

In the UK, the terms counterfeit and forgery are interchangeable, with a slight bias towards the use of counterfeiting for coinage and forgery for banknotes and documents. In the USA, counterfeiters produce contemporary fakes; forgers make fakes aimed at collectors.
This book follows the U.K. usage

ALTERED DATE
A famous example of fakers altering dates is where 1932 or 1935 George V pennies have been tooled to look like the rare 1933 date.

ARTIFICIAL TONING
Giving a coin a false patina by such means as chemical coating, burying, exposing to cigar smoke, 'cooking' inside potatoes, etc.

BARBAROUS
Very poor contemporary copies of Greek and Roman coins, from 'baa-baa', the sound of foreign tongues to the ancient Greeks. Many of these copies emanate from the barbarian tribes bordering their territories.

BARBAROUS RADIATES
British and Continental copies of antoniniani of the late third century A.D., particularly the issues of Claudius II and Tetricus I & II.

BLACK MONEY
Because of the colour of base metal silver imitations, such as the French silver deniers of the fourteenth century, black money became a general term for them. Also sometimes applied to counters, jetons and brass tokens imitating silver coins.

BRACTEATE
This is a thin medieval coin, usually in silver, with the obverse design showing through to form the reverse design, as a mirror image. Also termed 'hollow pennies'. The term is from a latin word meaning thin silver foil.

BUNGTOWN COPPERS (Bungtowns)
Imitations of British copper coins, particularly George III halfpennies, emanating from Britain and the Americas. Derivation thought to be from the slang term *bung*, meaning bribe or swindle. These crude, illegal copies circulated in Pennsylvania and other North-Eastern states of America when it was still a British colony in the late eighteenth century. Amongst them are to be found examples with risible legends. Because of these non-standard legends, the coins could be claimed not to be direct counterfeits of genuine coins, and for this reason they were also called Regal Evasions.

CHISEL CUTS
The little nicks that crop up on ancient coins were most probably made by traders checking the coin metal for plating.. Counterfeit *and* genuine British Iron Age staters and Roman denarii often have these small nicks on their edges.

CHOP MARKS
Individual countermarks or Chinese letters impressed on coins by Asian merchants and bankers (Hong Kong in particular), to indicate that the coins were genuine. Also to save the merchant having constantly to recheck coins already checked, as they passed through his hands again. The commonest coins so marked were Mexican and Latin American dollars. Also found on Hong Kong, Straits Settlements and British Trade dollars. The Indian equivalent is *shroff marks* (q.v.).

CLICHÉ
Forgeries made by soldering together two embossed discs of silver foil with tin or tin-lead solder. The impressions were made on the silver foil by pressing it on a genuine coin. Also used to describe single-sided electrotypes and stereotypes.

CLIPPING
The illegal practice of cutting away parts of the edges of coins (mostly silver and gold), to sell as bullion or to use for counterfeiting. Apart from clipping, there was an odd procedure called 'sweating the coins' which involved long periods of shaking gold or silver hammered coins in a sack to gain precious metal from them without making them unacceptable. The sack would then be burnt to retrieve the metal residue.

COIN FAKERS
U.S. expression for counterfeiters aiming their products at collectors.

COIN WEIGHT
Coin-like object in base metal, having the precise weight of the particular precious metal coin it was to be used to check, as indicated by the inscription or design on it. Its primary use was to check that the coin had its full weight of precious metal, unclipped and not too worn. Its strong secondary use was as a counterfeit check.

COINERS and COINING
Used to describe counterfeiters and counterfeiting, although the terms referred originally to genuine coin producers and production.

CONTINENTAL STERLING
Continental imitations of English silver pennies *(see Crockards, Pollards and Rosarii)*. Because of its reputation for quality and consistency, English sterling coinage from the late twelfth century was well accepted on the Continent. This gave rise to the imitations that

were designed to look like this known standard to ensure their acceptability.

COUNTERFEIT
An imitation of a genuine coin, made to deceive. A forgery. The word can be traced back through the old French, contre fait, to the medieval latin, contra factum. It is used in the U.K. and increasingly in the U.S. for pieces intended to enter circulation, *and* for those intended to fool collectors.

COUNTERMARK
Impression (device, letter or figure) added to an existing coin after its initial issue, making it legal tender in other than the original issuing country or confirming or altering its value. Also, rarely, to confer official status on counterfeits.

COUNTERSTAMP
Alternative term for Countermark, q.v.

CROCKARDS, CROCARDS or CROCCODONE
The term probably stems from the latin Crux, meaning a cross. They were late thirteenth century Continental imitations in debased silver of English silver pennies. Similar to Pollards (qv), except that the head is wearing a chaplet with three roses (hence the alternative name, Rosarii) instead of a crown. Two of any type were generally taken to be worth one English penny, making them useful as small change until they were banned in 1310.

DANDIPRAT (also spelt Dandyprat)
Early sixteenth century term for any tiny coin.

DEBASEMENT
Reduction in the precious metal content of officially issued coins.

DIE-AXIS
Coin and medal alignment/rotation. Take any decimal coin. Hold it right way up at the top and bottom and swivel it round. The design on the other side will also appear the right way up. This die-axis arrangement is called *medallic* and is usually indicated in texts by one or two upward pointing arrows. If the second side had appeared upside down, this, known as *coin* alignment, would be indicated by an upward and a downward arrow, or by just a single downward arrow. For imprecise axes, the second arrow always points to the top of the reverse when the obverse is upright. Some texts express this as a clock time, e.g. 4 o/c.

DODKIN
Term used for poor metal foreign coins. Henry IV and V issued edicts against their use as currency. These editcts proved ineffectual.

DOIT
Tiny Dutch copper coin filling a small change gap in England from the late sixteenth to the early nineteenth century. Also termed Doitkin.

ELECTROTYPE
Product of an electrolytic process, similar to industrial electroplating, producing separately the two sides of the coin being copied. These shells are then fixed together, either by glueing or soldering, with a filler such as lead in between. Although quality replicas and counterfeits can result, they are possibly the easiest to detect because of the difficulty of completely masking the edge join. Examples are known with the joins plated over. There is also usually a reduction from the norm in both size and weight.

ELECTRUM
A naturally occurring alloy of around three parts gold to one part silver, copper, etc. It was the first metal used for coinage in the West - by the Lydians. The term is also used for similar, artificial alloys. Also known as white gold. In its natural form, it has an inconsistent gold content and no lead. The artificial gold-silver alloy has a consistent gold content, plus lead and copper.

'ENIGMATIC' STERLINGS
Imitations of Esterlings (qv).

EPIDEMICS
Where counterfeits, imitations and/or tokens become so prevalent that they represent a significant percentage of the total circulating coinage.

ESTERLINGS (also EASTERLINGS, EASTERLINS, ESTRELINS or even STERLINGS)
Small, low-grade silver Continental imitations of medieval English silver pennies - from the thirteenth century. *See also Crockards and Pollards.*

EVASIONS
Lightweight copies of George I, II and III copper coins. They were 'near' copies, but not near enough to be classified as forgeries. Mostly halfpence, but also farthings, made lightweight in order to achieve a profit. With the face of King George on one side, the illiterate would accept them at 'face' value, regardless of how inappropriate was the accompanying legend, e.g. *Guglielmus Shakespeare.*

FACSIMILE
Another word for replica or reproduction (qv).

FAKE
(v) To tamper with, contrive, in order to deceive.
(n) Copy of existing coin to fool collectors. More generally, something that looks genuine but is not.

The word fake is old thieves' slang, probably of Dutch or German origin. It may stem from the word feague, which meant boosting the sale value of a horse by making it look younger or stronger. On the other hand it may have come from the German *fegen*, meaning to furbish up. It is widely used.

FALSE DATES
Where coins bear a date different from the actual year of issue. George V sovereigns dated 1925 were issued by the Royal Mint from 1926 to 1949. Beraha dated his 'sovereigns' 1926. U.S. Dollars from 1798 to 1803, were later produced - for undiscerning collectors - with the date 1804.

FANTASY
Any coin design dreamt up by a forger or replicator that does not match a real coin. Most are unlikely to be mistaken for real coins, despite many being intended to fool collectors.

FLAN
The metal disc ready for striking, to convert it into a coin. Also termed blank and planchet (U.S. & Fr.). Sometimes used to mean the surface of the stamped metal disc.

FORGERY
Fraudulently making or altering anything; that which is forged or counterfeited. Copy of a circulating or obsolete coin intended to deceive.

FORGING
The act of a criminal forger. Also, to confuse matters, the act of a blacksmith producing, say, an iron die, for *forging* coins, i.e. for their legitimate production.

GALLEY HALFPENCE
Italian wine-merchants of the fifteenth century were known as Galley-men, and so the small base metal 'silver' coins (Venetian soldini) they brought into England were known as Galley halfpence. Like the Lussheboumes of the previous century, they copied English coins and circulated in England, despite legislation banning them. They appeared mostly from 1400 to 1415, and 1519 to 1520.

GRAINED EDGE/GRAINING
The serrated edge on coins (often incorrectly called milling).

HAMMERED
Hand-struck coin.

IMITATIONS OF VALUE
Copies made to the same value and in the same precious metal as the originals by different authorities, because of the general acceptance of the originals outside the country of origin, e.g. Maria Theresia thalers.

LIMESFALSA
Lightweight cast Roman bronzes, also known as 'frontier forgeries'.

LOST WAX
Casting method, whereby a wax model of a coin is encased, the wax melted away and the hollow filled with molten metal. (Fr.) *Ciré Perdue.*

LUSSHEBOURNES
In Edward III's reign, merchants brought into England base metal coins nicknamed Lussheboumes, because most of them originated in Luxembourg. Sometimes spelt LUSHEBOURNES, and also known as LUSHBURGS and LUSHBOROWS. John the Blind started it all, imitating the English sterling penny, including the crown on the monarch's head, unlike crockards and pollards (q.v.). His efforts have his name as EIWANES, which he hoped that illiterate English merchants would take to be EDWARDVS. Copyists of his idea during the fourteenth century were, notably, Robert of Bethune, William I of Namur and the bishops of Toul.

MARIA THERESIA DOLLAR
Austrian Thaler of 1780. The most frequently restruck coin.

MEDLEYS
Alternative term for EVASIONS (q.v.)

MILLED
Machine-made coin.

MILLING
Producing machine-made coins, *not* graining (q.v.). Also a U.S. term for the raised rim round a coin that facilitates stacking and protects the design from undue wear.

MINIMI or MINIMISSIMI (singular = MINIM or MINIMISSIMOS)
Tiny bronze barbarous radiate (3rd century A.D.) or diademed (4th century A.D.) copies of Roman coins degenerating down to pinhead size.

MINT
Where the coins were/are made.

MINTMARK
Identifying mark on a coin, indicating its source, i.e. the particular mint at which it was struck.

MONEY WEIGHTS *(see COIN WEIGHTS).*

OBSIDIONAL COINS
Emergency money produced in besieged towns. Also called siege money or siege pieces.

OBVERSE
The more important side of a coin (usually 'heads' for obvious reasons).

OFFSTRUCK
Coins resulting when the die strikes the flan off-centre.

PADUANS
Renaissance copies of Greek and Roman coins emanating from sixteenth century Padua in Italy. Cavino was the most famous producer of Paduans.

PLATED COINS
Base metal counterfeits covered with a precious metal skin, wash or coating. There are some exceptions to this rule, where silver or platinum is the metal underlying a gold exterior. Also where an iron core has been covered with a copper alloy. The ancient Greeks knew how to plate coins. Plated Iron Age staters were copper covered with a very fine plating of gold, requiring a high skill level. By the time of the Romans, plated coins were around in large numbers, mostly counterfeit, but some could have been due to official debasements of the coinage. In the Roman era, from Gallienus's reign, all the official 'silver' coins were plated or silver-washed.

PLUG/PLUGGED MONEY
Anti-counterfeit e design combining two different metals. An example is James II's tin coins with a central copper plug.

POLLARDS
Base silver Continental imitations of medieval English pennies with bare headed busts. See also Crockards and Lusshebournes. In Edward I's time, these imitation pennies were imported into England in quantities that drove out the good English silver, leading to sanctions.

POTIN
Cast Celtic coin, sometimes called Speculum, after the metal used.

PRIVY MARK
Concealed mark in a coin design inserted for security and other reasons. Some identify the moneyer, others the specific die. The term is sometimes misused to mean MINTMARK (q.v.).

PYX, Trial of the
Sample checking of the coins being produced by a Mint, to ensure that the prescribed precious metal content was being maintained.

RADIATE
Roman Emperor's crown of sun's rays. Occasional examples suggest that this could be an erroneous description of a barred crown.

REPLICA/REPRODUCTION
Copy made for commercial purposes, display or study.

RESTRIKE
A coin made from genuine dies after they are obsolete. Restrikes can be official or unofficial and can be the same as or different from the original issues. Struck from untouched original dies or modified ones. Mints have been known to cut new dies of old coins, but whether these should be called restrikes is a moot point. Official restrikes are endemic with Indian coins.

REVERSE
The less important side of a coin (usually 'tails').

SCISSEL
Waste metal strip with holes where coin flans have been stamped out.

SHROFF MARKS
Indian merchants or bankers' countermarks on coins, to test for plating and also act as a record of the test when next seen, to save repetition. The Chinese equivalent is *Chop Marks* (q.v.).

TOKENS AND TOKEN MONEY
When an official coin does not contain an appropriate value of metal, it is token money. This is not the same as tokens. Token money bears an official design to show that it is authorized. Tokens can resemble coins and token money closely, but are issued without general approval, although they have on occasion been favoured with an official 'blind eye'. They were issued by trades-people, individuals, local Councils, etc. They may or may not contain an appropriate amount of metal.

TOOLING
The act of re-engraving, either to improve a coin's appearance, alter or remove detail, or add faked detail to enhance a coin's value.

TOUCH NEEDLES
Gold and silver rods of known alloy percentages, used for checking coins by the touchstone method.

TOUCHMARK
The mark left on a touchstone by a precious metal object or a touch needle.

TOUCHSTONE
A siliceous stone used for checking the precious metal content of objects and coins.

ABBREVIATIONS
gm = grams gr = grains mm = millimetres

Index

Illustrations in bold
Counterfeiters in italics

The Counterfeit Coin Library

THE COUNTERFEIT COIN STORY is the first book to be published in a series of books and booklets on different aspects of coin counterfeiting, a hitherto comparatively neglected area of numismatics.

Other titles soon to appear include:

COUNTERFEIT COIN DETECTION FOR ALL

THE COUNTERFEIT COIN COMPANION

COUNTERFEIT COIN BIBLIOGRAPHY

COUNTERFEIT COINS AROUND THE WORLD

FAKE POUND COINS

COUNTERFEITERS ENCOUNTERED

COMIC COINS AND FUNNY MONEY

COUNTERFEIT COIN DETECTION FOR ALL
There are many ways of detecting counterfeits and this book sets out to provide a comprehensive guide to all methods not requiring expensive equipment, expertise or rare skills!

THE COUNTERFEIT COIN COMPANION
The heart of this reference book is a listing of hundreds of known counterfeits, with numerous illustrations.

Other major sections include coin hoards and museum collections containing counterfeits; coin and counterfeit metals; ancient methods of counterfeit detection; modern detection methods reference; imitative issues; coin replicas; checklists of specific clues to counterfeits; apparent coins; word centre of counterfeit and relevant coin terms and phrases, including slang, crooks' cant, archaic and foreign. On the Net.

COUNTERFEIT COIN BIBLIOGRAPHY
An impressive reference to books, journals, magazines, newspaper articles, etc. relevant to coin counterfeiting. Key books and articles are highlighted. The comprehensive listing is also separated into different sections such as detection methods, counterfeiters, prevention, eras, techniques and so on, to render it as useful as possible.

COUNTERFEIT COINS AROUND THE WORLD
Many examples are described and illustrated to show the extent to which counterfeit coins occur in the majority of the world's coin issuing countries. The first part of the book looks at the ancient world, and the second part from the sixteenth century to date.

FAKE POUND COINS
With over 20 million fake pound coins in circulation, the pound in your pocket may not be as genuine as you may imagine. This booklet will show you how to spot the 'wrong-uns'.

COUNTERFEITERS ENCOUNTERED
The early coin counterfeiters are almost entirely unknown. Then, from the fifteenth century, figures began to emerge who achieved notoriety, lasting down to the present day. The products of some have become collectable in their own right! They make up a fascinating collection of tales. An amplification of the chapter herein on The Coiners, it concentrates on the fakers aiming their products at collectors, giving much useful information on how to spot these nuisances. There is information on the range of coins produced by the individuals, supported by numerous illustrations. The final section of the book looks at replica makers, with particular reference to those whose products could mislead.

COMIC COINS AND FUNNY MONEY
There are many amusing stories associated with counterfeiting. As the little girl actually said, "of course the coins are hot. Daddy's only just made them!" Cartoons add to the fun, to make a book present to delight any coin enthusiast.